In the Land of the Ayatollahs

The ink of the scholars was weighed against the blood of the martyrs and outweighed it.

A saying of the Prophet Muhammad (al-Khatib, *Tarikh*)

In the Land of the Ayatollahs
Tupac Shakur is King

Reflections from Iran and the Arab World

Shahzad Aziz

AMAL PRESS
BRISTOL • ENGLAND

Copyright © 2007 Shahzad Aziz
All rights reserved.

Amal Press, PO Box 688, Bristol BS99 3ZR, England

http://www.amalpress.com
info@amalpress.com

ISBN 978-0-9552359-2-4 paperback

Cover design: White Canvass Media Solutions

For Umi, Abu and Saba

CONTENTS

ACKNOWLEDGEMENTS

FIRST AND FOREMOST, eternal gratitude to all those I met and spoke to on my escapade, including the many who did not make the final cut—without their contribution this book simply could not have been written. With equal parity, eternal gratitude also to my wife, for having the kindness and patience to endure what no woman should endure during the first years of her marriage. Many, many thanks also to the following people: Valerie Turner for her copy-editing, commentary and courage to tell me when my jokes weren't funny; Taher Moosavi and Afolabi Euba, for their thoughtful and constructive observations on the manuscript; Zahid Ali for his counsel on the 'sensitive' chapters; Jawad Babar, Ghulam Ahmed and Tanveer Qureshi for being my sparring partners; N.J. for his ceaseless attempts to open up my 'doors of perception'; Muhammad Ilyas Gul for playing yin to my yang; Cyberium.co.uk for uncovering what I could not; Gary Clarke (MBC) for caring when others would not; Ali Khan, Mahmood Zar, Juber Ahmed and Moin Uddeen Maniar, for providing me with a fertile intellectual environment for my two brain cells to grow in (at least you guys tried); Abdallateef Whiteman for his small but priceless act of generosity; Malcolm X and Muhammad Ali for reasons which may or may not become obvious; Aftab A. Malik and all the publishing team at Amal Press and finally, a special thank you to my parents, to whom I owe everything but my own failings.

PROLOGUE: FROM THE MARABAR TO THE TORA BORA CAVES

> There are some exquisite echoes in India; there is the whisper round the dome at Bajipur; there are the long, solid sentences that voyage through the air at Mandu, and return unbroken to their creator. The echo in a Marabar cave is not like these, it is entirely devoid of distinction. Whatever is said, the same monotonous noise replies, and quivers up and down the walls until it is absorbed into the roof. 'Boum' is the sound as far as the human alphabet can express it, or 'bou-oum', or 'ou-boum'—utterly dull. Hope, politeness, the blowing of a nose, the squeak of a boot, all produce 'boum'.
>
> *A Passage to India*, E. M. Forster

PROLOGUE? WHAT ON earth are you doing reading the 'prologue'? Prologues are for geeks and nerds. Unnecessary verbal clutter annoyingly laid to rest at the very opening of a book. Worst of all, for a book of this type, they provide the author with an opportunity to act sanctimonious and come across as sophisticated (Ooo! la de da de da!), as he speaks of the noble reasons behind why he wrote the book (as if the reader really cares), or even worse, he meticulously guides you through the methodology he has adopted (boring! boring!).

Are you still here? Well ... I suppose I had better get on with it then ... I suppose I had better get on with explaining what this book is about.

The central event in E. M. Forster's *A Passage to India* is the mysterious incident that takes place in the Marabar Caves between the dashing Dr Aziz and the English rose, Adela Quested. Dr Aziz is an Indian medical practitioner who displays all the best virtues of Muslim hospitality that Forster had so come to admire from his experiences in British India. Adela is a fresh-off-the-boat English lady who is appalled at the snobbery and distance with which her country folk were ruling India. The final and most important 'character' in the scene is the ancient Marabar Caves themselves. Dark and dingy and with echoes that 'threaten meaning and overturn reason,'[1] these uninhabitable caves provide neutral territory for East and West to meet. Something happens in those caves. What? We know not. But a meeting between two essentially decent people, one from the Islamic East, one from the West, ends up with one accusing the other of sexual assault. Dr Aziz vehemently denies any improper conduct. He is, however, charged and detained, and the matter eventually goes to trial. This trial represents a political discourse between British and Indian,

Eastern and Western. In true Platonic style, the Marabar Caves strip people of their sensory perceptions of sight and sound. Each side is therefore left to construct the 'truth' about what happened—about the echo that Adela's experience generates. Each side is left to decipher the meaning of 'bou-oum' and 'ou-boum'. The purpose of the trial is to determine the meaning of 'bou-oum' and 'ou-boum'. What 'bou-oum' and 'ou-boum' mean to the British and to the Indians are two very different things.

For the British, the assault on an English lady simply reinforces all their preconceived opinions of Indians, that in common with the other 'darker races' they were an uncivilised lower species who were not only less intelligent, but also less attractive than white Britons. At Dr Aziz's trial the prosecutor opens the case by enunciating what he asserts is a general truth, "that the darker races are physically attracted by the fairer, but not vice versa—not a matter for bitterness this, not a matter for abuse, but just a fact which any scientific observer will confirm". For the British, the meaning of 'bou-oum' and 'ou-boum' could be decoded by these two simple universal truths; Adela was British, therefore she was civilised and incapable of being attracted to someone of a darker race; Dr Aziz was an Indian, thus uncivilised and attracted to the fairer race. It was therefore not only not surprising, but wholly inevitable, that such an incident as alleged by Adela would occur when an English lady and an Indian man are thrust together in such a place.

For the Indians, the incident reinforces all their preconceived opinions of the British. Dr Aziz's treatment (from arrest to trial) under a criminal justice system established by the British, perfectly highlights the institutionalised and endemic racial bias so deeply entrenched in British rule in India. It was a system of rule that promoted itself as being fair and transparent, but was, as every Indian knew, one that ultimately favoured a British citizen over an Indian citizen. In Dr Aziz, we had a man of impeccable character. One who was intelligent, hardworking, hospitable and polite to people of all communities and all races. He was even better looking than Adela. For the Indians, it was clear that someone of such character was incapable of committing such an awful act. Adela on the other hand was new to British India. Nobody knew her character, nobody except that nice Mrs Moore (the elderly lady who brought her to India)— and Mrs Moore, knowing both Dr Aziz and Adela, believed in Dr Aziz's innocence. She would have established the Indian man's innocence at his trial had the British not mischievously and conveniently shuttled her out the country before the trial (a wholly wrong assumption, as Mrs Moore left India for altogether different reasons). Once again, for the Indians, it was clear that Adela was of dubious character; this was proven by the fact that the only person who really knew her, disbelieved her. Yet this racist British system of rule, on a mere unsubstantiated allegation by a British women of untrustworthy character, had damned and stained the longstanding reputation of an innocent and good Indian man.

In the buildup to the trial, Forster wonderfully illustrates how neither community is concerned with establishing the truth, establishing what actually happened in that cave. Instead, once Adela has made the complaint and Dr Aziz is arrested, a herd mentality takes over the British and Indian communities. Each is driven into opposing camps, each constructs their perception of the truth through preconceived assumptions.

For those who have not read the book, the story deserves completion. During her evidence, Adela admits that she was wrong to accuse Dr Aziz of such a serious allegation and that the truth was that she herself was unsure of what happened in those dark, menacing and sense-stripping caves. Dr Aziz is acquitted, but neither community changes its perception of what happened.

The fictitious Marabar Hills are said to be based on the Barabar Hills that lie in the northeastern part of India. On the other side of 'old India', 'pre-partitioned India', just across its western border (now Pakistan's border) lie the Tora Bora Caves, located between two mountain ridges. I have often imagined that the Tora Bora Caves share some characteristics with the Marabar Caves. Like the Marabar Caves, I imagine they are dark and menacing and strip humans of their sense of sight. More importantly, I also imagine their echo to be the same monotonous 'bou-oum ou-boum' sound that reverberates around the Marabar Caves. A little over three-quarters of a century after Forster wrote his novel, another meeting is taking place between East and West, between the Muslim world and the Western world—this time in the Tora Bora Caves. American soldiers are on the hunt for Osama Bin Laden and al-Qa'ida fighters.

The presence of al-Qa'ida and American soldiers creates a 'bou-oum ou-boum' echo in the Tora Bora Caves. But what does 'bou-oum' and 'ou-boum' mean this time? Well, as in Forster's novel, it means two very different things to the East and the West, to the Muslim world and the Western world.

As in the novel, neither side is concerned with establishing the truth. Neither is committed to honestly exploring all the underlying reasons behind what caused the 9/11 attacks and the subsequent 'War on Terror'. Instead, just as in the novel, a herd mentality takes over the Western (specifically the US) and Muslim worlds. Each community is driven into an opposing camp, each side blames the other, each explains the American presence in Afghanistan and the War on Terror through their own perception of the truth, through their preconceived assumptions about the 'other'.

The United States sees itself as the leader of the free world—no nation has done more to promote and preserve 'democracy' and 'freedom' than America has—from fighting fascism in Europe, to defeating the wider global threat posed by the communist bloc. The attack on 9/11 was an attack not only on its citizens; it was an attack on its values. It was an attack on 'democracy' and 'freedom'. That is why American soldiers found themselves searching the Tora Bora Caves. That is what 'bou-oum' and 'ou-boum' mean.

Just as the British approached the incident in the Marabar Caves through flawed, preconceived assumptions about itself and the Indian community, the United States likewise approached the 9/11 tragedy through flawed, preconceived assumptions about itself and about al-Qa'ida. Somehow, it was beyond the administration's collective conscience that the *reason* they were attacked on 9/11 had little to do with al-Qa'ida holding intense ideological convictions against democracy and more to do with US motives behind its intervention and presence in the Middle East. No! That could never be the case. America is Good, it fights fascism, communism, it never does anything Bad.

For many Muslims around the world, the US presence in Afghanistan reinforced all their preconceived opinions of America—that the United States is a greedy imperial power that needs more and more oil to feed and sustain its ever-increasing and indulgent economy; that throughout the twentieth-century US presence and intervention in far too many Muslim lands, especially in the Middle East, has almost always been connected with attaining easy access to these countries' natural resources; that in order to gain access to this 'black gold', it has been willing to interfere in the internal politics of these states so as to support, aid, and even prop-up US-friendly regimes. Afghanistan is not, therefore, about seeking justice for 9/11. For too many Muslims, in too many Muslim lands, it is about that greedy imperial power wishing to trespass upon the sacred soil of yet another Muslim country and set up yet another US-friendly puppet regime. In this instance, the goal is to obtain greater access to the natural resources of central Asia. So convinced are *some* Muslims that this is the *only* reason why the United States went into Afghanistan, that this has become the real meaning of 'bou-oum' and 'ou-boum', that even the 9/11 tragedy has been interpreted so as to fit their preconceived image of the United States.

Both within the Muslim community in the United Kingdom and on my travels in the Middle East, I have often heard the most crazy and absurd stories designed to distance Muslims from 9/11. For 'we' Muslims could never commit such an evil atrocity. No! We are decent and God-fearing people. Islam teaches compassion, peace and love, not violence and terrorism. No Muslim could have done this! I have heard stories that 'the Jews did it', because they wanted the United States to attack Muslim nations, as this would be in Israel's interest. There was even corroborative evidence to support this assertion; 'the Jews definitely did it, because, did you know that on the morning of 9/11 none of the thousands of Jews who worked in the Twin Towers turned up for work? This was because they were told by the Jewish hijackers not to turn up!' When I ask about the source for this story, remarkably, it turns out to be a mystery as unsolvable as the one in the Marabar Caves. The most incredible story I heard (and heard several times) was that, 'the United States did it themselves'. So greedy was America for the oil in central Asia that the American government (most likely the CIA) set up the events of 9/11 and made out that it was Muslims in Afghanistan that had done it, thus giving themselves the perfect pretext for invading Afghanistan. For these well-informed Muslims in the know, the fool is the one who believes everything America tells him.

As difficult as it is for some Muslims to accept, the harsh reality is that unfortunately, within the global Muslim population, there are individuals and groups whose hatred of the United States is so great and so virulent that some of them are indeed both willing and capable of indiscriminately killing large numbers of civilians (both Muslim and non-Muslim, as events have shown) in order to further their political ideology. The painful truth is that regardless of whether or not there is any substance to the conspiracy theories about 9/11, there exist Muslims who, if given the means to carry out a terrorist attack, would do so (as subsequent events appear to prove). And yes, events in the Tora Bora mountains of Afghanistan and the actions of the American soldiers in those dark menacing caves are at least partially a result of an American desire to exact retribution upon those whom the United States felt were responsible for the deaths of thousands of its civilians.

Most travel literature attempts to capture the 'essence' of the society the writer has visited; to paint as accurately as possible a detailed picture of the culture and society the traveller has interacted with. Whilst this book is written in the format of a travel diary, it does not seriously attempt to do any of these things (although brief introductory descriptions are given about each of the cities and countries that I visited). This is not the purpose of the book.

Contained within this travelogue are my visits to a number of major cities in the Middle East. During my short stays in each city, I spent as much time as possible talking to as many of the locals as possible, getting their views and opinions on a number of contemporary issues affecting the

Arab/Muslim world and relations between Muslims and the West in the post-9/11 era.

Before I embarked upon my journey I already had in mind the types of issues that I would discuss. I mention this because the reader will quickly become aware that while the information I received from the people that I spoke to is revealing and important to the content and structure of this book, it is the analysis of the data and my opinions that form the substance of each of the chapters.

Given the complexity and diversity of Arab and Persian culture, I did feel it very important that in a project of this type, I do not simply quote from one stratum of society. Therefore, I have deliberately attempted to include viewpoints from as many sections of society as possible, to ensure that the final draft reflects class, gender, faith and educational differences within Arab and Persian communities. However, I do accept that it is very difficult for any project like this to completely reflect all opinions, take into account all social categories and make sure that the balance of both opinions and social categories is reflective of that society. For example, gender segregation is deeply entrenched in the Middle East, and this meant that I was able to interview more men than women.

Whilst sifting through the data it very quickly became apparent that much of the material that I had collected was often very critical of Middle Eastern governments. I am only too acutely aware that Western writers often write about Middle Eastern societies through a 'West is best' mentality. As the reader will soon see, the West hardly comes out in glowing terms in this book. Furthermore, in defence of these regimes (be it a limited form of defence), I would ask the reader to bear in mind that even as we constantly moan and complain about our government and their policies, 'government-bashing' seems to be a universal trait. One should not, therefore, automatically assume that simply because the people that I spoke to were often critical of their political rulers, that this means they desire regime change through revolution or US military intervention. My personal opinion is that most of the people that I spoke to want political reform—reform that takes place through an evolutionary rather than a revolutionary or military process. And one should certainly not assume that Arabs or Persians who are critical of their states want a secular liberal Western democracy. As the differing communities within post-conflict Iraq show, Middle Easterners very much differ on the type of government they feel is best suited for them.

Whilst I have attempted to summarise as accurately and as fairly as possible the sometimes lengthy conversations that I had with people, there have been some deliberate changes to the text. The names of the people that I spoke to have either been changed or I have simply referred to them through the position they occupy in that society (for example, 'the professor from Damascus University', or 'the taxi driver from Tehran'). On a few occasions I have felt it necessary to slightly alter background facts in order to protect the identity of a person.

Finally, the conclusions that I draw on the topics and issues that I discuss are not meant to reflect an objective view of the subject matter. I don't think this is possible. When it comes to debating issues such as the Arab-Israeli conflict, nothing even remotely resembling an objective view exists. Neither, it must be stressed, do my views reflect the Muslim viewpoint. With well over a billion Muslims worldwide, a single or united voice or stance on the issues that I explore is probably impossible to achieve. Having said this, I cannot distance myself from the fact that I interpret and make sense of the issues that I discuss very much through the eyes of a Muslim, or more accurately, a British Muslim. The conclusions, however persuasively you may or may not think I have argued them, therefore simply reflect my personal opinions.

Personal opinions are, as we all know, not formed within a vacuum. In the same way that identities are not formed within a vacuum. Their construction is dependent not only on the present, but also on our history (or histories as may be the case). As Shakespeare so eloquently put it, "What's past is prologue". The cryptic and not so cryptic references to pop culture and Western literature that are peppered throughout the pages of this book and embedded in the chapter titles are not simply done for presentational effect. They are also designed to reflect and remind the reader of the competing discourses, of the 'other present(s)' and the 'other 'history(ies)', that Muslims living in the West have to deal and engage with, but increasingly (as globalisation takes effect), Muslims of the Eastern lands do as well.

It is of course important that all communities have their voice (or voices) heard. For the British Muslim community (as with other minority communities in the United Kingdom), having their voice heard has been fraught and besieged with difficulties. For my parents' generation, many of whom entered the British labour market in low-skilled, manual labour jobs in the 1950s and 1960s, the priority was putting bread on the table (and sometimes bread on two tables, as money was sent home). Since many were initially allowed entry on a short-term basis, to work or study, the Indian subcontinent was always their home, to which they would return one day.

In such circumstances the development of a distinctly British Muslim voice (or voices) that could constructively contribute to the major contemporary debates of the day through politics, the arts, literature, journalism, the professions, etc. . . . was somewhat hampered. The 'myth of return' remained simply a myth and, like many other communities that emigrated from the Commonwealth at the same time, they remained in the United Kingdom and made it a home for themselves and their families, scattering themselves in and around the inner cities of the towns of Great Britain.

The Thatcher years of the eighties in which I and many second-generation British Muslims grew up, were a decade of excess, of unprecedented economic success, of the loads-a-money, love-it-and-laud-it yuppie culture in which we were all upwardly mobile. All, except those who happened to live in the inner cities. The Thatcher-Lawson economic miracle seemed to pass us by; the Thatcherite dismantling of the welfare state did not. Forgotten, ignored, discriminated against, marginalised . . . from Brixton to Handsworth and Lozells (where I grew up) many of these inner cities went up in flames (in what would later be called the race riots of the eighties), in protest . . . in anger . . . in rage! Some ethnic communities had clearly had enough. It wasn't simply Afro-Caribbeans, Asians, or Muslims who were ignored. Morrissey of The Smiths spoke for a generation of marginalised white youth when in their hit song, *Panic*, he sang aloud,

> Panic on the streets of London,
>   Panic on the streets of Birmingham,
> I wonder to myself could life ever be sane again . . .
>   Burn down the disco, hang the blessed DJ,
> because the music that they play,
>   it says nothing to me about my life.

In the end, they didn't have to hang the DJ because her own party did it for us.[2] But at least the working-class white community had a voice that could be aired and heard. For the British Muslim community, coupled with the social and economic deprivation of the inner cities, internal issues about identity raged on. In her novel *Brick Lane*, Monica Ali sums up the internal conflict in a scene set in the mid-eighties between Chanu and Dr Azad's wife:

> Chanu: " . . . behind every story of immigrant success there lies a deeper tragedy. . . . I'm talking about the clash between Western values and our own. I'm talking about the struggle to assimilate and the need to preserve one's identity and heritage. I'm talking about children who don't know what their

identity is. I'm talking about the feelings of alienation engendered by a society where racism is prevalent. I'm talking about the terrific struggle to preserve one's sanity while striving to achieve the best for one's family."

Dr Azad's wife: "Crap ... Why do you make it so complicated? ... Assimilation this, alienation that ... Listen when I'm in Bangladesh I put on a sari and cover my head and all that. But here I go out to work. I work with white girls and I'm one of them. If I want to come home and eat curry, that's my business. Some women spend ten, twenty years here and they sit in the kitchen grinding spices all day and learn only two words of English ... They go around covered head to toe, in their little walking prisons, and when someone calls to them in the street they get upset. The society is racist. The society is all wrong. Everything should change for them. They don't have to change one thing. That ... is the tragedy." [3]

As the eighties drew to an end, two events, the collapse of the communist states one after another like dominos and the *Satanic Verses* affair, suggested that at the end of the decade of decadence, one enemy of the West (communism) was about to be replaced by another (Muslim fundamentalism). The first Gulf War in the early nineties cemented this geopolitical shift in the *hostes hostium*.[4] It was almost as if in one part of the world the Iron Curtain was coming down, whilst in another, an 'Iron Veil' was going up. Against this backdrop of shifting patterns in international and global politics, British Muslims, quietly and unassumingly, slowly began to filter into the universities of Great Britain in greater numbers than ever before. Like other minorities, they were making it despite and not because of the system. Remarkably, I was fortunate enough to be amongst this group, choosing to go to London to study law. One of the reasons I chose London was because it includes (then as now) the most eclectic and diverse range of Muslim intellectuals in Europe, free to ply their trade attending the lecture circuit of the university Islamic societies of London. These intellectuals probed us to think, to debate and argue amongst ourselves about the world around us, about the kind of society we wanted to live in and the role that we could play in bringing about change. For us, student politics wasn't dead, it was alive and kicking and wearing a chequered kaffiyeh scarf.

By the time we graduated and seeped into the professions, the political climate worsened. At a national level, the British media increasingly sought to concentrate on the few London-based speakers (I shall refrain from using the term intellectual to describe them), whose non-stop barrage of anti-West ranting played right into the hands of a right-wing British media looking to put a face to the new enemy.

In the summer of 2001, race riots in the northern England towns of Bradford, Oldham and Burnley flashed across our screens in scenes reminiscent of the bad old days of the eighties. The difference this time was that it wasn't young Afro-Caribbeans expressing their anger and rage, it was Muslims. Young British-born Muslims who, for whatever reason, felt the only way they could express their grievances was to send their cities up in flames.

Then, just as things were calming down, 9/11 knocked on our door, and life as we knew it was never to be the same again. It turned the world upside-down. It ruptured the fabric of the political order created in the aftermath of the fall of communism. It generated a political earthquake of such seismic proportions that its after-effects may shape many of the major political and military events of this new century. At the time of writing, there have already been two wars conducted by the United States against Muslim nations and there is a realistic likelihood that more may follow. The response by Muslim extremists (for want of a better word) thus far has been suicide bombings in occupied Afghanistan, in occupied Iraq (since 9/11, the greatest number of civilian victims of this method of killing have been Muslim) and beyond, in Bali, in Madrid and more recently in London.

We live in strange times. Our world has never been more connected—we truly live in a global village. The great cities of the West have never been more multi-cultural, multi-racial and multi-religious. And yet oddly, our misunderstanding and ignorance of each other has never been so great. Our global TV networks provide us with twenty-four hour coverage of news and events, debated over and over and over again. So many voices demanding to be heard, all speaking at the same time, all wanting their fifteen minutes, all claiming to be speaking the truth, a non-stop bombardment of our senses through audio, visual and digital mediums, all becoming louder and louder until they blur into each other forming a single monotonous sound ... with an echo that reverberates on the world's airwaves and which, as far as the human alphabet can express it, sounds something like 'bou-oum' or 'ou-boum'. What is this book about? It is one individual's journey to find out the meaning of 'bou-oum' and 'ou-boum'.

1. GENESIS AND EXODUS: THE ISLAMIC REVOLUTION AND PERSIAN DIASPORA
(Birmingham–Frankfurt–Tehran)

"ALL WELCOME, INCLUDING gays, Jews and paedophiles", read the words firmly imprinted at the bottom of the poster advertising the university Islamic society's next lecture. At the time I remember shaking my head and thinking to myself that they'd really done it this time. This time, they'd well and truly overstepped the mark. A few weeks later the university temporarily banned the student Islamic society. This came after the umpteenth warning requesting that they refrain from making either anti-Semitic or homophobic remarks. Secretly, I'm sure that some non-Muslim students and staff alike felt that the ban was long overdue, that the university student union had been dithering over the issue for far too long, that if any of the other student societies (especially those comprised of mainly white members) were to publicly espouse anti-Islamic, racist or bigoted views, they would have been banned on the spot.

At the Friday sermon immediately after the ban, those running the Islamic society (the same people responsible for the poster) expressed outrage at the decision. The speaker used the sermon to illustrate how the ban reflected the hypocrisy of the West, which boasted of the sacrosanct status of freedom of speech, yet increasingly sought to deny 'us' Muslims the right to speak freely on issues such as the atrocities Israel was committing against the Palestinian people (although I did not quite follow how linking Jews to paedophiles forwarded this particular argument). This was the 'hypocrisy of democracy', the speaker sought to remind us. What the incident reminded 'us', was not so much the hypocrisy of democracy, but more that 'we' (or more accurately, our 'apathy') had voted the bigots into power. The more the speaker tried to convince us that 'they', the elected members, were the innocent victims in this whole scandal, the more it reflected the depth to which they had alienated themselves from the mainstream Muslim student population.

The radicalisation of some sections of the British Muslim community is just one of a number of ever-increasing factors that give Islam and Muslims a higher profile in Britain and other parts of the Western world. The Salman Rushdie affair, the first Gulf War, 9/11, al-Qa'ida, Afghanistan, Bali, the second Gulf War, Madrid, London, the list grows ever longer. Why? Why Islam? Why Muslims? When the collapse of the communist bloc resulted in most of the developing world navigating a path towards liberal democratic ideals, the Muslim world appears to shun the increased prosperity and concern for human rights that such societies seek to afford their citizens. Not only do the customs and rituals of the developing Muslim countries appear strange and out of place in the modern world, but more worryingly, an increasing number of its followers appear to gravitate towards extremism and fundamentalism.

As appealing as these Western propositions appear, they are fundamentally flawed. Truly liberal democratic societies are still a rare species outside North America and Western Europe (many are democratic simply in name). And this phenomenon we call fundamentalism can be found in virtually all societies. Christian fundamentalism, Jewish fundamentalism, Hindu fundamentalism, even secular fundamentalism, are but a few of many. The reason the West is not as preoccupied with these other fundamentalisms is because, with the exception of Christian fundamentalism, Westerners are rarely affected by them. Ironically, in the case of Jewish and Hindu fundamentalists, it is Muslim communities that appear most at risk of incurring their wrath.

The incident with the poster occurred several years ago whilst I was a university student in London. Even then it was becoming evident that in the coming years relations between the West and the Arab/Muslim world would become increasingly strained. At the time I wanted to visit the Middle East to write a book that explored some of these tensions and further attempt to tackle some of the misconceptions that each society appears to be developing about the other, but I had neither the finances nor the time to complete such a project. Now, several years later, I found myself in the living room of my home in Birmingham, reminiscing about the poster incident whilst waiting for the taxi to the train station, from where I would catch a train to the airport, from where I would catch the first of two flights to the Middle East. Finally, I would write a book that might shed a little light on some of the issues that currently affect relations between the West and the Arab/Muslim world in the now post-9/11 era.

The taxi driver who took me to the train station was a young Muslim man of Pakistani origin. Like many private-hire drivers of Pakistani descent that work in the city, the inside of his taxi was decorated with sticky-back emblems depicting various calligraphed Quranic verses. This use of aesthetic symbolism to publicly espouse the religious component of one's ethnic identity is rare amongst English taxi drivers. Where cultural markers are used, they tend to express profane rather than sacred components of the English identity (such as affiliation towards football clubs). It may appear to be a miniscule and unimportant cultural difference, but this difference wonderfully highlights the extent to which religious faith continues to dominate the cultural identity of Muslim communities the world over.

During the short journey to the railway station, the radio was tuned into the news. Bin Laden dominated the headlines. Although the United States had been unable to capture him, the Afghan military campaign was coming to an end. America was successfully completing the first phase of its self-proclaimed War on Terror. Those critics who predicted the campaign would take months, possibly years, had been proved wrong. I asked the taxi driver what he thought about the war in Afghanistan. Neither the substance of what he told me, nor the vehemence with which he delivered his answer surprised me. I had heard such arguments before. They were shared by many British Muslims. He felt that the US bombing campaign had led to the killing of innocent civilians. Whilst he did not condone the events that took place on 9/11, those unjust attacks on US soil were the result of its unjust foreign policy in the Middle East. America still had not learnt the lessons of 9/11 and he believed further attacks on its soil would follow. His comments reminded me of Malcolm X's, "chickens have come home to roost", speech made in the aftermath of Kennedy's assassination. Was Uncle Sam simply reaping what it had sown? Or was there a failure by this taxi driver to sufficiently recognise and condemn unjustifiable acts committed in the name of a religion that he was going out of his way to tell his passengers he belonged to?

The plane to Frankfurt was small and not very impressive. Not at all the jumbo jet that I had imagined would transport me to the exotic land that is Frankfurt Airport. On board, I found myself seated next to a very important-looking German businessman. Having had only a light breakfast, I was feeling hungry and looking forward to being fed once we were airborne. Sure enough, a few minutes after take-off the cabin crew began serving lunch. The male flight attendant serving us informed me that lunch would consist of a ham baguette and a small carton of yoghurt. I politely told the attendant that I didn't eat ham, and could I have the vegetarian option instead. The flight attendant gently smiled back at me and politely informed me that, as he had already mentioned, they were *only* serving ham baguettes. He handed me the lunch pack and said that I could simply have the fruit-flavoured yoghurt if I didn't eat ham. I was not happy. I looked at the miniscule carton of peach yoghurt before me. After one spoonful I decided to read the list of ingredients on the side of the carton. GELATINE—the words shot up at me from the side of the carton and smacked me in the face. I didn't eat gelatine. I placed the carton back on the tray. It tasted disgusting anyway.

My tummy was still rumbling. My conscience decided to call an emergency debate on whether or not it would be permissible for me to remove the ham from the baguette and just eat the salad filling. It would no longer be a ham baguette then, just a lettuce- and two-tomatoes baguette. The motion was rejected, as my conscience issued a fatwa declaring that such an act would not be permissible. My epic journey to the Promised Land would have to be undertaken on an empty stomach. I needed to be up for the challenge, to rise to the occasion. It was moments like this that defined great people. I would prove I was up to the challenge, and with the help of three glasses of apple juice, I managed to make the first leg of my trip to Frankfurt Airport.

The Iranian Revolution of 1979 sent shock waves throughout the world, turned American foreign policy in the region on its head and changed the face of the Middle East.

Iran (formerly Persia) is steeped in history and culture. Their people are part of a civilisation that dates back several thousand years; theirs is a society whose contribution to human civilisation has been immense. By the late 1970s though, the country was in trouble. Its people were under the rule of the Shah of Iran, Mohammed Reza Pahlavi. He was blessed with an oil boom that had flooded the country with millions of petrodollars. This in turn brought untold wealth and riches to a country desperately trying to recapture former glories. But like many other Middle Eastern countries that benefited from the discovery of oil under their soil, this newfound wealth did not trickle down to the masses. And the masses were not best pleased.

As the decade came to an end, large sections of the population felt alienated from a regime they saw as corrupt, unjust and out of touch with the people. As the voices of protest grew louder, the Shah began to adopt increasingly violent measures to repress anti-government sentiment. These voices of protest came from all sectors of society. They emerged from the rural areas where many of the poor lived. It was the villagers who had least benefited under the Shah's rule. They also came from the urban middle-classes who were faced with glass doors and glass ceilings in the high-income employment sector. Many felt nepotism and government corruption were the reasons. The frustrations of the poor and middle-classes filtered down to university campuses and the student population formed another significant group that was committed to deposing the Shah.

Anti-government feeling also spanned both ends of the ideological spectrum. Groups ranged from Islamic parties that emerged from the religious schools in the holy cities of Qom and Mashad and were committed to a theological polity, to the secular, leftist groups that flourished on university campuses. These groups sought inspiration from Marxist doctrines and the communist states. Whatever their differences, all were united in their aim to depose the Shah. And in February of 1979 they succeeded. Ayatollah Khomeini returned from exile in France and eventually took over from the Shah who was forced to flee the country in fear for his life; in danger from the very people he had ruled.

Victory had been achieved. Or had it? On 1 April 1979, in a national referendum, the country voted for an Islamic republic. Ayatollah Khomeini went on to become the supreme spiritual leader. Many of the secular groups that formed part of the Revolution had supported him in the referendum in the hope that he would adopt a Broad Church approach to his rule. But within the first few months after power had been secured it became apparent that Khomeini and his group of religious clerics were attempting to create a theocratic state: one in which the godless secular and Marxist groups had no place. Khomeini's rise to power as the head of a Muslim country was unusual. Most Muslim populations in the Middle East expect their leaders to be God-fearing and religious (or at least give the impression that they are), and this was a quality that many Iranians felt the Shah lacked. But Khomeini wasn't simply a 'religious man'; he was also a 'man of religion'. Even throughout Islamic history, very few men of religion had succeeded to become the head of state.

Iran's fledgling theocratic state passed laws that laid down the ideals by which people ought to live their lives. One of the most controversial (certainly the most highly publicised) of these new laws was the requirement that all women wear the *hijab*, or veil, in public places. Those who could not tolerate life in such a society and had the means to leave did so. And in the days and months after the Revolution thousands of Iranians left Iran, seeking exile in Europe and North America.

It is not easy for anyone—any people—to go into indefinite exile from their home country. It is not simply a case of living abroad; the social umbilical cord from the mother country has been cut. The process is immensely painful. Not only must one adapt to living in a radically new environment, one must also deal with the condition of being in exile from the motherland. Most of the Iranians that I was seated with in the departures lounge for the Frankfurt–Tehran flight were part of this 'Persian diaspora'. These people resided mainly in Europe and North America, but occasionally returned home for short holidays.

I began talking to one such Iranian. He went by the Anglicised name of Robert. A short man of light build, he was probably about forty years in age, wore small, rounded glasses and spoke in a gentle manner. Currently, he was working in the IT sector in California. His story was not uncommon, in that during the 1979 Revolution he had been studying in the United States. In the months that immediately followed the Revolution he watched with keen interest the religious state that Khomeini was trying to create. Observing from afar, he witnessed Khomeini turning the secular into the sacred. It was clear to him that he could not live in such a society and so he decided not to return home. The decision was not easy. From the way he spoke to me I got the impression that it was as if Khomeini's new government had forced him to remain in America, that in reality, he never had a real choice between going home or staying in the United States.

I asked him why he had chosen the United States over Iran. He told me that he had never been a religious man. Even as a child he had never believed in Islam. For him, all religions were simply a collection of fairy tales. The Revolution had nothing to do with religion and everything to do with money, he told me. The people of Iran wanted more prosperous lives; that was their real grievance. This I could understand, but he went further and added that the United States was also a sympathetic partner to the 1979 Revolution. This I could not understand and so I asked him to explain. The Shah was initially a great friend and ally of the West, he said. But by 1979 the internal difficulties the Shah faced with his people were such that he began making difficult demands on the United States. They could not go on supporting him indefinitely. In the end, they got fed up with his regime and thought that change would be good for them as well. I could appreciate why the United States would display frustration with the Shah's increasing demands (especially if they were politically sensitive). What I found difficult to grasp was why they would either support, or remain indifferent to the anti-revolutionary movements in Iran. The majority of these groups were either Islamic or communist in origin. From America's point of view, whatever the defects of the Shah, surely he was better than the alternatives? Robert did not agree. A Middle Eastern foreign policy based on divide-and-rule could accommodate states that were opposed to their presence and influence in the region. Nations that chose to oppose US foreign policy would be made to suffer through the imposition of economic and trade sanctions (nations such as Iran, Libya and Saddam's Iraq). This would significantly diminish their political and economic power in the region and they could be used as examples to warn other nations of what could happen to them should they choose to oppose US policy in the region. In the grand scheme of things, countries such as Iran were used to reinforce US presence and control in the region.

All this theorising about US foreign policy still did not fully address why he chose to remain in the United States. I asked again. He answered with the reply of millions of immigrants throughout the history of the United States: his complete anathema towards any form of state-enforced religious orthodoxy meant that he would find it intolerable to live in Iran. What he had really despised about the new regime was its obsession with imposing its religious ideology on the everyday lives of ordinary people. Why should he be forced to obey laws that were based on a religious doctrine he had no respect for? What right did the ruling ayatollahs have to interfere in his personal life and control it in ways they deemed acceptable? What gave them the right to tell him how he ought to live his life? Whatever the faults of the United States, at least he was able to live his life free from this obsessive state interference. It was this freedom from government control that had enabled him to live his life according to his own ideals and further allowed him to pursue a successful career in Silicon Valley.

Boarding time arrived before we had a chance to finish our conversation. As I made my way onto the plane I thought about what he had told me. Whilst I was taken aback by his vehement disbelief in Islam (after all, it was my faith!), I could, nevertheless, empathise with his position. Whatever my religious convictions, what right did I have to enforce certain codes of religious behaviour on individuals who simply did not share them? The extent (if any) to which a government ought to separate religion from the state is a problem facing many Muslim countries. It would be an issue that I was sure I would revisit on my journey.

On the way to my seat I noticed that most of the men were well-dressed, many of them in Western designer clothes. Very few women were wearing the *hijab* and again, most were in fashionable Western clothing. I must have seen about sixty copies of *Cosmopolitan* being read by these fashion-conscious Iranian women. American accents emanated from every corner of the plane and this reaffirmed my view that these passengers were Iranians who had either lived in the West, or had spent a significant portion of their lives there. Shortly after take-off, the cabin crew offered us complimentary drinks. Alcohol was served and consumed by some though not all of the passengers.

Sitting amongst these people I could quite easily have convinced myself that I was travelling to the United States and not to the land of the ayatollahs, to an Islamic state where laws on female apparel and alcohol are strictly enforced. What Robert had told me made a little more sense. These passengers' lifestyles were so at odds with the ruling ayatollahs of Iran that I simply could not envisage how the two groups of people could coexist. One of the problems that the Shah and the wealthy elite had faced was how much more Westernised they had become from the rest of the population. The adoption of Western attitudes had been resented by large sections of the population, who viewed such behaviour as both decadent and a betrayal of their Islamic heritage. When the Revolution came, this wealthy elite either had to change their ways or leave. I was sitting amongst many who had (or whose parents had) chosen the latter option.

When we entered Iranian airspace all remaining alcohol was confiscated by the flight attendants and we were told to prepare for landing. For the women on our flight this included putting on the legally-required headscarf.

Our flight landed at Tehran Airport at about 1:30 a.m. This was not an ideal time for me to arrive. I needed to convert my currency into Iranian rials. The banks in the United Kingdom had refused to do this for me. A few days before my flight I even made an enquiry with an Iranian bank in London. They were also unable to conduct the transaction. I was however, advised that Tehran Airport had a facility where I could exchange money at any time of the day.

The airport itself was large, rather dowdy looking and very quiet. Well, quiet that is until I walked through a set of doors that led me to the arrivals lounge. Instantly, I was hit by a deafening wall of noise generated by a very large and boisterous crowd—the relatives and friends of the passengers on my flight. The heavy mixture of high-pitched verbal commotion combined with a healthy dose of pushing and shoving (the purpose of which was to get to loved ones), made the whole experience very disorienting.

As my brain began the process of social acclimatisation to this alien environment, it became apparent that within this crowd was a group that, in the land I came from, were commonly referred to as taxi drivers. They could be separated from the relatives/friends category by their slightly cheaper clothes and dodgy moustaches. From my backpack and rather lost look, they quickly realised that I might be one of the few fares they would get from this flight. And as I began my search for the *Bureau de Change* they followed me—almost all of them. I felt like the Pied Piper leading the dodgy moustached men to the tune (or the scent) of my American dollars. It wasn't long before I got fed up with the herd of moustaches harassing me. I started to shout at them to leave me alone, but it was a futile exercise. They had become entranced, hypnotised by the lure of green dollar bills.

Fifteen minutes later, I was still unable to find this damn money exchange place. In frustration I took off my backpack, slammed it on the floor and just stood in despair. The taxi drivers had now turned into vultures and were squabbling amongst each other on who could offer me the cheapest fare. Dazed and confused and surrounded by twenty hyperactive dodgy moustaches, the plight of these people suddenly struck me. The Revolution had never been about those wealthy people I had been on the flight with. The Revolution was about the poor, the working-classes. It was about creating a more equitable society so that ordinary people would have a better chance to succeed. The Revolution was about the people who stood before me. Over two decades had passed, yet the rich remained rich. I knew this from observing the passengers on my flight. I was not in Iran in 1979 when the Revolution took place, but looking at the faces of these desperate taxi drivers, I doubted very much that their positions had changed materially during the last two decades. I had only been in the country a few minutes, and my thoughts were premature, but at that moment I felt that the Revolution had surely failed to make the kind of fundamental changes to these people's lives that it had hoped for and promised.

One of the taxi drivers approached me and in broken English said he would take me to the money exchange (he guessed that was where I wanted to go). I agreed. He led me towards the exit door whilst at the same time angrily ushering away the other taxi drivers in case they should steal his prized catch. As soon as we exited the main doors, I immediately saw the money exchange to my left and hurriedly walked towards it.

I expected the taxi driver to politely wait outside whilst I was in the exchange. To both my amazement and anger, he followed me in and calmly leaned himself up against the counter. Short of telling him to get lost (which I was sorely tempted to do), I had no choice but to continue with my transaction. I spoke to the man behind the counter and we quickly agreed on how many Iranian rials I would get for my US dollars.

The agreement made, I nervously handed over my money. At this point the now grinning taxi driver leant over to get a closer look at my US dollars. I could have punched him. I was told that I would get approximately four million Iranian rials for my US dollars. You would think I might have been happy to have become an instant Iranian millionaire. Not so. As the wads of Iranian notes were being steadily stacked on the counter, it quickly dawned upon me that I might not have enough space in my inside pockets to put away all this money. I was right. In no time at all the inside pockets of my jeans were overflowing with cash. Yet the wads of cash kept stacking up. I had no choice but to place the remainder of the money in my outer coat pockets, something I did not wish to do for obvious safety reasons.

During this rather anxious period it had not escaped my attention that the dodgy taxi driver was standing a few feet away and watching the whole spectacle with a broad smile on his face. It would have been simpler if I had walked into Tehran Airport with a T-shirt bearing the words, "Attention! Foreign idiot with American dollar bills in pocket, mug with ease!"

Having secured all my money, I then followed the taxi driver who ushered me outside to his waiting taxi. I nervously watched his every move so that I could assess the suitability of this man to take me to my hotel. Why was I being so sceptical? What reason did I have to distrust this man who had done nothing but assist me? I started to feel guilty. I had almost convinced myself that it was okay, that I had nothing to fear, that I was getting paranoid about nothing. Then I saw his car. The car looked even dodgier than his moustache. My mind was made up. There was no way I was getting into his taxi and I told him so in no uncertain terms. I started to walk away from him and head back towards the airport entrance. He followed, pleading with me to get in. But it was too late. My mind had been made up. A white car whizzed past almost knocking me over. Was there no end to my misfortune? My anger turned to joy when I turned around and saw the words 'Airport Taxi' emblazoned on the side of the car. I was saved. I saw the airport taxi office immediately ahead of me—I truly had been saved. I walked over to the official taxi office and immediately ordered a cab to my hotel.

My official airport taxi driver was a nice man. He was very polite and had a pious look about him. I took an instant liking to him. On our way to the hotel he asked me where I was from. I told him I was from the United Kingdom. He asked me which part of the United Kingdom I came from. I told him I was from Birmingham. "BIRMINGHAM" he shouted loudly, followed by, "Aston Villa, I support Aston Villa". He then went on to tell me that he had been a lifelong Villa fan. When I told him that I had been to the Villa Ground to watch them play he almost fainted. What a weird world, a lifelong Aston Villa fan living in Tehran. This city would be full of surprises and contradictions. I was sure of it.

I had reserved a room at a four-star hotel in Tehran's central district. Although I was on a very tight budget I did allow myself this one luxury in the beginning, so that I could ease myself into Iranian society. Hereafter, I would only allow myself to stay in cheap two-star hotels.

After I had booked in I was taken to my room on the third floor. I threw my luggage onto the floor, quickly changed and collapsed onto the bed. It was almost 3 a.m. and I was exhausted. I had done it. I had arrived in Iran.

2. BIG BROTHER ON SUGAR STREET (Tehran)

> You must worship the government first and foremost if you wish your life to be free of problems.
>
> *Sugar Street,* Naguib Mahfouz

IT WAS CLOSE to 9 a.m. when I awoke the following morning. I stumbled out of bed and opened the curtains. Before me stood the great city of Tehran. The morning rush hour was in full swing, people hurriedly making their way to work. The untidy streets and concrete buildings were not overly impressive, but neither had I expected them to be. The weather was dull and overcast and not too unlike the weather I had left behind in England. I quickly changed and made my way to the hotel's dining area to have breakfast.

The hotel's website had promised a 'free American buffet breakfast' for every guest. The fact that this Iranian hotel chose to Americanise one of its services was both odd and intriguing. After all, was this not the country that tops the world league in anti-US rhetoric? A nation that once famously branded America the 'Great Satan'? Such is our impression of Iran in the West that I half expected to see anti-American demonstrations the moment I touched Iranian soil. Yet here I was on my very first morning in Iran having American culture shoved down my throat (quite literally!). Well, not quite. The American buffet breakfast turned out to be a selection of Iranian pastries. Not that there was anything wrong with the pastry mind you. However, I did wonder why this Iranian hotel would choose to package this part of their service in this way. In part, I assumed the hotel establishment thought it might appeal to foreign guests, especially from the United States. But that could not be the whole reason. I could see the odd European and Japanese guest in the dining area, but I did not see any Americans. The overwhelming majority of the hotel guests were native Iranians. I assumed they were middle-class businessmen in Tehran on business. It was these people such services were designed to attract. I was sure of it.

As trivial as it may seem, this aspect of the hotel's marketing is in fact significant. Despite all the anti-American rhetoric that has emanated from the Iranian regime over the past few decades, America still appeals to certain sections of the Iranian population. If the name attracted sufficiently negative connotations would the hotel use it? I would argue not. There must be something in the word America, which the hotel management believes will act as an inducement to certain sections of the local market. If this is the case, then what is it about America—the brand name (not the country)—that certain segments of the population find so appealing? Why is it that despite over two decades of hostility and unfriendly relations between the world's superpower and this nation, parts of the population are still drawn to America? What is it about this unique brand that enables it to survive and flourish in the most hostile of environments? These questions are important because America has been able to transplant various aspects of its culture into foreign lands and integrate them into alien cultures in a way that is unparalleled in human history. Even amongst nations and cultures where America, the country, is deeply unpopular (such as Iran), aspects of American popular culture (whether it be drinking Coca-Cola, wearing jeans or watching a Hollywood movie) still manage to fuse themselves (to varying degrees) into the everyday lives of ordinary people, without them even stopping to think about the apparent contradiction. I am not inferring some sort of hypocrisy on their part, but a curious bafflement at the unique power of this discourse that creates such a paradox.

In some ways Tehran reminded me of communist eastern Europe; the heavy police presence; the box-shaped cars dating back several decades; the unattractive concrete buildings and streets, many of them not well kept. In other ways Tehran reminded me of Lahore, Pakistan; a sprawling metropolis bustling with life and activity; vibrant market places that constantly bombarded the senses with an eclectic and colourful blend of exotic sights, smells and sounds; slow-moving traffic forever expelling exhaust fumes into the air whilst its drivers sounded their horns endlessly, for no apparent reason.

If there is something aesthetically pleasing about Tehran's landscape, then it is unquestionably the snow-capped mountains that hug the northern part of the city. On a clear day they can be seen from the city centre and greatly enhance its scenic location.

One aspect of Tehran that makes an immediate impression on the British tourist is the sight of heavily armed police. Compared to the United Kingdom, there is a much larger police presence on the streets. Tehran's streets may well be safer because of this police presence, but they certainly didn't arouse a feeling of safety and well-being in me. I held my breath and quickened my pace every time I passed a stationary officer slouched up against a wall with his gun lazily pointing in my direction, paranoid that his lethal weapon might go off at any moment.

Without a doubt though, the most unforgettable aspect of Tehran is the appalling and reckless standard of driving one encounters. There is only one golden rule of driving that everyone must be aware of: that there are no rules—no speed restrictions, no adherence to traffic signals or road signs (they are just there to make the place look pretty), no lane discipline on multi-lane roads (again the dividing lines are simply there for show), even the distinction between road and pavement is blurred with motorbikes travelling on both.

If one looks carefully enough, sometimes the difference between a wealthy Tehranian and a poor one is apparent. Many working-class Tehranian men wear counterfeit Western designer clothes. Heaven forbid their rich counterparts be seen in anything other than the real thing.

As required by law, the women were all dressed in various forms of the *hijab*. Women from poorer backgrounds tended to cover from head to toe in black robes. This is the image the West has of Iranian women. Women from the upper-classes tended to fulfil their legal obligations by simply wearing headscarves. Many also were heavily made-up. Their clothes, less likely to be hidden under black robes, were again of Western origin—no skirts, but plenty of jeans and designer tops.

There was a vast array of counterfeit Western designer clothing for sale in the market stalls. European designer labels dominated the imitation couture market with Versace, Armani and YSL heading the list. It was only in the booming counterfeit sports clothing area that American labels such as Nike seem to outsell European counterparts such as Adidas (which also sold very well).

One of my main tasks on that first morning was to locate the British Embassy to register myself. The embassy was conveniently located in Tehran's central district and only a short distance from my hotel. Britain's empire is long dead, but I have always felt that it is in its foreign embassies that remnants of empire still survive. Walking through the British Embassy's plush surroundings in Tehran only reaffirmed this view.

After finishing at the embassy I went back to the hotel for lunch, where I struck up a conversation with one of the hotel waiters. We agreed to meet up again later that evening after he had finished his shift.

That afternoon, I continued my tour of the sights and sounds of Tehran. I got lost several times and on more than one occasion I had to ask for directions. Unlike many of the other countries I would visit, Iran does not receive a high influx of Western tourists. The low number of tourists from Europe and North America has nothing to do with a lack of interesting sites to visit (on the contrary, the country is immensely rich in culture, history and natural beauty), but everything to do with the negative image Iran has in the West. This image is one of fanatics fuelled by religious bigotry and an immense hatred of everything Western. It may have been only my first full day in Iran, but already such stereotypes were severely challenged.

On one occasion when I got lost a young man who spoke in broken English said he would take me to the office of an English translator a few doors down from where we were standing. The office was situated in the basement of a clothes store. It was small and dingy and crammed full of papers. The translator was an elderly man busy working on his typewriter. He was genuinely pleased to see me and asked if I would stay a short while. I agreed to do so.

Whilst in conversation with the translator a young boy in his mid-teens entered the room and joined us. Although he spoke no English, the translator told me he wished to ask me a question. His question, when translated, was more of a statement than anything else. He told me that it was a very big dream of his to come and live in England (everyone referred to 'England' and not 'Great Britain' or the 'United Kingdom'). He wasn't old enough to work or go to university, so I asked him why. He said that he wanted to live in England so that he could listen to Western pop music, something that he could not do in Iran (certainly not legally). Most people emigrated to the West for economic or political reasons, but this non-English speaking boy wished to leave his motherland and live in the West simply so that he could listen to English-language popular music. I looked at him and started mentioning the names of Western pop stars; "Michael Jackson, you like Michael Jackson?" He smiled and nodded his head. "What about Madonna, you like Madonna?" Again he nodded his head. The lure of America's cultural discourse was much stronger than I had anticipated. In the West, we assume that people who live in countries such as Iran are attracted to America or the West for some deep ideological reason, a respect for democratic values or freedom of speech. In reality, the lure of the West for many does not lie in placing a tick on a ballot paper every four years, or having access to a newspaper whose editorial is critical of government policy. For many, the real lure of the West lies in the appeal of its lifestyle and leisure opportunities, many of which are forbidden in their own country. It is Western decadence they want, not Western democracy.

That evening I met up with the hotel waiter as agreed. He told me his name was Fahim. He was thirty-six years of age, unmarried, of short medium build, with curly hair. His English was good and I was extremely impressed when he told me that it was self-taught. We decided to go for a walk around Tehran's now neon-lit city centre.

I was eager to hear Fahim's views on the Iranian state, so I began by asking him whether he considered himself to be religious. "Yes and no", he replied. Yes and no, what did he mean by this? I asked. He explained. From childhood to early adulthood he had considered himself to be someone of strong religious conviction. He had grown up in a poor suburb of Tehran and even though the kids in his neighbourhood were disadvantaged, his religious teachers had always taught him that a strong faith in God would allow one to overcome the obstacles that his background had burdened him with. He never questioned or doubted their authority or the sincerity of their message. To be able to realise one's dreams was possible, even for a poor kid, provided he had belief in God and he followed the ways of his religious teachers. Throughout his childhood and teenage years he listened to and obeyed the message of the ayatollahs. Yet somehow God appeared to bypass all his prayers and hard work. He spoke in very vague terms, not elaborating on what career he had wished to follow and in what way he was prevented from pursuing it. Fahim wasn't the only one who felt let down by the religious scholars. He added that almost all of his childhood friends went through similar experiences, never quite getting the financial support that would allow them to study at university or begin an apprenticeship with a good employer. Then about ten years ago, he began to doubt his faith. The very thing that he had always sought inspiration from he was now questioning. I asked him why he blamed his faith for a failure in the system that caused he and his friends to suffer. After all, there existed a whole array of political and socio-economic factors that could explain why the poor in Iran were under-represented in higher education or why there was little social mobility between the working-classes and middle-classes. He quite vehemently pointed out that one of the main objectives of the Revolution was to fuse the political and economic systems of Iranian society with the religious doctrines of the ruling ayatollahs. Religion was at the very heart of Iran's political, economic and social structures. Any discussion of a failure in the system could not therefore ignore religion, or at least the form of religion advocated by the ayatollahs.

Ten years on, he had regained his faith in God. But now when he heard the ayatollahs speak he was not sure how much of what they said was God's word and how much of it was their interpretation of God's word. I asked him to explain what he meant by this. He said that for all their promise of creating a meritocracy, he found it very strange that the religious texts were interpreted in a way that seemed to reaffirm the power and authority of the religious elite. Fahim was not naïve; the sarcasm in his voice was barely concealed.

Iran's religious revolution had promised much to people like Fahim. Yet the goals of any fiercely idealistic ideology are very difficult to achieve. It would be unfair to use economic prosperity as a barometer to measure the success of the religious revolution in Iran. The ruling ayatollahs' portfolio extended far beyond increasing the country's economic output. Their policies were a socio-cultural as well as a political-economic reaction against the Westernisation policies of the Shah. He had attempted to implant a foreign ideology onto the people and culture of Iran. This policy of Westernisation failed because it alienated large sections of the population. When the ayatollahs came to power, they replaced the policy of Westernisation with one of Islamisation. Yet could it not be argued that they too had attempted to implant a foreign ideology onto the people and culture of Iran—by forcing a twentieth-century Persian community to live according to an interpretation of how a seventh-century Arab community had lived—and that such a policy had an impact on Iranian society similar to that of the political system that it replaced: the alienation of large sections of the population.

Iran's religious revolutionaries had noble aspirations for their country and for their people. Moral ideals, which they valued and saw as beneficial to the individual and to society, could best be realised through control of the state machinery. But any political ideology that aims to create a morally upright and noble society by using the state apparatus as some sort of social conditioning mechanism is almost bound to encounter enormous difficulties. Firstly, they will immediately offend individuals in that society whose definition of a morally upright and noble society is very different from theirs. People like Robert, who I met at Frankfurt Airport, are a prime example of this. The second difficulty is the assumption by the ruling elite that their system of government and the laws that they pass will have the intended or desired effect on the people being governed. They may not. The communist experiment in eastern Europe and the former Soviet Union are very good examples of this. Human nature is extremely complex and an assumption that 'x' law or policy will have 'y' effect is a very dangerous assumption to make. Fahim and virtually all the other people that I had met on my trip so far were perfect illustrations of this. If anything, my initial conclusions were that this system of religious laws was having the opposite effect on people and turning them away from a faith they may otherwise hold more dearly.

3. IN THE LAND OF THE AYATOLLAHS TUPAC SHAKUR IS KING
(Tehran)

DURING MY MEETING with Fahim I had expressed a desire to visit the mountain range on the northern outskirts of Tehran. I was aware that this was possible, as several telecabin services ran from a number of locations in the north of the city. He also thought it was a good idea but advised me to leave in the early morning as the following day was Friday. Friday is both a holy day and the weekend holiday in many Islamic countries and Iran was no exception. Friday's telecabins would be full of young Iranian families making the most of their day off.

As advised, I got up early. Fahim had already started his shift and so ordered a taxi for me. When it arrived the driver got out of the vehicle, gestured towards me to get into the front passenger seat and then hurriedly walked over to Fahim who was standing by the hotel entrance. I did as I was told and got into the car. The vehicle's outer bodywork was riddled with dents and scratches. The inside was no better, with bits and pieces that were missing, or looked as if they were about to fall off. The taxi very much resembled the one owned by the dodgy moustached man that had helped me at Tehran Airport. In retrospect, maybe I had been too harsh and judgemental of both him and his car. As I was soon to discover, most taxis in Tehran resembled stunt cars.

Once inside the vehicle I composed myself. I needed to. I was about to be driven through Tehran during the morning rush hour. I had forgotten to bring along my driver's helmet and this particular make of car was not fitted with an emergency escape pod (standard feature on all new models, I assumed). Instead, I would have to revert to plan B. Tried and tested, plan B had been used from the very dawn of the motor vehicle industry. Plan B was to reach over to my side and fasten my seat belt. This I tried to do, only to discover that the seat belt was broken. Apprehensive and void of any further ideas to secure myself in this death trap, I immediately began work on plan C, hoping I could come up with something before the taxi driver returned. Whilst I was fretting away about my future safety and the chances that I would die in an auto crash, my driver had somehow managed to engage himself in a heated conversation with Fahim. I could hear raised voices and began wondering whether it was a good idea to remain seated in the car. Why were they arguing? I had no idea. Maybe Fahim was trying to negotiate a good price for my fare or maybe it was something else. In any event, the argument ended abruptly with the taxi driver, in mid-conversation, suddenly turning around and storming over to his vehicle. He looked far from pleased.

I had come up with plan C. I would get out of the car, thank the taxi driver for his attendance that morning, regretfully inform him that because his vehicle failed to comply with one or two Iranian highway code regulations, it would be in neither of our interests to continue with the transaction. So whilst I was grateful for his assistance, it would, nevertheless, in the circumstances, be more prudent if I ordered another taxi. Unfortunately, the circumstances had changed somewhat since I formulated plan C, what with raging bull charging towards me. When he entered the vehicle I thought it wise not to raise the issue with him. Much better to risk my life than cause unnecessary fuss.

As soon as he got into the car his demeanor changed. In a relaxed and reassuring manner he turned to me, smiled, and said he would take me to the telecabin port. And with that, we were off. He moved away at speed and without checking his rear view mirrors. Having barged his way into one lane of traffic, he then proceeded to turn at the next junction and join another stream of heavy traffic without either slowing down or looking for a gap in the lane of traffic he was about to merge with. If I were a Christian, I would have asked for the last rites. We weaved our way through the traffic at such reckless speed and with such disregard for others on the road, including pedestrians, that I began to question the driver's mental state. My only comforting thought was that everybody else was driving in a similar manner (really not much comfort on further thought). I reconciled myself to the proposition that since he was not the only one practicing this Mad Max driving, there had to be some method to the madness; what I was witnessing was surely a superior and more sophisticated form of driving than my limited intelligence could appreciate.

We drove along, narrowly missing other vehicles and pedestrians with alarming regularity. The driver found my involuntary nervous reactions to these near death encounters extremely amusing. At one point I shrieked as we almost ran over an elderly woman. This caused him to laugh out loud and give me a look that I am sure read, 'you big girl's blouse, this is how a real man drives'.

Mad Max was able to converse in broken English and asked, "Where are you made?" I gave him a confused look, not sure what he was trying to say. He elaborated: "made in England?"; "made in USA?"; "made in Canada?" I smiled back and said; "made in England". Leaning over he quietly uttered, "My car is British car", before nodding his head and leaning back again.

This wasn't simply a throwaway line. The way he expressed these words gave one the impression that there was a deeper meaning to his remark, but what? Aware that I had not fully understood the hidden cultural meaning he was trying to convey, he pointed to a passing Japanese car, laughed out loud and said, "I don't have Japanese rubbish". I looked at him in bewilderment. He then pointed to a German car and said, "I don't have German rubbish". What parallel universe was he living in? He knew he had gone too far with his last remark, so he corrected himself by saying, "German cars okay" (only okay!), before again turning to me, smiling and again uttering, "I have British car". Particular emphasis was placed on the word British. I finally understood what he was trying to say. He did not own any old car; he owned a BRITISH car.

I asked him what car he had (not at all recognising the make or model). Voice filled with pride, he said loudly and slowly; "this . . . is . . . a . . . Hillman". Unless I am mistaken, a Hillman is a car Britain had stopped making several decades ago. How strange, a species of car that had become extinct in its home country a generation and more ago still exists in the faraway land of Iran.

What I found most intriguing about this man's boast was that although he was showing off the brand of car he was driving, it wasn't the manufacturer that was the brand name. It was the country of origin of the manufacturer that had become the brand. Like the hotel's use of the term American buffet breakfast, one could read much into the genuine pride this ordinary working-class Iranian took in owning a British car (albeit an extinct one). His attraction towards the vehicle had little to do with the fact that it was reliable or of a prestigious make. If this had been the case he would not have made the comments he did about Japanese and German cars. The reason he took such pride in owning a product of British origin and was able to rationalise it as superior to Japanese and German cars was because there was something about Great Britain that appealed to him, and by owning a British car he could associate himself with what he found so appealing. Like the United States, the United Kingdom had become a brand name. Yet what was unusual about this man's fondness of Great Britain was that it was constructed from the discourses of a previous era. It was the Great Britain of the colonial period that appealed to him. An era in which it was the greatest of all the European colonial powers, with a supposedly more superior, cultured, refined and sophisticated lifestyle to that of the colonised people.

If it seems that I am adding two and two and coming up with eight, then consider my walk through Tehran that week. The most popular brands of cigarettes being sold on the streets had names such as Dorchester,

Winchester, Kent and Churchill (Marlboro was the only popular American brand on sale). It wasn't simply that these popular brands of cigarettes had English-sounding names. It was the type of English name they had that was significant. These names all resonated with a grandeur and type of lifestyle associated with the upper class English gentleman made famous during the colonial era. I was sure it was the resurrection of these dead discourses that enabled the taxi driver to differentiate and rationalise his British car as being superior to Japanese and German cars.

As our taxi penetrated the north of the city, both the quality of the houses and the cleanliness of the streets markedly improved. It wasn't west London, but it was obvious that I was driving through the more prosperous part of the city. The driver dropped me off at the base of one of the mountains. He pointed to a steep track by the mountain base and said it would lead me to the telecabin port. I could either catch a special bus or simply walk. I got out of the vehicle and noticed that the air was both cooler and cleaner than downtown Tehran. It would have to be the latter option. Although still early morning, many people were already making their way up the steep track. I joined them.

It was obvious that the majority of these people were from the middle- and upper-classes. The abundance of genuine designer clothes gave the game away. The couture range included Ralph Lauren's Polo brand. I noticed this brand in particular because of the American flag imprinted on their clothing range. Indeed, I saw several sweatshirts with the trademark American flag quite clearly and visibly printed on them. Wasn't this blatant display of the American flag illegal? At the very least it must be risqué behaviour. Surely in a country such as Iran there are greater social connotations attached to the public display of the American flag than in a country such as the United Kingdom? These people must have been aware that by wearing such clothing they risked bringing themselves to the attention of the authorities. Were these people being careless or could the authorities not care less? Either way, it again challenged my perceptions of Iran.

Everything that I had assumed about this country was being challenged and when I thought I could be shocked no more, I was wrong. I heard a sound. It was in the distance but as I continued to walk up the steep track it slowly got louder. I had heard this sound before. But I must surely be mistaken; such a sound would never be heard in public in Iran. I continued walking. The sound became louder and louder until I could no longer deny what I was hearing. Yes, it was the sound of gangsta rap. I saw the source—a ghetto blaster carried by a young Iranian man (probably in his early twenties). He was surrounded by a group of boys and girls his own age. Several of them were bopping their heads to the sound of the ghetto fabulous. Surely this was illegal? I had been told that popular Western music was forbidden in Iran (although classical music was tolerated). Gangsta rap clearly fell into this prohibited category. My trip was supposed to be a spiritual journey to Islamic lands. I was returning to my cultural roots only to discover that they were slowly being dyed red, white and blue. I was getting concerned. Where were all the religious people? I had met none so far. Where were the ayatollahs? The group of people bopping along to the music seemed to be more interested in what Tupac Shakur had to say than any ayatollah.

When I finally arrived at the telecabin ticket office I bought my ticket and joined a rather long queue. It was clear that I would be waiting some time. I stood patiently, cursing myself for not leaving earlier.

When the telecabin finally arrived, I got in and sat next to an elderly man. The journey to the top of the mountain would take about twenty minutes. The elderly man politely asked me where I was from. His English was good and we chatted away during the ride. He was self-employed with a small business. He had a son who was studying to be a dentist at Tehran University; he hoped his son would be able to develop a successful practice after he completed his studies. But this was not inevitable. Graduates in Iran had an uncertain future, he told me. He had worked hard in order to fund his son's education. He and his wife had endured much hardship in the hope that their only son would have a better life than they. But he was not sure whether the sacrifices they had made would pay off. He did not appear too optimistic and I was genuinely saddened by his story. I told him that many parents in the West also struggle to fund their children's education. Contrary to what he thought, his experiences were not dissimilar from those faced by many parents in the West. Not surprisingly, he did not believe me.

Intrigued as to why I was in his country, he asked where I would be travelling after my stay in Tehran. I told him that I hoped to visit Qom next. "Qom" he shouted out in disbelief, "why do you want to go there?" Why did I want to go there? Did I need to explain? The holy city of Qom is steeped in history. It is one of the ancient centres of Shia learning. Even today, it has a stranglehold on the political and cultural landscape of the country. Why would he express shock at my desire to visit this most important and sacred of Iranian towns? So I asked him. "We don't like Qom", he replied. By 'we', I initially assumed he meant the rest of the people in the cabin, all of whom had been listening intently to our conversation and were now nodding their heads in approval of what this elderly gentleman was saying. I was genuinely shocked and sat in silence trying to digest the significance of what he had just said (and it was significant). I looked through the windows of the telecabin. The great city of Tehran was below us. Maybe I was wrong, maybe the words, "we don't like Qom", extended beyond the confines of this small cabin and included the people below us. The idea did not sound fanciful. I had seen enough on my visit to give credence to this interpretation of his comment.

I had never visited a snow-capped mountain before and so when we finally arrived at the top, I was taken by surprise at the spectacular views. When I first dreamed of travelling to the Middle East I had visions of deserts, Bedouin tribes and unbearably hot weather. Beautiful as it was, this was the last thing that I had expected to see.

I spent the morning taking photographs and enjoying the breathtaking landscape. At morning's end, I began my journey back down. It was Friday and I had planned to recite Friday prayers at Tehran University. The sermons that are delivered on Fridays are infamous for their anti-American rhetoric. Finally, I would get my chance to witness some real life hatred of the West.

At the base of the mountain I was greeted by hoards of people making their way up to the telecabins. So great was the number of people that at times I physically struggled to get by the tide of men, women and children heading in the opposite direction. This mass of human traffic surprised me. It was Friday and you could hear the call to prayer on numerous strategically placed loudspeakers. Yet it seemed that I was the only one who was planning to answer the call to prayer. The remainder of the people seemed intent on enjoying their day out. This was weird. I wasn't casting any moral aspersions on these people. I was just totally baffled as to how this country could have gone through a religious revolution. Where had all the religious people gone?

Outside the gates of the university I paid the taxi driver and headed to the campus. I was not the only one; there were about seven zillion others flocking to attend the congregational prayer. So there were religious people in Iran after all. And they came from all sectors of society; the rich, the poor, the old, the young, men and women, students and professionals, all united in a common faith.

The prayer hall was an enormous arena that resembled a large tent. I had been to Friday prayers with large congregations before. I had even been in larger congregations than this. But what seemed to separate this congregation from others was that it had atmosphere. By atmosphere, I mean a degree of audience participation in the ceremony that I had simply not encountered before. After prayers were concluded a number of individuals stood up and incited the audience to chant anti-US and anti-Israeli slogans. The crowd responded and the arena was soon filled with the chants of "death to

America" and "death to Israel". I watched with close scrutiny the faces of the people in the audience whilst they participated in this collective outpouring of anti-US and anti-Israeli feeling. I may be wrong, but my gut feeling was that many in the crowd were shouting these angry slogans because it had become custom to do so, not because at that particular moment in time they all suddenly and collectively developed extreme anger at US and Israeli policy in the region and that the only way they could express this anger was by way of collective chanting that denounced the two nations (although I would not question the fact that many of these people may hold grievances about how the United States and Israel operate in the region).

The ceremony over, I decided not to catch a taxi but to walk back to the hotel. It would give me time to digest the events of that afternoon. I began to think about Marx's famous dictum about religion being the opiate of the masses. Many in the West would look at the ceremony that I had just attended and come to a similar conclusion. No doubt some of these people may argue that what was going on amounted to a form of brainwashing, a theocratic propaganda machine that exploited the masses by conditioning them to think in a particular way. Robert, the man I had met at Frankfurt Airport, had expressed this very view. I had little doubt that many of the Westernised Iranians who I had encountered on my expedition to the north of the city today would agree with him. Yet this was too simplistic an analysis. After all, the theocratic propaganda machine seemed to have little effect on the thousands I had to walk past at the mountain base earlier on. But even more significant than this was the sight of Western counterfeit goods being sold immediately outside the university premises. One minute a worshipper was angrily chanting 'death to America', the next he was happily buying a fake pair of Nike trainers. The phenomena would appear to suggest that many worshippers were somehow managing to reconcile their hatred of Western governments with their love of Western products. These underlying contradictions seem to suggest a complex web of social discourses at play.

If it is still argued that these worshippers are being brainwashed, then who is to say that the same is not happening to Westernised Iranians (if such a division of Iranian society is possible given the contradictions that I have just mentioned)? The brand products of the West that many Iranians are so seduced by reflect idealised forms of a Western lifestyle that do not exist. For example, the gangsta rap that the young Iranians at the mountain base were listening to idealises the African-American ghetto experience by giving it a veneer of ultra-coolness. The music manages to glamorise the lifestyle of the African-American male in a way that many young white American youth (and some middle-class Iranian youth as well) find appealing. Yet the hypnotically cool lifestyle of the ghetto that is being portrayed is far removed from the poverty, suffering and hardship that many there face on a daily basis. The experiences of the ghettoes and of the African-American people who live in them may be many things, but glamorous they are not.

The same can be said of the cigarettes being sold on the streets of Tehran with names that are reminiscent of aspects of the English gentry. The manufacturers are clearly trying to develop a brand image that is based on a stereotypical image of the lifestyle of the English gentleman. These illusions of grandeur that smokers of these cigarettes are supposed to experience truly are illusory. They promote a grand lifestyle that is an illusion; it does not exist.

And what of those Iranian women on my plane journey from Frankfurt to Tehran who were reading *Cosmopolitan* and similar lifestyle and fashion magazines? These magazines are part of a culture industry that homogenises female notions of beauty and idealises specific female body forms (as depicted by the models in the magazines). Leaving aside Iranian women for a moment, the majority of Western women are simply unable to attain these idealised depictions of female beauty. The magazines do not reflect Western female beauty; they reflect what Western female beauty ought to be.

In all three examples, various sub-cultures of Western society are packaged and then sold to the Iranian consumer on the pretext that this is a part of Western culture that they can experience and be part of, if only they purchase the product. And yet in all three examples the product is not in any way a genuine experience of the Western sub-culture. Who, therefore, is being brainwashed here, the worshipper of Islam or the consumer of Western products?

I had wanted to visit the tomb of Ayatollah Khomeini, which is situated just outside Tehran. The day's events just increased my desire to go there. When I got back to the hotel I told Fahim to book a taxi to take me there later that evening. He was puzzled as to why I would want to visit such a place, but nevertheless acceded to my request.

The taxi arrived on time and Fahim very kindly agreed on a reasonable fee with the taxi driver to take me to Khomeini's tomb and bring me back.

Traffic was heavy and it took us forty-five minutes to reach our destination. Security at the complex was tight and only Muslims were allowed inside the mosque itself. My complete lack of Persian meant that the taxi driver had to assist in getting me past the security guards. This was no easy feat and I endured an anxious wait as the security officers made telephone calls before I was finally allowed entry. Once inside, I again marvelled at the beauty of Persian architecture. The place was full of people and a sermon was being delivered. Khomeini's tomb was enclosed within a cube-shaped glass structure. Men and women of all ages surrounded it, jostling amongst each other in order to get a better view. That they revered this man was beyond question; one only needed to look at the emotions clearly etched on their faces to appreciate how much he meant to them. Many were in tears. Some even broke down hysterically and had to be quietened by the security guards. To many outside Iran, Khomeini's rise to power is an anathema. In the West particularly, the Iranian Revolution appeared as a regressive revolution. Modern societies were simply not supposed to evolve in this way. Khomeini's genius lay in his ability to empathise with the grievances of a generation of poor Iranians and also articulate their hopes and dreams in a way that appealed to them. When state corruption and state brutality were at their peak in Iran, he, more than anyone else, was able to present a vision of a just and fair society in a way that many could understand. This is what the West fails to appreciate. Whether he delivered this vision is, of course, another matter, but looking at the hoards of people surrounding the glass enclosure, I finally began to appreciate the enormous depth of their feeling towards this man who had achieved super-saint status. Khomeini may be dead, but the country still lives under his shadow. He may not have the support of all of the people, but he still rules.

4. CARELESS WHISPERS IN THE STATE OF GRACE
(Tehran–Qom–Esfahan)

QOM MAY WELL be the religious and ideological heart of Iran, but there is little for one to see in this small but significant town. I visited on a day trip. From there, the plan was to catch an evening coach to the ancient Persian city of Esfahan.

Before I left the capital, I still had one small task to complete: to purchase an airline ticket to Damascus (the capital of Syria). It had been a great wish of mine to travel to Iraq. Unfortunately, the Iraqi Embassy in London was not amenable to the idea. At the time, the Iran/Iraq border was not the easiest or safest to cross. It was with great regret that I therefore had to bypass Iraq on my travels. There is no border between Iran and Syria, so I would either have to travel by coach via Turkey (a journey of approximately three days), or fly directly to Syria (a trip of a few hours). I chose the latter option. Travel agents in the United Kingdom had quoted extortionate prices for the Tehran to Damascus flight. Several people had advised me to buy my ticket in Iran, as I would be able to purchase it at a much more competitive price. Fahim, who had assisted me no end during my stay in Tehran, said he would ring several travel agents on my behalf in order to get the least expensive quote. This he did, managing to get one from a travel agent based near the city airport who was offering a one-way ticket from Tehran to Damascus for a hundred and forty dollars, almost half the price I had been quoted by some travel agents in the United Kingdom.

The taxi driver on the way to the travel agent took an instant liking to me. He was a thin, middle-aged man with a receding hairline that was fast turning grey. His name was Yusuf and he had been plying his trade for over twenty years. Fahim had already told him that I was from the United Kingdom and as soon as I got into his car he proudly announced that he was learning to speak English. To prove his point he opened up the glove compartment and took out a book on learning to speak English. I told him that his English was very good and this seemed to please him immensely.

He began by telling me that he was a big fan of the British singer, George Michael (I suppose prohibition can make just about anything seem appealing!). Was Western pop music not banned in Iran, I asked? Yes it was, he replied, but added that people still listened to it in secret. Again, to prove his point he opened up the glove compartment and this time took out a tape cassette, which he inserted into his car stereo. He played four songs for me; George Michael's *Careless Whisper*; The Beatles, *Hey Jude*; Simon and Garfunkel's *Bridge over Troubled Water* and Frank Sinatra's *My Way*. Whilst these songs were playing, he told me that Iranians, rich and poor, did all sorts of things that were prohibited by the state. Provided they weren't careless and kept their activities undercover, they could get away with almost anything. Some of these songs were poignant reminders of the situation he and many Iranians were in, I thought. Provided there were no 'careless whispers', Iranians could indeed do it 'their way'.

Without any prompting, Yusuf told me that he did not have a problem with Westerners; that, contrary to what I may have presumed, most Iranians did not have a hatred of the West or of Christians. "We have many Christians in Iran", he uttered. And as if by magic, he pointed out a church that we just happened to be driving past. We turned onto the next street and this time he pointed to a shop selling Christmas trees. Christmas was only a few days away. The sight was surreal, Christmas trees being sold openly in Tehran in the run-up to Christmas!

Yusuf wasn't the first Iranian to have gone out of his way to assure me that he had no ill feeling towards Westerners. I felt guilty that he felt the need to remove a stereotype given him by the West. If anything, I ought to have been the one apologising to him for the negative and unfair way in which we portray his country and people.

When we arrived at the travel agency he kindly offered to accompany me and assist in purchasing the ticket. I was grateful and indeed his assistance was required as the travel agent spoke poor English. I purchased the ticket and left the agency a very relieved man. I could continue my travels without worrying about how I would get to Syria.

On our journey back to the hotel I made a conscious decision to commence discussing more serious issues. He had told me earlier on that he was forty-three years old, so I began by asking him whether he preferred living in pre-revolution Iran or post-revolution Iran. The former he said, because there were far fewer restrictions and intrusions into one's life under the Shah's rule, although he did add that in the last few years things had gotten much better and that the Iranian government was slowly becoming less restrictive and granting Iranian people more freedom. Moreover, he was confident that this process would continue.

Did this mean he had opposed the Revolution? "Not at all", he replied. On the contrary, he had been a big supporter of the Revolution because life under the Shah was "bad". 'Bad', what did he mean by this? I asked. He meant that corruption was rife and that the Shah did not care about his people. From the way he said this I took 'his people' to mean the poor, as opposed to Iranian people as a whole (although I did not ask him to clarify the point). The Revolution, or what he perceived the Revolution to be about, encompassed ideals that he cherished. That is why he had supported it. He did not come across as particularly religious, so I asked him what were these ideals that he so valued. He listed four things; democracy, equality of opportunity, fairness and the absence of corruption. I had quite wrongly and quite patronisingly passed Yusuf off as someone of limited education. The answers he gave me and the way he expressed them strongly suggested he was well-read, and cared a great deal about the aims and goals of the Revolution.

He continued without interruption from me. When the Revolution finally took place, he said he was overjoyed. Iran could begin from scratch and create a society in which everyone had rights—rights that were properly protected by a state that spoke for everyone and not just a ruling elite. He asked me whether I was aware of the UN Declaration of Human Rights. I said that I was. It was the ideals that were laid out in that 1948 charter that he hoped would be incorporated into the new Iranian constitution. The world was witnessing so many rights-based movements during that period that he thought the Iranian Revolution was simply part and parcel of the same genre of movement as the US civil rights movement and the feminist movement of earlier years. (How wrong he was!)

In his opinion the biggest single defect of the post-revolution governments was their failure to separate state and religion. He resented the interference, the assumption that they knew best. The Revolution had sought to take rules and laws that were created fifteen-hundred years ago (a reference to the revelation of Islam) and incorporate them directly into a twentieth-century society without properly revising them or adapting them to meet the requirements of a modern society. It was not that Islam should be made redundant, he argued. On the contrary, he felt Islamic values should have a strong presence in a Muslim society and pointed out (with genuine pride) that Islam had given both black people and women equal rights long before the West had. In today's modern society we needed experts in each field of government activity, he commented. The problem with the Revolution was that it put into power orthodox religious scholars who were simply ill-equipped to deal with the machinery of modern government. I sat in silence, listening intently to what he was saying. From what I had seen of Iran so far, I thought many Iranians might agree with a lot of what he had to say.

We had almost reached the hotel when he came out with a most extraordinary remark. "I admire Abraham Lincoln", he said in a quiet voice. At first I thought I had misheard him. I asked him to repeat what he had said. "I like Abraham Lincoln, he was a great man", he uttered, this time a little more loudly. That this ordinary working-class Iranian would admire an American president from the nineteenth century (albeit a famous one), both amazed and bemused me. "Why do you like him?" I asked. "Because he freed the black man, I respect him for that", he replied. I suppose old Abe probably appealed to his belief in universal human rights. Still, it was difficult to apprehend that in today's Iran an ordinary working-class person could or would semi-idolise a dead American president.

The vehicle stopped at a set of traffic lights and a young Iranian woman walked past us. "Iranian woman very beautiful", he said looking at me. I smiled and replied, "I'm saying nothing". This seemed to upset him and he asked, "You not think Iranian woman beautiful?" If I did not answer this time I knew he would be offended. I replied in the affirmative and he seemed pleased with the answer. Contrary to what I might think, he told me, men and women did mix in Iranian society and some of them even had relations outside marriage. He himself had approached and chatted up many women in his time. I should do the same, he suggested. They would be after me because I had a British passport. (Oh how wonderful!) I need not worry he said, resting his hand on my arm. It was all very simple. First I needed to pick out a woman that I liked. If she did not have a child with her then it was generally safe to approach her. I should walk up to her and say, "me like you . . . you like me? Let's go park and do some nice things". A fail proof technique he assured me. A hundred percent success rate he assured me. Somehow, I remained unconvinced.

We arrived at the hotel. Just before I got out of the vehicle, he asked if I wanted to go to his house for a quick drink. I smiled, thinking to myself, he had no idea how such a comment would be interpreted in the West. Oh how naïve I was. He knew exactly what it meant. He clarified by saying he was inviting me round to his place for an 'alcoholic' drink. I was rather offended, but instead of chastising him on his sinful proposal, I foolishly questioned the truthfulness of what he told me. He assured me he was not lying, that he was offering me an alcoholic drink, that alcohol was available in Iran (be it illegally), you just needed to look in the right places. I was aware that the rich had access to alcohol, but that the working-classes also had access to the forbidden fruit seemed less plausible. Offended by my scepticism, he started up the engine and informed me that he was going to take me to his house just to prove that he was not lying. "I believe you, I believe you", I shouted whilst urging him to switch off the engine. He obliged. I told him to wait whilst I collected my luggage from the hotel. I was headed to the bus station to catch the coach to Qom. He had agreed earlier to give me a lift there.

Inside the hotel, I collected my luggage, paid the hotel bill and said my goodbyes. Before leaving, I thanked Fahim for all his assistance. We shook hands, wished each other well and I departed. Yusuf took me to the South Terminal Bus Station, from where I boarded a coach to Qom.

I arrived in Qom just after midday. Yusuf had urged me not to visit the place. Like Fahim and the elderly man in the telecabin, he felt that I would find it dull and boring. After arriving in Qom, I began to understand why I had been receiving such advice. Apart from the magnificent tomb of Hazrat-e Masumeh, there is little else to see. The place lacked both natural and architectural beauty. For some reason I had expected Qom to be a Middle Eastern version of Oxford or Cambridge. The presence of gowned ayatollahs walking around the town centre indicated that it was a centre of academic learning. Architecturally though, the town is a world away from the two institutions I imagined it would resemble. I yearned to speak with one of the ayatollahs, but I knew that in the short time I had this would be both extremely unlikely and possibly unwise (given that I would have felt obliged to ask why it was that during my travels in Iran I had encountered so many people who disliked the religious elite).

Instead, I spent the afternoon hours walking around the town's vibrant market places, taking in the unique atmosphere of the stalls and shops whilst quietly contemplating the role of religion and state in Islamic societies. Qom was, after all, one of the most ideal places to mull over such an important issue.

The Christian West is more or less comfortable with a separation between state and religion. Modern-day politics have been rendered and surrendered unto modern-day Caesars, with names like Bush and Blair. Most Islamic scholars would however, regard such a division as inconsistent with the teachings of Islam. On one level this difference in attitude is strange because, as the Arab scholar Muhammad Haykal has correctly pointed out, "Christianity and Islam entertain the same view of life and ethics."[1] If Islam and Christianity share similar systems of morality, why is it that one religion places a greater emphasis on the state to enforce this morality than the other? Why the differing approaches? The scholar Karen Armstrong, in her assessment of the issue, comments:

> In the Christian tradition . . . there is a strong tendency to see political activity as extrinsic to the religious life . . . In Europe we have gradually evolved an ideal which separates Church and state and we usually blame Islam for 'confusing' two areas that are essentially distinct. But the Christian experience should not prejudice us against other cultural and religious traditions which have developed under different conditions. When Muhammad brought his revelation to his people, Arabia was outside the civilised world and its political and social order was disintegrating. Christianity however, came to birth in the Roman Empire, which imposed, however brutally, a certain peace and social security. Jesus and St Paul did not have to worry about the social and political order because it was already set up. . . . Unlike Jesus, however, Muhammad did not have the luxury of being born 'when all the world was at peace'. He was born into the bloodbath of seventh-century Arabia where the old values were being radically undermined and nothing adequate had yet appeared to take their place . . . There was an urgent need for a political solution and in the seventh century such a solution would inevitably be religious.[2]

The Orientalist scholar Maxime Rodinson takes a similar stance:

> Christianity was born as a little sect in an outlying province of an immense empire. The founder of Christianity did not have the least intention of founding a state and always insisted that state structures should be respected. . . . In contrast, the Muslim community . . . originated in a stateless, tribal society and was more or less compelled by circumstances to organize itself into a state almost from the beginning. The community of the faithful was at the same time a political structure, a state. By becoming a Muslim, one joined both a religion (*dīn*) . . . and a political organisation (*dawla*). At one stroke one became a believer and a subject.[3]

Historical circumstances therefore appear to be the reason for the two differing positions. But if today's Christian communities seem to be more or less at ease, both with how Christianity's ancient doctrine impacts the polity of their country's constitution, and the effect such a secular polity has on their everyday lives, then the same cannot be said for the effect that Islam's doctrines have on today's Muslim societies. Some adhere to Islamic law more strictly than others. A small number of Muslim countries are strongly theocratic; Saudi Arabia, Iran and the former Taliban Afghanistan are good examples of countries where Islam is strongly fused with the political system of the state.

Others, such as Turkey, are puritanically secular. Most of the rest occupy positions somewhere in between. To complicate matters even further, many Muslims who live in secular states, or states that are undergoing secularisation, seem to deplore religion's expulsion from the polity of their country and blame many of society's social ills on the breakdown of this bond. But equally, many Muslims who live in theocratic states resent their government's religious interference and yearn for the freedoms that those who reside in secular countries enjoy (as my experiences in Iran seem to illustrate). The differing approaches between Muslim states and the differing opinions of the people who live within these states suggest that contemporary Muslim societies are not at all decided about the extent to which religious life ought to be intrinsic to the political systems of their countries. Why is this so? These matters are enormously important because they can hugely impact the stability or instability of a country. In order to understand why the contemporary Muslim world is able to churn out both secular countries such as Turkey, and theocratic regimes such as Saudi Arabia, let's refer to Armstrong and Rodinson's comments. There is some substance to what they are saying. The Prophet Muhammad (God bless him and grant him peace)[4] proved to be a highly effective and successful political leader during a difficult period of history. Many of the social and welfare reforms he implemented in order to tackle the awful problems his community faced necessitated his control of the state machinery. At one level it is therefore quite understandable why a secular Islamic state appears to be an anathema. How can a Muslim state wishing to implement the Prophet's teachings ignore or alter the fact that significant portions of his teachings were implemented through the machinery of the state?

But as any student of contemporary Islamic history knows, what is equally an anathema is a modern theocratic Islamic state that enjoys the long-term popular support of its people. Just look at the histories of the three theocratic states I have mentioned. While I have not conducted a MORI poll, it is abundantly clear that the religious elite in Iran do not have the support of large sectors of their society. If it were not for US and other military aid from the West, the House of Saud would almost definitely have faced a serious challenge to its authority (it may still). As for the now extinct Taliban in Afghanistan, even during their short reign they were constantly at war with factions such as the Northern Alliance, and without the help of Pakistan and Messrs Bin Laden and friends it is difficult to see how the regime could have survived long-term. Why do theocratic Muslim states face such difficulty in sustaining the long-term popular support of their people? Well, ironically enough, it might be, in part, the result of

Islam's success as a world religion. At its birth, the Prophet of Islam was the head of a small community in the Arabian Peninsula. His followers believed that he had received direct revelation from God, thus the legitimacy of his rule was never questioned. Since the Prophet's death and nearly fifteen-hundred years later, that small Muslim community has grown to well over a billion followers worldwide. Today's Muslim community originates from all four corners of the globe and encompasses a whole array of races, peoples and cultures. This enormous community is inevitably heterogeneous in nature, both culturally and ideologically. A large and culturally diverse religious community without a leader in direct communication with the Almighty is going to have problems establishing ideological unity, especially in relation to the interpretation of commands considered to be divine texts. Without ideological unity, any society that allows one group to heavily enforce its viewpoint (however sincere they may be) upon others is at serious risk of sleepwalking into tyranny. One only needs to look at the enormous differences that exist between Shiite Iran and Wahhabi Saudi Arabia. Both are theocratic states in which there is a strong fusion between state and religion. Yet the ideological gap between these two countries is so vast that some Saudi scholars even go so far as to suggest that Shiites should be considered non-Muslims. Strong words indeed! Needless to say, such comments do not go down very well amongst the ruling ayatollahs of Iran, who fought so hard to establish the Islamic Republic of Iran. But many of Saudi Arabia's own critics (internal and external) speak from an Islamic platform and denounce the regime for not being truly Islamic (Messrs Bin Laden and his al-Qa'ida group are one such organisation).

I may be wrong, but given the heterogeneous nature of Muslim societies and Muslim thinkers (which it could be argued is not a bad thing), it is unlikely that any Islamic group stringently implementing its ideology through the state machinery will ever have long-term popular appeal. Such regimes will provoke resentment from those Muslim citizens who feel they are being forced to practice their religion and there will be an even greater resentment from devout Muslims of differing theological backgrounds who feel that they are being subjected to laws that they do not perceive as Islamic. Given the vast and almost permanent ideological differences that now exist in Muslim societies, it is nearly impossible for any Islamic state to completely fuse religion and state without dissent arising from its population.

The solution, one might argue, is to highlight the sources of political conflict and tension, remove them from the political sphere and confine them firmly to the private sphere. But that is the road to secularism, and a division between religion and the state for many Islamic scholars is tantamount to religious heresy. One simply cannot confine to the private sphere issues that the Prophet Muhammad dealt with through the political sphere. A solution needs to be found to this very real issue, which faces not only Iran, but the whole of the Muslim world. Otherwise, Muslim societies put themselves at the risk of continuing political and economical instability.

I wanted to speak to someone who lived in Qom before I left and the opportunity arose late that afternoon when I entered a small convenience store to buy a drink. The shop assistant was a young man who told me his name was Ali. He invited me to join him for tea, and I accepted. We took tea (or coffee in my case) on a small table and two stools situated just outside the shop (which I presumed were there for just such purposes). He told me he was twenty-three years old and had come to Qom several years ago, from a small village, to study Islam. He needed to work part-time in the shop in order to supplement his meagre living allowance.

We spoke for over an hour about a variety of subjects that ranged from marriage to employment. The most interesting aspect of our conversation concentrated on my presence in Qom. Ali made it clear to me that the reason he had invited me for tea was because he enjoyed speaking to people from different cultures and that he was someone who liked people of all nationalities. Once again, I felt this unsolicited comment was made in order to rebut some perceived assumption I was supposed to have about him. But before I could respond to the comment he went on to ask whether I had faced any hostility in Iran. 'No' I replied. My answer came as no surprise to him and he assured me that I would find Iranian people hospitable, whichever part of Iran I travelled to. However, I might encounter some hostility in Qom from some of the more 'religiously conservative people' (on account of my being a Sunni Muslim), and this is why he had initially asked whether I had been subject to any hostility. The words 'religiously conservative people' are mine. The exact words Ali used were, 'people of low culture'; a phrase he used several times before I stopped to ask him to what and whom he was referring. Some of the religious teachers and students of Qom were intolerant and bigoted towards outsiders, he said, before adding that they were a minority in Qom and Iran.

By the time we finished our conversation it was getting dark and I really needed to be on my way. The bus station was too far to walk to and so Ali ordered a taxi for me.

The bus to Esfahan was empty. I was its only passenger. I had had a long and exhausting day. I was tired, I hadn't eaten since morning and I desperately needed a shower. After finding a seat on the bus, I rummaged through my backpack, found one of my "emergency-only flapjacks," gobbled it up and then fell asleep.

We arrived in Esfahan in the early hours of the morning. The bus driver and his assistant had refused to take money from me when I boarded the bus. They took me to my destination and tracked down a taxi for me, and again refused to accept any money. It was only after much perseverance that they reluctantly accepted my fare. I thanked them, got into my taxi and asked the driver to take me to my hotel.

I moved from a four-star hotel to a two-star hotel. They only charged four dollars a night (down from the forty dollars a night I paid at my last hotel). What an amazingly low price! I congratulated myself for my prudence in seeking out such a fantastically cheap deal. Then I saw my room. The bed was broken, creepy crawlies roamed around the floor, the washbasin looked like it hadn't been cleaned for forty years and when I turned on the tap a brown substance that was part solid, part liquid came out. A communal toilet adjoined my room. I paid it a visit. Even before I opened the toilet door the intoxicating smell of stale urine swirled around my nostrils. The toilet, or what remained of it, had its seat removed and there was faeces stuck to the basin. I changed my mind about using it, returned to my room, quietly got out my sleeping bag, placed it on top of the bed, unzipped it, got into it, zipped it back up to the top and then fell asleep.

5. COCA-COLONISATION
(Esfahan)

And when we look in through the windows, all we see are shadows. And
when we try and listen, all we hear is a whispering. And we cannot understand the whispering, because our minds have been invaded by a war. A war
that we have won and lost. The very worst sort of war. A war that captures
dreams and re-dreams them. A war that has made us adore our conquerors
and despise ourselves.

The God of Small Things, Arundhati Roy

DURING THE SIXTEENTH century Esfahan was the jewel in the crown of the
Persian Empire. With both trade and the arts flourishing, the town experienced a renaissance that changed the face of the Islamic world. So important
had the city become during these times that people referred to it as *Esfahan
nesf-e jahan* (Esfahan is half the world).

Having spent the morning and afternoon of my first day in Esfahan
taking in its sights and sounds, I soon discovered why this great city was
once referred to as 'half the world'. Magnificent palaces, awe-inspiring
mosques, beautiful gardens, ancient bridges; the city is sprinkled with some
of the most breathtaking architecture in the whole of Iran. Esfahan is a truly
beautiful city. At the town's centre is the majestic Meidun-e Emam
Khomeini Square (the name was changed after the Revolution). Beautifully
laid out with gardens and water fountains and surrounded by some of the
best of Persian architecture, the aesthetic surroundings created a relaxed and
genteel feel. I was so taken in that I visited the square every day during my
stay in Esfahan.

On a lunch break one afternoon I visited an Internet café run by a
group of university graduates. One of the owners of the café was a woman
and I spoke to her briefly. Her position as co-owner of this modern establishment did not surprise me. I had been pleasantly surprised to see many
Iranian women in the public domain. From the moment I stepped on
Iranian soil (where I was dealt with by a female customs official), I had
witnessed Iranian women participating in all walks of life. In our short conversation I mentioned this observation to her. She agreed with me and
added that whilst things were not perfect, in many ways Iranian women

were much better off than women in many other Middle Eastern countries.

Before leaving for Iran, I read the book by the Nobel prizewinner V. S. Naipaul. Entitled, *Beyond Belief: Islamic Excursions among the Converted People,*[1] Naipaul documents his visit to Iran, Pakistan, Indonesia and Malaysia during the mid-nineties. The book in fact represents Naipaul's second trip to these countries. His first visit (undertaken shortly after the Iranian Revolution) was famously recorded in the now critically acclaimed (at least in Western literary circles), *Among the Believers: An Islamic Journey.*[2] I remember reading *Among the Believers* many years ago and being immensely annoyed at Naipaul's inability to observe his subjects through anything other than the spectacles of a Western imperialist (a trend that he continues in his second book). This pseudo-imperialist attitude towards the natives begins from the very first page of *Among the Believers* where, in describing his first meeting with his driver soon after arriving in Tehran, he says of him:

> He was in his late twenties, small and carefully dressed, handsome, with a well-barbered head of hair. I didn't like him. I saw him as a man of simple origins, simply educated, but with a great sneering pride, deferential but resentful, not liking himself for what he was doing. He was the kind of man who, without political doctrine, only with resentments, had made the Iranian revolution.[3]

I too made first impression comments about the impact the Iranian Revolution arguably had on the lives of Iranian taxi drivers (and maybe it was premature for me to make such remarks), but this is wholly different from undertaking a psychoanalytic assessment on a man one has just met. And there was I, thinking I had been too judgemental of the dodgy moustached taxi driver.

The Western literary establishment warmed to both books. *Among the Believers* stands out as a modern classic. Jason Cowley, writing for the *Times,* commented on his second book: "No other writer has his moral courage, his willingness to travel to find a subject, to listen and report, without prescription, the opinions of so called ordinary people . . . "[4]

'Without prescription', without prescription! The fact that a Western critic writing for a reputable and well-established newspaper believes the book is written 'without prescription' is deeply disturbing indeed.

Growing up in Britain in the eighties and nineties I was one of many British Asians/Muslims who felt let down by a generation of British-Asian and Anglo-Indian writers who, having gained a Western audience, used it to reinforce the negative and stereotypical images and perceptions that many who live in the West have of the third world. What is most saddening is that *Among the Believers* was published a few years after Edward Said's, *Orientalism*.[5] A landmark in modern critical literature, *Orientalism* will quite rightly go down as one of the most significant books of the latter part of the twentieth century. Said's most important work, it wonderfully elucidates the windows of partiality through which the West has studied and observed the East. The book has had a huge impact upon a number of the Western social sciences, especially those engaged in the study of Islam and Muslim societies, where there was a recognition that previous generations of Western writers and scholars had constructed a distorted image of Islamic societies. And yet when *Among the Believers* was published, Western critics appeared to suffer collective amnesia about what Said had said. For British Muslims such as myself, the warm response that Naipaul's two books received strongly suggests that the West has now entered a 'neo-Orientalist' stage in its history, where the world is still divided into a 'rational' West and an 'irrational' East. The events of 9/11 will no doubt cement this analogy because one of the side-effects of the tragedy is that it has created a climate where such discourses will be allowed to proliferate with increasing tolerance. Particularly distressing about Naipaul's books is that some of the pioneers of this neo-Orientalist tradition are people who originate (racially at least) from the 'other' or the 'third world'. The origins of the author can act to enhance the authenticity of the work and this in turn can act as a 'discourse of power' over and above anything he has written.

I mention Naipaul's work because in *Beyond Belief* he makes some rather controversial comments on Islam being an imperial ideology that seeks to eradicate the histories of its non-Arab followers and converts. In particular, he opens the book by commenting:

> Islam is in its origins an Arab religion. Everyone not an Arab who is a Muslim is a convert. Islam is not simply a matter of conscience or private belief. It makes imperial demands. A convert's worldview alters. His holy places are in Arab lands; his sacred language is Arabic. His idea of history alters. He rejects his own; he becomes, whether he likes it or not, a part of the Arab story. The convert has to turn away from everything that is his.[6]

It was these comments that were running through my mind one afternoon as I continued my tour of the city by visiting the old bazaar that surrounds the magnificent Jami Mosque. This ancient shopping precinct must be centuries old. When I first walked through the bazaar's crowded and narrow streets the place certainly felt strange, exotic and untouched by Western civilisation. I was wrong. I did not need to look too hard to discover how this most overtly anti-Western country was struggling and failing to repel the influences of Western culture. My simple search for a drink to quench my thirst established as much. In addition to Coca-Cola, Pepsi and other Western soft drinks that were on sale, there was a whole array of cheap Iranian imitations. For Pepsi-Cola there was Parsi-Cola. For Coca-Cola there was the very rude sounding Foca-Cola. And for Fanta lovers there was the even ruder sounding Foca-Fanna. I opted to buy something called Coffee Cola, which oddly enough tasted nothing like coffee or cola but exactly like 7-UP. It wasn't simply in the soft drink industry that the West had achieved market penetration. Its imperial tentacles were able to touch many aspects of Iranian popular culture: drinks, food, clothing, fashion, motor vehicles, music, language—the list was endless. As I mentioned in an earlier chapter, with so many of these Western products and their Iranian imitations, one is not simply purchasing the product *per se*; there is a partic-ular sub-culture of the Western lifestyle that is being sold along with it and it is often this lifestyle that the Iranian consumer really wishes to purchase.

When the religious elite took over the country, strident measures were taken to ensure that the population was not exposed to what they consid-ered to be undesirable Western influences. Therefore, the vessels through which Western culture was transmitted were banned. Everything from Western satellite stations such as CNN and MTV to Western fast food restaurants such as McDonalds and Burger King were banned. Yet the aya-tollahs had overlooked the fact that there exists a whole array of other sources that subtly and discreetly transmit facets of Western culture. Why is it that a pair of Western designer jeans is so popular that counterfeit ver-sions of the product are being sold by the truckload? To your average teenage Esfahanian, is there something that is appealing in a pair of Versace jeans other than the quality or cut of the fabric? Yes, the fact that it is from the West makes it more appealing. Western culture is blocked from being transmitted to Iran via channels such as MTV, but it still makes its way into the mindset of the country's youth through a piece of denim. The advent of the Internet means that no state will be able to create a filtration system that effectively blocks out influences from other countries.

So what does all this have to do with Naipaul's comment that Islam is an imperial ideology? Well, what Naipaul failed to observe on his visit to Iran was how that other imperial ideology, the one that originates from the West, is also slowly eradicating the culture and history of countries such as Iran. The ancient bazaar that I walked through may look and feel very Iranian, but even remote and isolated societies such as these are slowly succumbing to the influences of Western cultural colonialism (I was astonished at the number of shops and stalls under the shadow of the Jami Mosque selling Liverpool and Manchester United football tops). These market places are not simply a barometer of how the Iranian soft drink market is gradually becoming monopolised by fizzy drinks from the West. They are also useful in gauging the increasing number of consumer products and services that are being Westernised. There may be no McDonalds or Burger King in Esfahan, but those cold fizzy drinks I seem to be obsessed with are now being sold in an increasing number of Western-style fast food outlets. There was one such joint near my hotel which sold burgers, hotdogs and pizzas. I visited the place several times and on each occasion had a long wait. People aren't drawn to these places simply in order to satisfy their hunger. I'm afraid the ayatollahs of Iran have not even begun to eradicate the sources through which Western culture is being both transmitted and consumed.

I spent that afternoon in the courtyard of the breathtakingly beautiful Jami Mosque thinking about this subject. Whilst trying to formulate my thoughts, two of Andy Warhol's famous paintings kept coming to mind. The first was his simple painting of a tin of Campbell's soup. As time goes by, that rather strange and seemingly pointless painting makes increasingly more sense. Consumerism is homogenising the world's cultures in more ways than even Warhol could have imagined. The second was his painting of several dozen bottles of Coca-Cola. I kept imagining this picture becoming larger and larger as the number of Coke bottles multiplied endlessly.

Naipaul's comment about Islam attempting to dismiss and eradicate the histories of the 'converted people' is deeply flawed. Firstly, it ignores the fact that many Iranians are aware and very proud of other aspects of their non-Islamic identity, such as their Persian heritage. The Persian civilisation predates the coming of Islam to Iran by several thousand years. From my short stay in the country, it was apparent to me that Iran's Persian heritage, far from being eradicated by Islam, still appeared to form a very important component of the average Iranian's ethnic identity. Secondly (and most importantly), Naipaul ignores the extent to which the culture of the so-called Arab religion of Islam grows as it permeates non-Arab societies. The relationship is not one-way and is much more complex than Naipaul's simplistic and rather primitive analysis allows. The Persian influence on Islamic architecture is one example. This non-Arab people transformed and influenced a central part of Islamic culture, the architecture of its holy place of worship, the mosque. In fact, Dr Umar Faruq Abdallah's detailed research into the history of Islamic societies draws an almost opposite conclusion. He argues that it was the ability of Islam's universal norms to harmonise themselves with indigenous forms of cultural expression that allowed the religion to grow and flourish in its own unique and distinct way in so many different parts of the world;

> In China, Islam looked Chinese; in Mali, it looked African. Sustained cultural relevance to distinct peoples, diverse places, and different times underlay Islam's long success as a global civilization. The religion became not only functional and familiar at the local level but dynamically engaging, fostering stable indigenous Muslim identities and allowing Muslims to put down deep roots and make lasting contributions wherever they went.[7]

Finally, Naipaul's comment about Islam's purported imperial ambitions can be applied equally to all imperial ideologies, religious or secular. Can the same not be said of Christianity's influence as it spread through pagan Europe? Christian Europeans altered their calendar so that it began (supposedly) from the birth of Jesus. In doing so, have they not also readjusted their own history and dismissed what came before it? Does a European Christian's view of the world not change upon conversion? Are there not also European Christian holy places in or near the Arab lands? Do a European Christian's conversion and the conversion of his society not mean that he also has become part of the remarkable story of a Jew from Jerusalem? All imperial ideologies demand that their culture be regarded as superior to that of the conquered natives (is that not true of ancient Rome or imperial Britain?). As I said, the qualities that Naipaul ascribes to imperial Islam can be applied equally to all imperial ideologies; including the one Naipaul seems to judge his subjects by.

That evening I decided to go to the cinema to watch an Iranian film. Iranian cinema is developing a reputation for making good films and I was eager to see what all the fuss was about.

I was hoping to watch something moving, challenging, something inspiring. Unfortunately, what I got was an Iranian version of *Lethal Weapon*, with a good-looking young cop and an older, more experienced, senior cop (who wasn't black, although he did have a dodgy moustache). From what I understood of the film, it started off with what looked like an important meeting between a woman and two men. Soon after the meeting, one of the two men is shot by some gangsters. This shooting immensely upset the female character who then called upon Iran's answer to Starsky and Hutch to track down the killers. After a lot of hoo-ha the officers finally manage to track down the killers who, in a strange twist to the story, appear to be related to the female character. The end. And the Oscar for best original screenplay goes to . . . !

6. PURPLE RAIN WHERE THE STREETS HAVE NO NAME
(Esfahan)

Every gun that is made, every warship launched, every rocket fired signifies in the final sense, a theft from those who hunger and are not fed, those who are cold and are not clothed. This world in arms is not spending money alone. It is spending the sweat of its labourers, the genius of its scientists, the hopes of its children. This is not a way of life at all in any true sense. Under the clouds of war, it is humanity hanging on a cross of iron.

Dwight Eisenhower

THE YEAR AFTER Khomeini came to power his country was plunged into a war with Saddam Hussein's Iraq that would last the best part of a decade. In the poignant words of one Western observer;

In 1980 one of the longest, bloodiest and most pointless wars in modern history began. The Iran-Iraq War lasted eight years, cost a million lives, sucked in neighbouring countries as well as the United States, led to Washington's dubious embrace of Saddam Hussein, spawned the Iran-Contra scandal, and saw the first serious use of chemical weapons in battle since World War I. When it was all over, essentially nothing had changed. The border between the two countries remained where it had been. Saddam was still in power in Baghdad, the Ayatollah Khomeini in Tehran.[1]

A major side effect of the war was that it severely disrupted Khomeini's blueprint for an Islamic state. He died a year after the war ended. The war had occupied almost all of his tenure as head of state. During his reign the country's resources and manpower went into fighting the Iraqi army. Because of this, it is almost impossible to properly assess his legacy. Had it not been for the war we might have been able to make a better assessment of his Islamic experiment. In the end, the baton was passed over to his disciples who, to this day, have a major influence on how the affairs of the country are run.

The factors that led to the outbreak of war provide a good example of some of the underlying tensions that exist amongst Iran and its Arab neighbours. Officially, the war began on 22 September 1980 with an Iraqi land

and air invasion of western Iran. The official reason Saddam Hussein cited for his country's act of aggression was that Iran had reneged on its promise to renegotiate the 1975 treaty on the Shatt al-Arab waterway, a strategically important waterway that forms part of the boundary between the two countries. Saddam just wanted to reclaim what was his. This interpretation of the treaty came as a slight surprise to the Iranians as they had been under the assumption that the 1975 agreement was a permanent and final resolution to the ongoing border dispute that had plagued relations between the two countries for many years.

Unofficially, there exist countless theories and counter-theories as to why Saddam and Khomeini went to war and why the war lasted as long as it did.

One aspect of the conflict was that it played up old Sunni/Shiite tensions. Khomeini came to power on a hard-line Shiite platform that had an evangelical element to it. He didn't want his revolutionary ideas to remain confined to Iran; he had hoped they would have a domino effect on surrounding Muslim countries (and this is why the United States was so concerned). Its neighbour Iraq had a delicate Sunni/Shiite balance, which both Saddam (who was of Sunni origin) and Khomeini were only too acutely aware of. The Baathist party spent many of its early years in office violently repressing their Iraqi Shiite opponents. Before the war, Khomeini lived in exile in Iraq; he was expelled in 1977. Soon after Khomeini came to power, the Iranian supported al-Dawah organisation was alleged to have made (failed) assassination attempts on Iraq's foreign minister and on its minister of culture and information. Rumour had it that Khomeini's government was assisting in the destabilisation of Saddam's regime.[2] Saddam was the head of a Marxist party and it was this type of heretical godless ideology that stood in opposition to everything Khomeini believed in. It was also this same heretical godless party that he had witnessed firsthand when they ruthlessly repressed his Shiite brethren.

Not only was Saddam a Sunni, he was also a keen supporter of the pan-Arab movement that came into fashion during the twentieth century, at a time when many of the Arab countries were gaining independence from their colonial rulers. A Middle Eastern movement based on uniting people of Arab origin would have given Saddam an opportunity to increase his influence in the region and stake his claim as one of the premier leaders of the Arab world (militarily, Iraq was fast becoming a major player in the region). A pan-Arab movement would also have the effect of sidelining Persian Iran.

Saddam's fixation on securing Iraqi income from oil may also have proved to be an important factor in starting an offensive against Iran. The

Shatt al-Arab waterway was very near Iran's oil-rich region of Khuzestan. It was thus no surprise that when the Iraqi invasion began, Saddam's army took an immediate liking to this particular area.

Saddam made sure that he attacked Iran when it was at its weakest. Iran had just gone through a revolution and had yet to fully stabilise. Shortly after coming into power, the new Iranian regime had begun executing leading members of the Iranian army in order to avoid the possibility of any military coups. This left a lacuna in the top ranks of the army. The ayatollahs, Saddam assumed, would be inexperienced in conducting modern military warfare. Furthermore, much of Iran's military hardware was US manufactured (inherited from the Shah's regime). Iranian relations with this ally had been severed and Saddam had calculated that the country would not be in a position to order much-needed spare parts for some of their military components. The timing of Saddam's invasion could not have been better.

Yet Saddam had greatly underestimated Khomeini's ability to rally his own people against the evil invader. So powerful and effective was his war cry that the ranks of the Iranian army soon swelled with men and boys from the breadth and depth of the country.

After Iraq initially made some inroads into the country, Iran slowly began to repel the Iraqi army back into Iraq. Fighting on the front lines was fierce and there was great loss of life, but by early 1982 Iran had successfully expunged the offending Iraqi troops from its borders. The war could have ended there, but Khomeini chose to go on the offensive and verge into Iraq to topple Saddam's regime, a decision that prolonged the war by six years. Saddam was now on the defensive. He had made a gross miscalculation (a pattern that he would repeat in later life). Now his regime was under threat. The roles had been reversed. To the Tehran government, it was the Baghdad regime that appeared weak and unstable (with its disaffected Shiites and Kurds). Khomeini sent his troops into Iraq confident that they would topple Saddam and, for a time, it seemed as if Saddam's regime was seriously under threat. But the Iranians didn't succeed. Saddam responded—by ordering the use of chemical weapons against the advancing Iranian soldiers. Jim Garamone in his article, "Iraq and the Use of Chemical Weapons" asserts that there were ten documented occasions in which the Iraqi military resorted to chemical agents.[3] When the war ended in 1988 and the Kurds started showing dissatisfaction at Saddam's rule, amongst other atrocities, he ordered his military to shower the Kurdish town of Halabja with mustard gas and sarin. The effects were devastating. The loss of human life ran into the thousands. Innocent men, women and children going about their everyday lives died what must have been excruciating deaths. The world sat back and watched as the human race plummeted to new depths of cruelty.

Iran wasn't a completely innocent party in this war either. Some of its tactics were likewise questionable. As the war dragged on, the body count began to rise for both sides. Yet both nations refused to back down and the fighting continued as fiercely as ever. Iran increasingly began to recruit young boys, many of them well short of their teenage years. These young children were thrown onto the battlefield of war and pitted against men, and men with fighting experience. But, in many ways, these boys were the most committed to the war effort; the seductive appeal of martyrdom is most potent on the young.

But actually, it is wrong to say that the outside world just sat back and watched; knowing what was going on, they competed to provide the arms that allowed these two nations to fight out a protracted anything-goes war. As Stephen Shalom comments:

> Khomeini had no qualms about sending his followers, including young boys, off to their deaths for his greater glory. This callous disregard for human life was no less characteristic of Saddam Hussein. And, for that matter, it was no less characteristic of much of the world community, which not only couldn't be bothered by a few hundred thousand Third World corpses, but tried to profit from the conflict.[4]

According to Mansour Farhang, at least ten nations sold arms to both sides (including the United States).[5] Iran's major suppliers were Syria, Libya, North Korea and China. The former Soviet Union, France and a number of Arab countries assisted Iraq in its war effort.

The position of Israel in this war is interesting. It was enemies with both countries. Yet its government made the incredible decision of agreeing to supply arms to Iran. The extent of Israel's involvement has always been unclear, especially after the "Report of the Congressional Committees Investigating the Iran-Contra Affair" issued in November 1987, which revealed that the United States was also using Israel as an intermediary to sell arms to Iran.[6] One investigation by the British *Observer* newspaper estimated that during the course of the war Israel's arms sales to Iran totalled five hundred million dollars annually.[7] The fact that the Iranian regime chose to accept arms from a nation it despised and had been hell-bent on destroying (through the funding of militant groups) indicates how desperate (or 'committed', depending on which way it is interpreted) it had become in its desire to defeat Saddam. That in itself was remarkable, but what was even more remarkable was the fact that Israel chose to supply arms to one of its fiercest enemies. A country that sought its destruction! Or was it so remarkable? Khomeini's march on Baghdad wasn't quite going according to plan. Both countries became entrenched in a drawn-out and protracted war of attrition. Neither side was willing to give up. As fighting dragged on without an end in sight, the economic and military prowess of these two mighty regional powers deteriorated and finally crumbled. This came in addition to the social costs of the enormous loss of human life. It certainly wasn't in Israel's interests to see a quick victor in this regional battle of the giants. It was in Israel's interests to see two of its most powerful enemies slowly bleed to death in a prolonged war. The longer it lasted the better it was because at the war's conclusion, both countries would be weaker and this ensured that Israel's continued military dominance in the region would not be threatened. Supplying arms was an intelligent and expedient way for Israel to ensure that the fighting would drag out just that little bit longer.

The position of the United States in this war is even more interesting. At the time of the Iraqi invasion, the superpower did not have diplomatic relations with either country. Relations with Iraq had been terminated since the time of the 1967 Arab-Israeli War. Relations with Iran were terminated shortly after the ayatollahs came into power in 1979. Officially, the Iraqi invasion provoked little response from the leader of the free world. Officially, Washington did not appear at all flustered by this act of international aggression (unofficially, there were rumours that Washington had given the green light to the invasion). As one State Department official eloquently summed up, "we don't give a damn as long as the Iran-Iraq carnage does not affect our allies in the region or alter the balance of power."[8] Two decades later, in the build up to the second Gulf War, the US administration went into overdrive telling a sceptical world that one proof of Saddam's evil was his invasion of his neighbours. It is almost as if the US government's moral conscience had a time delay mechanism.

During the early stages of the war, the official American position could best be described as one of 'relative neutrality'. Its ambivalence towards the two warring parties changed when Iranian forces expunged the Iraqi invaders from its soil, ventured onto Arab land and made a march towards Baghdad. At that point, the Iranian Revolution was seen to have a negative impact upon American interests in the Middle East. Under the rule of the Shah, Iran was their greatest ally in the region. Under the rule of the ayatollahs, Iran became their greatest enemy in the region. It was one thing for Iraq to invade Iran, but quite another for Iran to invade Iraq; that was a wholly different matter. An Iraqi victory over Iran was tolerable. It would result in a weakened Persian nation and this was definitely in American interests because whilst there would be an alteration in the balance of power in the region, it would be one that favoured American interests. But for Iran to be victorious against Iraq, a neighbour that had a significant and disaffected Shiite population; well, the consequences of an Iranian victory and a resulting Khomeini-influenced Iraqi regime did not bear thinking about. The United States changed its policy stance from one of relative neutrality to one that was pro-Iraqi, pro-Saddam.

In December of 1983, the Reagan administration dispatched a high level delegation to meet with Saddam's government (a delegation that included one Donald Rumsfeld). It proved successful. On 1 January 1984, the *Washington Post* wrote that the United States, "in a shift in policy, has informed friendly Persian Gulf nations that the defeat of Iraq in the 3 year-old-war with Iran would be 'contrary to U.S. interests' and has made several moves to prevent this result". In March of 1984, another US delegation was sent to clarify what 'moves' the United States could take to avoid an Iraqi defeat (again, Donald Rumsfeld was part of this delegation). By coincidence, it was around this time that news began to seep out about the Iraqis using chemical weapons against Iranian soldiers. On 5 March 1984, several days before that US delegation arrived in Baghdad, a US State Department report investigating these rumours concluded, "available evidence indicates that Iraq has used lethal chemical weapons".[9] Whilst the US delegation was actually in Baghdad, the UN published its own report on the allegations, concluding, "Mustard gas laced with a nerve agent has been used on Iranian soldiers . . ."[10] The US administration, armed with the knowledge that Saddam was using chemical weapons, still saw fit to arm Saddam for the remainder of the war. And arm him they did, supplying him with some of their best weaponry and military hardware, providing him vital intelligence information (such as Iranian troop positions picked up by US satellites) and urging other nations to adopt a similar pro-Iraqi, anti-Iranian stance.

If we fast-forward to the present, there has clearly been a material change in American attitude towards Saddam's conduct in the Iran-Iraq War on two fronts. Firstly, in respect to Saddam's invasion of Iran and secondly, in respect to Saddam's use of chemical weapons in the Iran-Iraq War. On the first issue, when Saddam invaded Iran in 1980 and started the Iran-Iraq War, the United States' response was not to condemn Saddam, not to tell the whole world what an evil man he was for invading Iran, not even to ask the world community to take some sort of action against this act of international aggression. On the contrary, the United States' response to a war that Saddam started was to help him, by providing him with all manner of military hardware and intelligence information and urging other nations to refrain from assisting the Iranians (even though the Americans themselves were secretly selling arms to Iran). Iran sought regime change in Iraq, but the United States not only opposed regime change, they did their best to ensure Saddam was not toppled from power. Two decades later, in the build-up to the second Gulf War, when it was the United States who sought the regime change of Saddam's government, Iraq's invasion of Iran was included in the propaganda portfolio constructed by the US administration and used to convince the world how evil Saddam was ("this is a man who invades his neighbours" the US administration told the world). There has been a dramatic reinterpretation of Iraq's invasion of Iran and the subsequent war that followed. The invasion that was not considered evil in 1980, became evil (or indicative of an evil man) in 2003.

There has been a similar readjustment in attitude towards the use of chemical weapons by Saddam in the Iran-Iraq War. Whilst the war was in progress, the United States was aware that Saddam had chemical weapons and they were aware that he had used them in the conflict. Knowing this, they still saw fit to supply him with more of these weapons of mass destruction.[11] However, in the build-up to the second Gulf War, sitting neatly alongside Iraq's invasion of Iran in the US propaganda portfolio, was Saddam's use of chemical weapons in the Iran-Iraq War. Again, at the time, Saddam's use of chemical weapons on Iranian soldiers in the Iran-Iraq War was not considered by the United States to be so evil that Saddam should be reeled in and held to account for his deadly deeds. The use of chemical weapons on Iranian soldiers was insignificant, or certainly not sufficient reason to prevent the US arming of Saddam's forces. By 2003 though, the use of chemical weapons in that conflict had become sufficiently significant, and was added to a growing list of factors that went to show what an evil tyrant he was and why he must be removed.

I could write at length about the morally abhorrent US foreign policy, happy to aid a regime it knew had used chemical weapons, about the blatant hypocrisy of an American foreign policy that at one period in its history finds no fault with Saddam's escapade into a neighbouring land and just two decades later not only re-moralises that invasion, but also miraculously discovers its moral conscience over atrocities Saddam has committed against his own people, both before and after the invasion of Iran. The gassing of the Kurds in 1988 and the brutal suppression of the Shiites in southern Iraq after their uprising at the conclusion of the first Gulf War suddenly gained a greater profile in the build-up to the second Gulf War. But these are not isolated incidents; the Baathist regime had been violently repressing these minorities and other dissenters throughout the seventies. The United States was aware of this when they armed Saddam in the eighties, but they didn't care, or they didn't care enough to prevent themselves from supporting his regime. Either this or they suffered from some sort of moral amnesia, which was, curiously enough, cured by Iraq's invasion of oil-rich Kuwait at the beginning of the nineties.

If the United States' support of Saddam wasn't deplorable enough, in 1986 the Iran-Contra affair blew up. After warning the world not to help Iran in this awful war, the Reagan administration secretly agreed to sell arms to Iran. Not only this, but in order to prevent a leftist insurgency in the upper echelons of the Iranian government, the United States also provided Tehran with intelligence information warning the ruling regime of threats from the left. On the issue of arms, in return for the illegal shipment of missiles to Iran the United States paid for the release of American hostages held by Iranian-backed terrorist groups in Lebanon. To complicate matters even further, since the dodgy proceeds of the arms shipments could not go directly into US coffers, they were instead redirected to Contra rebels fighting in Nicaragua. So in addition to violating their public stance on Iran, the US administration also violated its public stance on not dealing with terrorists, and violated the Boland Amendment passed by the US Congress (it placed severe restrictions on funding the Contras). When the details of the Iran-Contra affair became public knowledge, Reagan justified his administration's secret ties with Iran on the basis that they were trying to, "find an avenue to get Iran back where it once was and that is in the family of democratic nations".[12] This was a rather odd statement to make, since pre-revolution Iran could hardly be described as democratic. Mr Reagan wasn't completely wrong. It is true that Iran was once part of the family of democratic nations, but it ceased being part of this family in 1953, when the CIA assisted the Shah in overthrowing the democratically-elected Prime Minister Mohammad Mossadeq. Prime Minister Mossadeq had the audacity to anger the British and Americans by placing the interests of his people before that of the West, when he nationalised the oil industry and took control of it from Western companies.[13]

Stephen Shalom's summary of the United States' involvement in this war is perfect; he comments:

> The Iran-Iraq War was not a conflict between good and evil. But though both regimes were repugnant, it was the people of the two countries who served as the cannon fodder, and thus ending the war as soon as possible was

a humane imperative. Instead of lending its good offices to mediation efforts and diplomacy ... Washington manoeuvred for advantage, trying to gain vis-à-vis the Soviet Union and to undercut the left. The United States provided intelligence information, bogus and real, to both sides, provided arms to one side, funded paramilitary exile groups, sought military bases, and sent in the U.S. Navy—and all the while Iranians and Iraqis died.[14]

The reality is that the enormous oil reserves in the Middle East have meant that the United States must maintain friendly relations with as many oil-rich Arab nations as possible. As the oil crisis of the seventies revealed, without a continuous supply of cheap oil, the economies of the industrialised Western nations suffer enormously (especially in the case of the United States, the largest consumer of oil). One of the difficulties the United States has in developing friendly ties with oil-rich Arab nations is that the values and ideals that the United States hold dear and promote are miles apart from the values and ideals of the ruling Arab regimes. Practices that the United States ought to find morally objectionable are deeply entrenched in every oil-producing Arab state (the lack of democratic institutions, limits on the freedom of expression, the treatment of citizens who violate the limits set on freedom of expression, etc.). Not only do the ruling Arab regimes fail to measure up to America's political ideal of a secular liberal democratic state, but also, historically, many of the opponents of the ruling Arab regimes (if they haven't already been wiped out or suppressed by Arab rulers), have likewise also failed to hold dear the political values the United States considers sacrosanct. Most opponents are either Islamist, leftist or monarchist groups or organisations. All this has meant that in this most strategically important of places, the United States has had to develop relations with regimes it is, ideologically at least, in conflict with, or more accurately, ought to be in conflict with.

To complicate matters even further for US policymakers, the most oil-rich region in the world also happens to be one of the most volatile and unstable (as the last fifty years have shown); ruling regimes face challenges from within (as with the Shah of Iran) and/or from neighbouring regimes (as Iran and Kuwait faced from Saddam's Iraq). These conflicts often affect the geopolitical map of the region. The United States has historically sought to intervene in these conflicts, thereby changing or influencing the geopolitical map of the region. Herein lies the root problem: How to develop a foreign policy in this strategically important, but volatile region of the world, when nearly all the inter-state and intra-state conflicts take place between nations or groups that espouse ideologies that are vastly different from one's own. This ideological hurdle has not been nearly as difficult for US policymakers to overcome as it ought to have been. In such conflicts, US administrations have almost always tended to side with the group or nation that they consider best promotes/preserves their interests in the region. On one level such a stance is hardly controversial. World and regional superpowers have, since *time immemorial*, formulated policy that ensured the protection of their strategic interests. But in the modern world it is one thing for the leader of the democratic free world to develop a foreign policy framework that is heavily biased in support of regimes/groups that are sympathetic to US interests. It is a wholly different matter to support such regimes/groups when they grossly violate the political and human rights doctrines of the democratic free world. But to do all this, and then attempt to justify this self-serving intervention with a moral pretext, is to risk alienating the population of the region. That is, to argue that such intervention is necessary to eliminate the evil that the opposing regime/group poses, whilst at the same time overlooking the evils committed by the regime/group that one supports, will lead sections of the Arab/Muslim world to view (with some justification) the intervention as oppressive, exploitative and smacking of double standards. And if the regime/group that is aided by the United States is viewed by the individual Arab/Muslim as evil and oppressive, then it is not unusual that those who aid such regimes (i.e., the United States) will come to be viewed in similar terms.

An example would be the following; if Khomeini's rule and the Shah's rule were marked according to the political ideals the United States sees as sacrosanct, both regimes would fail, since neither regime was or is fully democratic (in the American sense) and both committed gross human rights violations. Therefore, to use political morality or political ethics as a barometer to judge which regime the United States ought to side with is futile; according to US standards both regimes fail miserably. In this oil-rich region what factor is then used by the United States to decide which regime to side with? Simple, which regime best promotes/preserves US interests? In this example, US interests quite clearly lay with the Shah and not with the disgruntled Islamic and leftist groups of pre-revolution Iran. Political morality or political ethics has nothing to do with it. Khomeini's regime failed America's politico-ethics exam and he was demonized for it. The Shah's regime would have also failed America's politico-ethics test, but it was supported with political, economic and military aid and his undemocratic regime's human rights abuses did not get the same scrutiny, nor were they given the same publicity.

The same test can be applied to the Iran-Iraq War. Once again, it is futile to use political morality or political ethics as a barometer to judge which regime the United States ought to side with. Seen through US spectacles, both regimes fail miserably. The United States supported Saddam in the eighties not for any moral or ethical reason, but because it was in their national interests to do so. An Iranian victory would have harmed US power and influence in this oil-rich region. And yet the United States sought to publicly justify their support of Saddam by framing the conflict in moral terms, in that the Iranian regime had to be defeated because it was evil. What was not considered evil (or evil enough) was Saddam's invasion of Iran, his use of chemical weapons or the ill treatment of many of his own citizens. Well, it wasn't considered evil until he invaded the undemocratic but US-friendly Kuwait (a.k.a. the country that holds ten percent of the world's oil reserves and borders another undemocratic but US-friendly and militarily weak country that holds twenty percent of the world's oil reserves). Suddenly, Saddam, the secular Arab leader who sought to crush the cancer of Islamic fundamentalism in the region, had metamorphosed into an evil dictator who had invaded a neighbouring oil-rich country for his own selfish purposes. Funny that, isn't it? Because back in 1980 Saddam did exactly this. I am reminded of the following line from the REM song, *Losing my Religion*: "... every waking hour, I am choosing my confessions".

One morning I decided to visit Golestan-e Shohada, the cemetery for those who died in the Iran-Iraq War. It was unlikely that it would provide me with answers to some of the questions about the war that were swirling around in my head, nevertheless, I felt I had to go. I left early in the morning. The cemetery was some distance from my hotel and I needed to catch a taxi to get there.

After arriving at my destination, I paid the taxi driver (who was slightly bemused that a Western tourist should wish to visit such a place) and entered the cemetery.

It is very difficult to describe how I felt about what I saw. What I do know was that this visit would prove to be the most difficult episode of my travels so far. The cemetery greeted me with row upon row upon row of identically-styled graves, each supplanted with a photograph of the deceased. I had never seen a graveyard like it before. In the cold silence of the morning, the vision was surreal. This pattern of placing a photograph of the deceased on top of each of those thousands of graves brought home the enormity of what happened in those years between 1980 and 1988.

I slowly walked around the cemetery, body and mind completely numb as I looked more carefully at some of the photographs of the people who had given their lives for their country. There were pictures of men, young boys and even women. Some of the boys looked no more than ten years old. Most distressing were the family portraits of deceased fathers together with their young children (probably taken just before they set off for war). Time and the elements were slowly draining away the colour from these photographs—it was as if these images harkened back to some distant time, more distant than the nearly two decades that had passed since the end of the war. Many of these small children would now be adults. It is only in their untold stories that the true cost of the war can be measured. Some of the graves had photographs of two people placed on them. I assumed they would have been siblings who had been buried together.

Given the outside world's participation in this conflict, it wasn't just Iranians and Iraqis who died in that war, a part of humanity died along with them.

I wanted to speak to somebody about the war. Nearby, I saw a gardener sweeping. I approached him. He did not speak English but did direct me to a school that adjoined the cemetery, where I was sure to find someone who spoke English. I entered the school and made my way through the heavily painted corridors until I came to an office. I knocked on the door and just walked in. This was crazy, I thought to myself, walking uninvited into a school in a foreign land. Fortunately, I was greeted by a pleasant old man. He spoke little English, but he did say he would talk to the school's English teacher and ask if he would be willing to speak to me. I stood outside his office as he walked off to find this English teacher. A small boy was pinned against one of the corridor walls. A teacher had him by his ear and was giving him a telling off. His crime I did not know, but that he had been a naughty boy, that much I did know. The scene brought a wry smile to my face as I recalled similar memories from attending the mosque as a child. The English teacher arrived. He was in his mid-thirties, wore glasses and was smartly dressed with a short, well-kept beard. He said he would be glad to speak to me and answer any questions that I had, if I could only wait until lunchtime, as he had a number of classes to teach before then. I agreed and headed off towards the town centre to waste some time by having a drink at a juice bar.

When I returned to the school at the agreed time he took me on a tour of the cemetery, explaining along the way the significance of some graves over others. The cemetery, it seemed, had the martyrs from the war, along with some very important religious figures. I wanted to ask him so many questions. "How did he believe the war started?" "Why did he think it had started?" "Was he 'for' the war?" "Did he fight in the war?" He refused to answer any of my questions. I persisted with my cross-examination until I detected growing signs of impatience in his voice.

Then, as if by accident, he let slip that many of his friends had fought and died in the war. He asked whether I wanted to see their graves. I nodded, not at all sure what the proper response to such an invitation was. He took me to the burial place of a childhood friend. Pointing to the grave he said that his friend was a good man. They had shared many happy memories growing up together in the same neighbourhood. When war broke out many young Iranian men in their area were conscripted to the army. When they called his friend up, he left behind his family, his education, his childhood, and went to fight on the front line—like the true patriot that he was. He was eighteen-years old when he fell. He died fighting for his country. His friend had given his life for his people. At this he broke down. I stood next to him in silence, feeling stupid and guilty for being so intrusive. I asked no further questions about the war.

He asked me who I was, where I came from and why I was here. This was much more comfortable terrain for him and so I obliged by answering his questions. Having provided a résumé of my background and career, I cautiously set about asking him about his profile, this time trying not to offend or irritate him. He told me that he had graduated from university with a degree in agricultural studies. Unable to find a job in his chosen field, he decided to take up teaching. He had been doing this for six years now. He asked me what I thought of Iran so far. I told him that I was really enjoying it, that everyone I had met had been hospitable and kind. He looked at me curiously as if to doubt what I was saying. There were some bad people in Iran he told me. I had to be careful. Many Iranians were Muslim only in name, not in their behaviour. I got the impression that this teacher was 'pro-regime'. He appeared to be one of the few people that I had met in Iran who fully believed in the ideals of the regime. The fact that some of his fellow countrymen could not live up to the high expectations set by their state seemed to appall him.

He advised me to be wary and always on my guard. I told him that I would. We ended on good terms. He flagged down a taxi and asked the driver to take me back to the town centre. Against my will and protestations, he paid for my fare.

That afternoon I revisited Imam Khomeini Square where I met a young man by the name of Mohammed. He was twenty-four years old, an electrical engineer and married to a doctor. Mohammed agreed to speak to me about his experiences of the war. I began by asking him questions about why he thought the war started. He replied by saying that he did not know. Mohammed was equally vague when I asked him about the merits of the war. This was getting frustrating; either he was genuine in his ignorance or, for whatever reason he was reluctant to talk openly about what he really thought about the war. What Mohammed was able to say was that his father had fought and died in the war; he was still only a child when his father was killed. Not surprisingly, the tragic event changed his life. Not only had he been robbed of a father figure, but the family had also lost its only breadwinner. He endured much hardship as he witnessed his mother struggling to raise the family. Fortunately, he came from a large extended family and they received help from his uncles during this difficult period in their lives. I pointed out to him that given his uncertain childhood, he had done very well to go to university and qualify as an engineer. He said that he had been very lucky. I found his humility reassuring.

He was less restrained in his comments when I asked him about the regime. On the whole, he was happy with the direction of the government. He came from a poor background and the state had helped him by giving him a scholarship that allowed him to progress on to a professional career. He was grateful for this help. He did wish to see more reforms and a further withering away of the enormous body of laws created since 1979. He was confident that this would eventually happen. 'Evolution not revolution' was what Iranians wanted he told me . . . in a round-about way.

Later on in the day I re-visited the Internet café I had been to earlier in the week and again bumped into the same woman that I had spoken to briefly on my previous visit. On this occasion we spoke for some time. We discussed the difficulties Iranian graduates faced in securing well-paid and rewarding careers. She confirmed what I had already begun to suspect, that Iran, to its credit, had a very good higher education system. Too good it seemed. Every year the graduates it produced greatly outnumbered the limited number of well-paid positions available in the workforce. This problem had existed for some years and was increasingly frustrating for young and highly-educated people; as her case so clearly illustrated. It was easy to sympathise with her story as she went into detail about the sacrifices that she had made in order to get a good education. She had graduated as a computer engineer but now found herself in a position where there simply wasn't demand for the skills she had gained.

It was her lack of success in finding gainful employment that led her to open this Internet café (along with several of her friends who found themselves in similar predicaments). I asked her whether anybody was to blame for the lack of decent opportunities for graduates. It came as no surprise to me when she pointed a finger at the government. In her opinion, many young graduates such as herself felt the government had failed to invest properly in the economy and in industry, in order to stimulate the kind of economic growth that would result in the need for an increased number of highly-skilled people. People were becoming apathetic. Most graduates now wished to move abroad to North America or Europe to seek employment. That was what she wanted to do. She wanted to leave the country because she felt that her talents were not being properly utilised in Iran.

7. MARTYRS BLOOD STAINS THE STAIRWAY TO HEAVEN
(Esfahan-Shiraz)

THE JOURNEY FROM Esfahan to the southern Iranian city of Shiraz is long and tedious. Our coach left Esfahan bus station in the late morning and did not arrive in Shiraz until late evening.

Halfway through the journey we stopped at a service station for about an hour. Word got out that our coach had a passenger on board from "England". Suddenly, I was being treated like a minor celebrity, or a freak, depending on which way you looked at it. A number of people came over to me, none of whom could speak English, and started to shout, "England ... England!" "Yes England", I replied, nodding my head. "Michael Owen", "David Beckham", they all shouted next. All together. All in verse. "Yes Michael Owen", "yes David Beckham", I shouted back. My responses delighted them no end and they continued with this primitive form of conversation, naming as many English footballers as they could. One individual in the small crowd went away and returned a few moments later with an Iranian newspaper. The back page contained a photograph from what must have been Manchester United's last game. Pointing to the United players in the photograph, he began reciting their names to me. So this was what ordinary Iranians associated Great Britain with—not its monarchy, Parliament or ancient institutions, not its great writers, thinkers or scientists, but Giggsy and the Neville brothers.

An extremely affable and pleasant middle-aged man occupied the seat next to me on the coach. During the course of the journey we enjoyed lengthy conversations about a great many things. When we arrived at the Shiraz bus station he kindly took it upon himself to order a taxi for me.

My hotel, although not five-star, was a noticeable improvement on my previous place of residence. It was run by an eccentric old man who felt an irresistible need to smother me with advice and assistance each and every time I saw him.

Shiraz is another of the great Persian cities. The country's capital from 1747 to 1779, the town is renowned for its arts, culture and above all, its poets.

I spent the day after my arrival in Shiraz visiting the city's many great sites. From speaking to its people, it was apparent that the town's rich history was a source of great pride for Shirazians. So much so, that at times it felt that modern-day Shiraz found it almost impossible to escape from the shadow of its great past.

Of the sites that I visited, I was most fascinated by the Shohada Mosque, which translates as the 'Martyrs Mosque'. The concept of martyrdom appears to be deeply embedded in Iranian culture. Throughout the country there were posters, paintings and postcards of famous martyrs—these were being sold on the streets and in the market places. Compare this with Western countries where it is the norm to find posters of celebrities, rock stars and screen legends in shopping malls and markets. To the Westerner (including myself), this obsession with martyrdom appears almost unhealthy.

Martyrdom exists in various guises in all societies. What distinguishes Iran from many other countries is the way in which Iranians appear (to the outsider) to perpetually revere their war dead. Other nations do not seem to engage in the year-round continuous hero-worship of their great warriors in the way that Iran seems to. In Iran, martyrdom is a big industry.

Why does Iran revere its war dead in this way? I didn't quite know. Maybe the answer, in part, lies in the fact that most Iranians are of Shiite decent and Shiites have through many periods in their history regarded themselves as a persecuted minority (persecuted mainly by Sunni Muslims, oddly enough). In periods when there was an absence of laws to sufficiently protect minority rights and the state was ill-prepared to enforce them, any persecuted minority that hoped to preserve its culture and way of life from hostile communities needed to make great sacrifices; otherwise its very existence was at risk. The greatest sacrifice to preserve the minority community and values is, of course, the sacrifice of one's own life. And the annals of Shiite history are littered with people who have done just that. None is more famous or important than the Prophet Muhammad's grandson, Hussein (may God be pleased with him). The story of his death and what it symbolised has become part of Shiite folklore. Hussein and his small band of followers were drawn into a war near Karbala (in Iraq) against the much superior forces of the corrupt Umayyad caliph, Yazid ibn Mu'awiya. His army, including Hussein, was massacred. However awful and distressing the details of his death may be to Muslim followers (Sunnis and Shiites alike), there is an eternal beauty to the story—that no matter how great the odds, this man was prepared to stand up and fight against tyranny, against injustice, against evil, even though it was sure to end his life. It may be argued that one effect of these stories is to generate a discourse in which history is seen as a self-perpetuating dialectic, in which devout Shiites see themselves as the standard-bearers and guardians of truth in a world that is hostile towards them and this truth. Take for example, the following quote found on the Islamic Republic of Iran Broadcasting website:

> Imam Hussein's martyrdom inspired reformers and revolutionaries and triggered freedom seeking uprisings throughout history. The most recent consequence of the heroic event of Karbala, was the triumph of the Islamic revolution in Iran under the leadership of Imam Khomeini.
>
> The martyrs create epics. Their blood is not squandered nor does it get dried on sands. In fact, the blood of martyrs remains fresh, is injected in the body of society and circulates in its arteries. ... Imam Hussein ... teaches that in all ages, people should stand up against injustice and oppression by waging Jihad which means a holy struggle, and if necessary they should guarantee the life of the society with the elixir of martyrdom.[1]

For a persecuted group, perpetual reverence of its great warriors may therefore be an important discourse of power in sustaining a common bond within a minority community during peaceful times and empowering members of that group when it is under real threat during times of war or violent persecution by another community. Perpetual reverence of martyrs can also be found in other groups that perceive themselves as being violently persecuted, for example, the Palestinian people.

That afternoon I paid a visit to Eram Park. Located just outside the town centre, Eram Park is an enchanting place full of beautiful gardens. From the number of families and school groups also visiting the park, it was obvious that many were drawn to the park's aesthetic qualities. Yet, as I was to quickly discover, it wasn't the park's aesthetic qualities that some were drawn to. Its small and narrow pathways, some of them hidden away under large trees and overgrown hedges, also usefully served other purposes, namely, to provide a retreat where Iranian boys and girls could secretly meet up. As I walked through the park, on more than one occasion my eye caught a glimpse of a teenage couple sitting together on a park bench, hidden from view by some enormous tree or overgrown bush, their eyes firmly fixated on the passing intruder, their bodies statuesque in pose (as if their forbidden act was frozen in time), expressions of worry and guilt clearly etched on their faces, no doubt in fear that someone would soon recognise who they were and report them to their parents. I thought back to what Yusuf, the taxi driver, had told me about pre-marital relationships. Maybe there was some truth in what he had said after all (although the most these young couples could be accused of was talking to each other and holding hands).

Towards the end of my walk in the park, I decided to take a rest and sat down on one of the park benches. To the left of me was another bench. Here I saw two smartly dressed teenage boys. Both were slouched down with their legs wide apart, trying to look as macho as possible. Their eyes were focused on two girls sitting on the bench opposite them. The two girls were seated in an upright Victorian pose; one of them had her make-up bag out and was applying something to her face; the other advised her on how she looked. Both were aware of the attention they were receiving and had that look (of which only girls are capable) of pretending not to be interested whilst actually being interested. So this was the Persian courtship dance, or so I christened it. Some aspects of human nature cannot be curtailed; regardlesss of state prohibitions, some activities will manage to find some avenue, some arena, in which to flourish.

Re-reading Lolita in Shiraz

Eram Park was very near Shiraz University and this was my next port of call. I had an appointment with a lecturer who taught in the university's humanities department. Given the open-ended nature of my travels I had been unable to agree on a specific time and date for our meeting. The best I could do was tell him on which dates I thought I would be in Shiraz. He knew I was coming, he just didn't know when.

After I arrived at the university, I spent the first twenty minutes wandering around the campus trying to find someone who could speak English. Security must have been made aware of my presence because two of their staff arrived to pick me up. They escorted me to a security cabin and here I met a female attendant who, much to my relief, spoke some English. She listened intently to what I had to say before suggesting that my best option was to enquire at the International Relations Office. This was a very good idea. Several months earlier, in the process of setting up this meeting, I had briefly corresponded via e-mail with the International Relations Office. If anyone would be able to assist me with my enquiry, it would be someone from this office. After seeking directions, I made my way there.

To my intense relief the international relations director I was introduced to was the very same man that I had been in brief e-mail correspondence with. A short, middle-aged man, he came across as very articulate and spoke with a slight American accent. He also had a very good memory because he knew exactly why I was there and whom I wanted to see.

Being fully versed as to the nature of my visit to the university, he made a quick call to the person concerned and was able to arrange an appointment for me to meet him at the university's restaurant at 7:30 p.m. I thanked him for his assistance. He invited me to have mid-afternoon tea with him and I accepted his kind offer.

His American accent intrigued me and so I asked whether he had lived in the States. He confirmed that he had indeed studied in America before returning to Iran to teach. He asked me what I thought of my stay in Iran so far. I replied by telling him that I was very much enjoying my time, especially since it seemed to continuously challenge the many pre-conceived perceptions I had of the country. As one example, I cited the large number of female students that I had seen on campus during my walkabout. I had not expected the number of female undergraduates to be so high. He confirmed that my observations were correct, adding that almost sixty percent of their students were female and that ten percent of their professors were women. If true, most Western universities would be proud of such statistics.

I also raised with him the plight of the highly educated, highly under-employed university graduates that Iran seemed to be burdened with, in particular, pointing out to him that an increasing number of them wished to leave Iran for Western Europe and North America. I suggested to him that this brain drain to the West could not be good for the long-term future of the country. After all, how could the developing world ever hope to catch up with the developed world when its brightest and best people immigrate to the developed world?

He recognised the problems that a brain drain to the West might cause to a society such as Iran, but believed that in the long run this movement of intellectual labour would be beneficial to Iran. I didn't quite understand the point he was trying to make. I asked him to elaborate. He explained. The long-term effects of such economic migration would be to enhance Iran's own economic productivity. The reason being that most of those graduates who went abroad would someday return home, bringing with them the new skills and experience that they acquired in Europe and North America. They would then pool all this new knowledge and experience into Iranian industries and businesses. His story held water only if, in fact, many Iranians returned to Iran and invested in the country. Whether this was happening in sufficient numbers to result in a net benefit to the country I did not know. Given the apathy and disillusionment those graduates in Esfahan expressed to me, I wasn't overly confident that once out of the country most young people would indeed be prepared to come back to the present economic and political climate.

Overall, I was very impressed with the director of the international relations office. His pleasant and polite nature tempted me to ask him about his views on the regime and the direction it was heading, but I refrained from doing so. He was in a position of authority and I got the feeling that if he were critical of the regime (and on the whole I got the impression he seemed quite supportive of it), he certainly would not disclose such information to a stranger like me.

After finishing tea and establishing that I hadn't any further appointments that evening, he invited me to accompany him to a graduation ceremony he was attending for some of the students at the university that evening. He was sure that I would meet people there that I would be interested in. Again, I had no hesitation in accepting his kind offer.

The ceremony lasted a couple of hours and was held at one of the university's lecture theatres. It wasn't that different from graduation ceremonies held in the West (with the exception of the traditional Iranian music that was played during the intervals).

At the conclusion, there was an informal get together of students, parents and lecturers. It was here that the director introduced me to a number of the teaching staff at the university. One of them was a female professor of English. She seemed much more open in our discussions. So much so, that I cautiously asked her whether the Revolution had enhanced the position of Iranian academics such as herself. She answered without any hesitation that the Revolution had benefited her career. During the Shah's reign, many of the academics in departments such as hers were foreigners, either from the United States or the United Kingdom. There was a perception amongst many Iranian academics (including herself) that there existed a two-tier structure in Iranian higher education under the Shah, with the best teaching positions frequently going to foreign, Western academics. The Revolution proved to be a blessing in disguise for her and many of her Iranian colleagues. When the Shah was toppled, most Western academics fled the country, opening up access to higher teaching positions for people such as herself.

Before I asked her this question, I had assumed she would answer in the negative: I believed instead, that she would probably argue that the ruling ayatollahs had curtailed intellectual freedom and stifled creativity in higher academia. It never occurred to me that some Iranian academics would feel that the Revolution had liberated them from the discrimination that was endemic in higher education before the Shah was deposed.[2]

I was also introduced to a professor of sociology who specialised in mass media communications. He was very critical of the way in which the Western media distorted its reporting of Iranian and Middle Eastern matters. The mass proliferation of Western-based international news organisations over the past decade had not led to people being better informed, but better dis-informed, he argued. This was especially true when it came to analysing the purposes and effects of US foreign policy in the region. In today's age of spin, political announcements (especially in foreign policy) were often couched, by Western governments, in moral and ethical terms. As an example, he cited Bush's War on Terror. He stressed that in many instances, if one looked carefully enough, the political terminology deployed by politicians to describe a particular policy objective was either incorrect or hid numerous other policy objectives that had nothing to do with pursuing an ethical foreign policy. The US media in particular often failed to properly scrutinise the political language used by the politicians and spin-doctors, and lacked these nuances. Again, he cited Bush's War on Terror as a good example of political language deployed by Washington to describe a particular policy objective, and adopted by the US media without proper, if any, scrutiny.

When I spoke to this academic, the Afghan phase of the War on Terror had ended. Whilst I was writing this book, the military phase (which excludes the reconstruction phase) in the Iraqi chapter on the War on Terror had come and gone. Like millions (possibly even billions) of others around the world, I watched the war unfold from the comfort of my living room. The international news networks provided me, and the global community, with twenty-four hour coverage of phase two of the War on Terror. Given this particular sociologist's expertise in mass media communications, it would have been interesting to know what he thought about the way in which the Western and now Arab news networks played out the second Gulf War. My guess is that he probably would have argued that the coverage reaffirmed the views he expressed to me. But would this be right? The enormous difficulties that British Prime Minister Tony Blair had in convincing the media (let alone the public) that war against Iraq was 'justified and lawful' seemed to suggest that the British media at least, weren't as susceptible to political talk as was suggested by the sociologist (whether the same can be said for one or two of the American news networks is another matter—I won't mention names, such as Fox News, a.k.a. the Republican Party Broadcasting Corporation).

If anything, it seems that the conflicts of the twenty-first century will need to be fought on two fronts, one military and the other in the media. The strategy the coalition forces adopted to conduct this war seemed simple enough: 'target military institutions only, keep civilian casualties to a minimum'. The difficult part of this strategy appeared to be in convincing a sceptical world that this was in fact how the war was being fought. 'Presentation' was more important than 'substance'. To this end, it was not at all surprising to see the daily reports and occasional video footage that emerged from the coalition forces telling us of smart bombs used in surgical bombing campaigns to destroy the military infrastructure of the evil regime of Saddam, but keep almost perfectly intact the lives of the innocent people of Iraq with whom the United States had no quarrel. The aim was, of course, to paint a picture in the mind of the viewer of a war conducted to 'target military institutions only, keep civilian casualties to a minimum'. By contrast, the Iraqi regime made sure that maximum exposure and coverage was given to the innocent civilian causalities, the unintended victims of coalition military aggression. They were, of course, trying to paint a picture of a war that was unjust and immoral. How better to do this than by allowing the international news networks to flood our screens with images of injured and maimed civilian Iraqis caught up in the coalition forces' self-proclaimed 'shock and awe' campaign. The story being told in their picture was one of innocent civilians (many of them children) unlawfully injured and killed by this evil crusader army and its weapons of awesome destruction. One war, two versions. But one should not become too downhearted; in this new era of modern military warfare, played out on a multi-media network before a global village, one ancient tradition of warfare still seems to have survived: the first casualty of war is truth.

The use of suicide bombers can be tied in with the issue of martyrdom I have discussed. When I first read the article on martyrdom from the IRIB (Islamic Republic of Iran Broadcasting) website, my immediate thought was that the article was specifically related to suicide bombers. This is quite clearly wrong. The author is speaking about martyrdom in the wider and more traditional sense (and may or may not include suicide bombing as one of many forms of martyrdom). Although suicide bombing is not peculiar to Muslim societies (the Indian Prime Minister Rajeev Gandhi was killed by a Tamil suicide bomber in the mid-eighties), the frequent use of this method by Palestinian groups has meant that it has become intrinsically linked with Arab societies. As this technique has now been adopted increasingly more often by Muslim groups within Muslim and non-Muslim countries, as the method of martyrdom, suicide bombings are being seen as peculiarly Islamic. This assumption, however persuasive, is incorrect. Suicide bombings have evolved not out of the Islamic canon (no pun intended), but are more a result of the disparity in military might between the suicide bomber and the power he is fighting. In other words, the enormous military power of Israel and the United States has probably had a greater influence on the development and use of suicide bombers by Hamas, al-Qa'ida or the Iraqi insurgents, than any Quranic verse or saying of the Prophet Muhammad. Or for that matter any deed of his grandchild, Hussein, who when faced with the same predicament of fighting an infinitely stronger opponent, did choose to target military personnel, rather than blow up civilians.

In the evening I met up with the lecturer from Shiraz University as agreed. We had a meal at the university restaurant and spent the evening exploring many of the issues that I discuss in this book. I was sad when the evening came to an end. It had been a fascinating day, one that had provided me with much food for thought.

8. ALLADIN SANE LOST IN THE LAND OF THE PHILOSOPHER KINGS (Shiraz)

THE RUINS OF the ancient Persian city of Persepolis lie just outside Shiraz. My hotel manager had arranged for a special taxi to take me there. There were many travel agencies that organised day trips to Persepolis, he told me. Most of them ripped tourists off. His hotel had wised up to this and so only negotiated with a few select companies that had been carefully vetted. There was one company the hotel regularly dealt with and he could negotiate a 'special discount' on my behalf. I agreed.

As requested, I was up and ready by 7 a.m. The hotel manager introduced me to the teenage guide who would take me to the ancient ruins. The guide introduced himself to me as the hotel manager's son. Hmmm! I was being taken on a ride in every sense of the word, but decided not to say anything.

The journey to Persepolis took about an hour. Mr Hotel Manager's son spoke very little English (I had well and truly been stitched), enough only to ask me whether he could play some music. I nodded my head to indicate my consent. He pushed the play button on his car stereo and the speakers belted out the sound of gangsta rap. Although he spoke almost no English, gangsta rap had touched him. The way he bopped his head to the tales of the ghetto fabulous told the story of a man who had been blessed by the music. Or perhaps he had no idea what they were rapping about, except he knew that to listen to such music made one very cool. That he could not understand what was being sung was irrelevant. I suppose it's similar to people who listen to opera in order to make themselves feel sophisticated or Western tourists who visit ancient ruins and think that it makes them look cultured. To young Iranians gangsta rap was their opera, Biggie Smalls was their Pavarotti.

Having arrived at our destination my guide told me he would not enter the fee-paying site. Instead, he would return to pick me up in four hours. I ought to have objected. After all, he was my guide. But I was glad to be on my own. His lack of English made meaningful conversation difficult and the long silences were already becoming uncomfortable.

The ancient ruins were in the middle of the Iranian desert and although it was still early morning, it was hot, very hot. I decided to buy a drink before I embarked on my expedition and headed for the cafeteria. The man serving me told me they had run out of bottled water and were awaiting fresh supplies. I bought some mango juice instead. With it, I made my way round the ruins, taking in the sights, appreciating the architecture, the culture, the history. It made me feel very sophisticated (a bit like when I listen to opera). Indeed, I must have looked the very embodiment of sophistication as I walked around the ruins, sucking on the straw to my mango juice, wondering if this wouldn't be a wonderful site to film an Indiana Jones movie.

Persepolis is both a strange and wonderful place. The ruins date back to 512 BC. The enormous array of stone columns create a surreal effect in the open Iranian desert and somehow reminded me of ancient Greece (ironically, it was the Greeks who invaded the city in 331 BC and destroyed it). As amazing as the ruins were, the place did not seem part of Iranian history. It was as if they had been transported from another land and just dumped in the middle of the Iranian desert. These ruins tell the story of a pagan Iran, of a once great civilisation that did not belong to the realm of Islam. One associates Iran with Islam, the very antithesis of paganism. That Iran preserves and promotes this pagan site in some ways seems odd. Though the ruins are an important part of Iranian history, it was difficult for me to take in.

I finished off my mango juice whilst standing next to an enormous stone carving of a king. Staring up at him I thought it was a good thing that he was not in Taliban Afghanistan. At that he turned his head down towards me and nodded in approval (well okay maybe he didn't quite do that!).

My four hours up, I returned to the exit area to be picked up by Mr Hotel Manager's son, for the drive back to Shiraz.

That afternoon I continued my tour of Shiraz, taking time out to visit sites that I had not yet seen. Keeping with tradition, I kept getting lost. On one such occasion I decided to enter a library to ask for directions.

The library wasn't very big, but it did look quite old. Its oak-like interior had an almost Victorian feel to it. I went to the reception desk where two girls were seated; as I relayed my enquiry several people turned around to have a look at the person with the foghorn voice who was speaking in English. For reasons I am not quite sure of, my speaking caused the two girls at the reception desk to look at each other and break into uncontrollable fits of laughter. Everyone in the library began to look in my direction. I felt like a freak, a circus act, who had descended onto this quiet, unassuming library in southern Iran, causing curiosity and intrigue amongst the locals. When the two girls eventually stopped laughing they said they could not answer my query, but they would call over the chief librarian as he may be able to assist me.

The chief librarian was a short, middle-aged, brown-skinned, bald-headed man who wore Gandhi-type spectacles. He was delighted to see me and immediately put out his hand for me to shake. He also spoke loudly, very loudly. For a librarian this seemed almost blasphemous—did they not teach him at librarian school to speak in a low voice? Does not the first commandment of 'librarianism' read, 'thou shalt not speak loudly in a library?' I looked at the two girls. They had started giggling again. I was sure they were laughing at me, but couldn't figure out why.

After providing me with directions he asked whether I could clarify something for him. "Sure" I replied, not at all aware of what he wanted clarifying. "What is the British Muslim community's contribution to the Palestinian cause?" he said loudly. I didn't know what to say. Iran has of course for some time been funding groups such as Hezbollah, which have been at the forefront of paramilitary campaigns against Israel (as recent events have shown). From the way he spoke it was apparent that he was very proud of Iran's contribution to fighting the Israeli state. If there was any one issue that the Iranian government and its people were in total agreement with, then it was this, that it is right and just to support the Palestinians in their struggles against Israel. On this subject at least, all philosophers had become kings and all kings had become philosophers.

Back to his question, I was stuck for words. I paused for several moments and tried to think of an appropriate answer. In the end I uttered, in a Hugh Grant kind of way, the only thing that came to mind, "yes, the British Muslim community supports the plight of the Palestinian people". I did not elaborate in what ways we provided support, but managed, even stuttering, to say the words with enough conviction to give the impression that whatever support we had provided, it was significant.

Mr Librarian drew amusement from my flustered state. I decided to go on the offensive and ask him the first question that came to mind. "Do you believe in suicide bombings?" I enquired, in my most Jeremy Paxman way. "Of course" he bellowed out, not at all ashamed or hesitant in his reply. I asked how he could justify the killing of innocent civilians. Quite simple, Israelis were not innocent civilians, he asserted. Aha! But the victims of suicide bombings were innocent civilians, I quickly retorted, further pointing out to him with a confidence that would have made Mr Paxman himself proud, that generally speaking, Palestinian suicide bombers didn't target military personnel. Nothing unnerved this man; he hit back with a most extraordinary reply. People have the right to resist occupation. The French did so during the Second World War. They resisted the Nazi occupation of their country. The world did not complain, instead they admired and applauded the gritty determination of the French people in their attempts to get rid of the evil and unlawful occupation of their country. The Jewish occupation of Palestine was the same as the Nazi occupation of France.

I was taken aback by this analogy (although when I thought about it later, I recalled that this argument had been put forward by a speaker at a lecture I attended many years ago). There was a crucial difference between the two scenarios, I pointed out. The French efforts at fighting German occupation were targeted at the occupying Nazi army. They weren't blowing up German civilians. To make an analogy between the two was therefore absurd. He did not think so. Yes, Israeli civilians were not military personnel, but neither could they be classified as 'innocent civilians'. He explained why. When immigrant Jews moved into Palestine, they knew they were settling on occupied land, land that belonged to other people, the 'original inhabitants', 'the Palestinians'. The effects of their illegal and unlawful migration into Palestine had displaced some of these 'original inhabitants' from their homes and many became refugees in foreign lands. Those Palestinians who were allowed to continue to reside in their homeland had to submit to the laws of the 'invaders'. He returned to his original example; if the Nazi army, after occupying France, displaced French people from their homeland and replaced them with the families and relatives of Nazis, then those German settlers were not 'innocent civilians'. They could also have become viable targets of paramilitary activity by French resistance fighters. It was this implicit acknowledgement that they had chosen to settle on land that was occupied by other civilians that resulted in them losing the designation of 'innocent civilian'.

It was an interesting argument and I had not previously analysed the issue from this perspective. I still disagreed with him though. Even if we were to accept that civilians who choose to occupy land knowing that some of the original inhabitants had been displaced in the process, whilst the remaining inhabitants were forced to submit to their 'rule of law', does that necessarily make them the legitimate targets of paramilitary/terrorist activity? It cannot. Unlawful occupation cannot give the displaced/occupied people an automatic right to blow up unarmed civilian men, women and particularly children (who may have no knowledge that their occupation and residency was at another's expense). In such circumstances the original inhabitants quite rightly have a legitimate grievance and a right to seek a remedy that equitably restores them to their original position. But that surely does not extend to a right to achieve redress by blowing up the new inhabitants. Even the victims must respond and work within a moral framework. In this particular scenario the resistance ought to be targeted at the machinery that enforces the unlawful occupation—the Israeli military—and not at the civilians who benefit from it. I ought to have relayed these arguments to Mr Librarian, but I was unable to articulate them at the time. Not that it would have done me any good. We were already beginning to go round in circles, neither party able to convince the other of his position. Before leaving, I thanked him for both the directions and the interesting and lively conversation.

I spent the remainder of the day on my sightseeing tour, but the librarian had started me thinking about the possible motives behind the Iranian government's policy of aiding paramilitary groups fighting Israel. One could theoretically argue that Jordan has a legitimate grievance with Israel, because it occupies land that it seized in the 1967 War. One could also argue that Lebanon has a legitimate grievance with Israel; they have turned the south of the country into a no-man's-land and are in quasi-control of some parts of it. One could also argue that Syria has a legitimate grievance with the Israeli state that captured and continues to occupy its Golan Heights and surrounding territories. But on the face of it, Iran does not have a direct grievance with Israel. Israel occupies none of its land nor does it threaten its sovereignty. Yet Iran has gone out of its way to assist paramilitary operations against the Israeli state. Why? Mr Librarian had taken genuine pride in the nobility of what his government was doing. If we leave aside the issue of whether or not assisting groups that manufacture suicide bombers can ever be described as a noble endeavour, we must ask, is the librarian's assumption that his government's policy is indeed noble and selfless correct? Is Iran's sole aim to assist an oppressed people or are there ulterior motives that, at the very least, might run alongside this 'noble objective'? At the very minimum, these 'noble objectives' must act as a political antidote to the anti-Shiite rhetoric that emanates from certain scholars in Saudi Arabia, and which is aimed at damaging their reputation. Iranian assistance can also forge allegiances with other political/religious and paramilitary organisations in the region and thereby increase Iran's own security in the region. Finally, if all the other major players (with the exception of Syria) are currently sitting back and watching the Palestinian occupation continue, too afraid to intervene in case it upsets the mighty United States, to the average Arab man on the street, angry at his own country's impotence, Iran may appear as a shining beacon against US-backed Israeli aggression. It would be wrong of me to suggest that there are only altruistic motives behind Iran's decision to aid Palestinian paramilitary groups. And equally wrong to suggest that Iran doesn't recognise the ways in which their efforts strengthen their position in the region.

9. SMOOTH CRIMINALS ON THE ROAD TO DAMASCUS
(Shiraz–Tehran–Damascus)

MY TRAVELS IN IRAN were coming to an end. With my seat on the evening Tehran–Damascus flight already booked, all that was left for me to do was go from Shiraz to Tehran. By coach, it takes the best part of a day. Fortunately, air travel within Iran is very cheap. So cheap, that I was able to purchase a ticket on the Shiraz–Tehran flight leaving that morning for a mere twenty-four dollars.

I was sad to be leaving Iran. I had arrived in the country with feelings of trepidation and fear. I would leave it with a vault full of memories of the generosity and kindness that the Iranian people had shown me. The BBC's international correspondent, John Simpson, who was in the country at the time of the Revolution in 1979, made the following comment on Iranian people:

> For those who know them, there is something deeply attractive about the people of Iran. The habitual, unselfish generosity which they show towards strangers is unusual even in the Islamic world. They also possess the rare ability to distinguish between individual people and the government of the country they come from. Even when the British government was being reviled daily in Iran, individual Britons were being treated with kindness and respect. Maybe it comes from the Islamic tradition of treating strangers as guests; maybe it is the result of the long centuries during which individual Persians have had no voice whatever in the way that they have been governed, and therefore wouldn't consider blaming someone for what their government did. Yet at a time when British officials were being rude and dismissive to Iranians who had fled their country to escape persecution, and when gangs attacked and occasionally murdered innocent Iranian refugees in the streets of American cities, British and American journalists were being treated with respect and kindness within Iran itself.[1]

I couldn't really disagree with this summation of the Iranian people. Iran and the Iranian people have great potential and much to offer to the world. Whatever the supporters of the Revolution may argue, I hope that the ruling clerics, for whatever reason, have simply been unable to fully tap into the enormous reservoir of human talent Iran possesses. I hope one day it is able to realise that potential. When it does, both Iran and the world will be the better for it.

The flight to Tehran was short and uneventful. The plane landed at Tehran Airport in the late morning. My flight to Damascus left mid-evening. Booking-in time for that flight was still some six hours away. I had already decided that I would spend this extra time by visiting the palaces of the former Shah, situated in the north of the city and then make my way to the town centre to visit the National Museum and Islamic Art Museum. Before setting off I dropped my heavy backpack at the luggage storage department of the airport and then made my way to the taxi office to book a ride to take me to the north of the city.

My taxi driver was a talkative and opinionated man who very much reminded me of a London cabby. He also spoke fairly good English. As soon as I got into his taxi he started to discuss the US war in Afghanistan. He was delighted by the removal of the Taliban, and expressed genuine admiration at the manner in which the US forces had executed their operations to remove what he described as 'the terrible regime'. This was not as surprising a remark for an Iranian to make as might first appear. The Tehran government had been uneasy about the Taliban taking power in a country with which it had a significant border. The Taliban doctrine was ideologically similar to the anti-Shia Wahhabi doctrine espoused by the Saudi regime. Their rise to power altered the geopolitical map of the region. I'm sure it did not escape the attention of at least some US administration officials that a Taliban government could act as a political counterbalance to one of its enemies in the region, namely Iran, who would find itself with an unfriendly neighbour on its western border (Iraq) and on its eastern border (Afghanistan). Of course, 9/11 changed everything. The United States and Iran finally had something in common; a dislike of the Taliban regime. They also re-evaluated their hatred of Saddam's regime. Two years after 9/11, the United States had removed both the Taliban regime in Afghanistan and Saddam's control over Iraq; both Iran's western and eastern borders were relieved of these unfriendly regimes.

Delighted at the Taliban's removal from Afghanistan, he went on to ask me why the British or Americans could not help the Iranian people. I didn't fully understand what he meant by this. He elaborated for me. The United States did not like the Taliban regime. They publicly went on record to say they would take a leading role in the War on Terrorism. In the case of the Taliban, this regime harboured terrorists and therefore had to be removed. Well, his government had been assisting terrorist groups for years, why did they not intervene and likewise remove them from power? The Iranian people would be very grateful for such a gesture, he reliably informed me. I smiled. He had made a persuasive case. Although, I wasn't quite convinced that many Iranians would be so grateful to see American troops on their soil, and they would certainly not rationalise a military attack as some sort of liberation.

Unlike some of the people that I had been speaking to in recent days, this taxi driver genuinely reviled the regime and wasn't afraid to speak about it. For the last time on my trip, I asked about whether he had supported the Revolution of 1979. 'Yes' he had, he told me. At the time he was a very big supporter of the Revolution. It was only after the Revolution had taken place did he realise the mistake he had made.

What was it about the Shah's regime that had caused him to rally against it, I asked? His reply echoed much of what I had heard during my travels in Iran; that corruption was rife, especially amongst the rich; that the police were harsh and brutal towards the people. But most of all, that there was no fairness in society. He wanted to see a society where all were treated equally. He had hoped the Revolution would eliminate the evils of the Shah's rule and create a truly egalitarian society. But he had made a terrible error of judgement. If people had thought life under the Shah was unbearable, what followed was even worse. He asserted that he wasn't alone in regretting his decision. Many of his friends and colleagues had likewise supported Khomeini in the belief that he represented ideals other than those that he eventually went on to implement during his rule. I commented that Khomeini was a religious cleric. Surely it would have been obvious that he would want to install a theocratic polity if he got into power? "No", he replied. As stupid as it sounded, he thought he was supporting a socialist revolution. It never occurred to him that the Revolution would result in the creation of a religious state. The speeches of Khomeini that were widely distributed prior to the Revolution had eloquently captured the failings of the Shah's rule. When opponents of the regime, religious and non-religious, heard these speeches, they could associate with what he was saying. What many (including himself) had failed to do was to read the small print. Once the Revolution had taken place it was too late to turn the clock back, the social contract between the state and its people had been signed.

Like so many Iranians that I had met, he seemed so idealistic in his vision of a post-Shah Iran. I asked him what it was about the new regime that he disliked. "Rules, rules, rules," he shouted out. Every month there were new rules to follow. New laws telling people what they could, but mainly what they could not do. The people quickly got fed up. This was not what many had dreamed and fought for. He looked at me and said if he voiced these things in public they (meaning the regime) would kill him. I nodded my head in quiet acknowledgement. He spoke with such vitriol and anger that it was obvious that such a vehement critique of the regime would not be openly tolerated. I cautiously put it to him that many people that I had spoken to felt things were getting better, that slowly but gradually, many of the restrictions placed on the populace were being lifted and people were enjoying greater freedom than at any time since the Revolution. Given the hatred he had shown for the regime, I didn't expect him to show any sympathy for the ruling elite. But to my surprise he shared this view and agreed that some positive changes were slowly taking place, although he did add that the pace of reform was slow and that he did not believe that it would go on forever.

The palaces of the former Shah of Iran are situated in an idyllic woodland setting, far from the hustle and bustle of downtown Tehran. Today, the palaces are popular tourist attractions, but they also provide ordinary Iranians with a window through which to view an important part of their recent past.

Not all of the palaces are open to the public. The government still uses some of them for state functions. Those that I did visit were European in architectural design. Even on the inside, the expensive furnishings and luxuries that filled the palace rooms mainly originated from Europe. The lavish furnishings tell the story of a ruling dynasty that had accustomed itself to a grand lifestyle. These riches were a world away from the impoverished lifestyle that so many Iranian subjects inhabited. So European were the surroundings, if I hadn't known better, I would have thought I was visiting the palace of a European monarch, not a Persian shah.

With much of the population living in poverty and surrounded by ever-increasing corruption, it was understandable that the people would begin to feel bitter and resentful towards the Shah. It was also understandable why the protests, when they did come, emerged from both secular and religious realms of society. Before my very eyes stood the physical evidence to corroborate what I had been told were some of the underlying reasons for the Shah's unpopularity (such as the tales of how his European lifestyle alienated him from his subjects or how the trappings of his wealth eventually resulted in his humble subjects ousting him from power).

I struck up a brief conversation with an administrator at one of the palaces. Iran had such a rich history of beautiful architectural design (which I had been fortunate enough to visit on my travels), was it not sad that its former rulers had sought out architects to construct palaces in an essentially European design? He nodded his head in acknowledgement. This was what the ruling monarch had wanted, he said. They had a tremendous admiration for European culture and decided to transport some of it to Iran. The effects of European colonialism on the minds of the rulers of colonised nations had indeed been very powerful, so powerful that sometimes they failed to notice the immense beauty in their own culture.

After finishing my tour of the palaces I caught a taxi to central Tehran to visit the museums. When I returned to the airport, I went to the storage section, collected my backpack and then moved on to the check-in desk. The plane arrived on time and I boarded the flight to Damascus.

The plane landed at Damascus Airport late in the evening. I managed to find both the currency exchange bureau and the airport taxi office without encountering any difficulty. The contrast with my stressful experiences at Tehran Airport could not have been greater. All that was left for me to do was to find a cheap and cheerful hotel.

There were plenty of cheap hotels to be found in Martyrs Square, my travel guide reliably informed me. Martyrs Square is in the very heart of Damascus. I asked the taxi driver whether he could recommend a hotel in the square for me. No he couldn't, he regrettably replied, he was new to the job and wasn't, as of yet, familiar with the hotels of central Damascus. What he could do for me was drive me around to a few of the hotels in the square and I could then pick and choose which hotel I liked best. This I thought was a very good idea and so accepted his kind suggestion.

Had I bothered to read my travel guide properly it would have been obvious to me that this man was extremely new to his job, because what he failed to tell me and what we were about to find out was that many of the cheap hotels in Martyrs Square double as brothels.

When I said I was looking for something 'cheap and cheerful' this wasn't quite what I had in mind. My only saving grace was that because I was unable to speak Arabic, it was the taxi driver who was going over to the hotelier/pimp to make the enquiries on my behalf. He didn't seem to be very good at it either, because he kept returning to the taxi to inform me that the hotel/brothel operated a 'no bonk,[2] no bed' policy. Or to put it another way, 'you don't bonk our prostitute, you don't get a bed for the night'.

The last straw came when one of the hoteliers standing at the door to his seedy looking establishment looked in my direction and said aloud, "You want ma-daam?" Several people who were walking by turned around to look at me. I turned the other away, pretending he was talking to someone else. I had had enough. I shouted at the taxi driver to return to his vehicle. I decided that I was going to pay that little bit extra and spend the night at a more 'well-to-do' establishment. I asked my driver to drive around until we located an expensive-looking hotel; we did, until we spotted one that seemed to fit the bill. I booked in for the night. The only extras they offered were half a dozen chocolate bars that I found in my refrigerator later that night.

I was able to negotiate an *en-suite* room with satellite TV. A porter took my backpack and escorted me up to my room. Once there, he lazily dropped the backpack on the floor and then demanded (yes demanded!) that I tip him. This I reluctantly did whilst muttering under my breath that he was a bigger prostitute than those I left behind at Martyrs Square.

Once he was gone, I opened my backpack to get out my sleeping clothes. WHAT! Somebody had been through my belongings! Things were missing! I emptied out the backpack and started to check what had been stolen. I immediately noticed that my handheld computer had gone. Thankfully, nothing else of expense was taken. Various items of toiletries were missing including my special anti-dandruff shampoo (in the days to come I would mourn this loss more than that of my computer). Where had the theft taken place? It could have been at any one of a number of places, Shiraz Airport, Tehran Airport, Tehran Airport Luggage Storage Department! or even Damascus Airport. I was depressed. I got the chocolate bars from the fridge and munched away in the hope they would treat my depression. It didn't work. There was nothing I could do. I got into bed and fell asleep.

10. MADAME TELLS A TALE OF TWO CITIES
(Damascus)

DAMASCUS IS ONE of the most important cities in the history of humankind. It plays a significant part in the stories of Islam, Christianity and Judaism. Only Jerusalem can make a similar claim. Like Jerusalem, the city is divided into the Old City and the New City. Damascus is also alleged to be the oldest continuously inhabited city in the world. People have been living in Damascus since 5000 BC!

The hotel I stayed in that first night was in the New City. When I awoke that morning I made up my mind; I simply could not afford to continue living in this expensive establishment. I was going to have to look for somewhere else to stay. I got out my trusted travel guide and started looking up hotels that were not so expensive that they would deplete my ever dwindling money supply in two days, or so cheap that I would need to engage in extra-curricular activities just to get a bed for the night. I was able to find one such hotel that seemed to fit the bill. I packed my bags, got ready and made my way downstairs to the reception area to pay off my bill.

Down at the reception desk I was greeted by two women, both in their mid-twenties and puffing away at cigarettes. I can't recall the last time I actually saw employees smoking openly at work. I paid my bill, said my goodbyes and was just about to leave when one of the women called me back. She had just received a phone call from one of the cleaners working on my floor. He informed her that six chocolate bars were missing from the refrigerator in my room. Did I know who had taken them? I shrugged my shoulders and with a Hugh Grant kind of stutter managed to utter that I might have taken one or two of the bars (well ok, it might even have been five or six, but hey, they were incy-wincey microscopic fun-size bars and I hadn't eaten all day). I told her that I thought the chocolates were free, which I genuinely did. "No they are not free", she said annoyingly back at me, before adding, "they are a dollar each". I needed to pay for all six missing chocolate bars. Six dollars! Six dollars! The bonk would have been cheaper. I paid the outstanding amount and walked out of the hotel.

This was not a good start to my travels in Syria. But when I thought that by leaving this hotel my disasters in Damascus would come to an end,

I was wrong. Next, I got hopelessly lost in search of this new hotel. I stopped into a lingerie shop to ask for directions (I swear I did not know it was a lingerie shop before I walked in). Once inside, I saw a man, who I assumed was the manager, talking to a person I assumed was an employee. I asked if anyone could speak English. The manager said he could. I asked him if he knew where the hotel was. To my relief, the manager said he did, and added that it would be easier if I caught a taxi there. He asked me to wait whilst he rang the hotel concerned to check if they had a room available. They did. He escorted me out of the shop and tracked down a taxi for me. I thanked him for his help, got into the taxi and headed towards my new hotel.

As soon as I walked into the new hotel, I liked it. It had a relaxed, cosmopolitan atmosphere, quite unlike the uptight and stuffy feel of my last hotel.

I hadn't slept properly last night either, my mind still upset by the theft. This search for a new hotel had tired me out even further. So I settled myself into my new room, and took a nap for a couple of hours before venturing out again.

I awoke two hours later and got ready to go out. I knew exactly where I wanted to go. The majestic Umayyad Mosque was the centrepiece of the Old City and this would be my first port of call.

My initial impression of Damascus was that the city was not unlike the Iranian towns that I had visited. Like Iran, it had a cool climate at this time of year. The roads appeared to be just as busy as they were in Tehran. Even the untidy concrete buildings looked the same as in Tehran. There was also an armed police/military presence on the streets which, like Iran, was intimidating for the visitor.

Closer inspection however, revealed that there were numerous differences between the two countries. In particular, the aroma of Western capitalism was much stronger here than in Iran. Syria is still regarded as one of the most closed societies in the world. Yet it was apparent that this country was more liberal than Iran and not so hung up about being open to Western influences. In addition to the presence of more Western/Japanese electronic and other consumables on sale, the streets in and around Martyrs Square had bars, clubs and even cinemas showing Western films.

The newspaper and magazine stands were stacked with European and American magazines—everything from *Time* magazine to *Cosmopolitan*.

Like in the West, a large proportion of Syrian magazines had attractive female models on their front cover, most wearing next to nothing (although there were no pornographic materials being sold). Posters of glamorous female models selling everything from mobile phones to fridges were plastered everywhere. As I had just arrived from a very conservative country, for the first time in my life the pivotal role that the 'female sexual form' has had in the success of Western based capitalism really dawned on me. It may have been men's brains that have inspired capitalist products, but it has been women's bodies that have been used to sell these capitalist products.

Even though the city had a greater feeling of material wealth than any of the Iranian cities I had visited, Damascus's New City lacked the aesthetic beauty of an Esfahan or even a Shiraz. The New City was littered with derelict buildings. Apart from making the place look ugly, it gave one the impression that the town had just recently been bombed.

The one advantage Damascus did have over Esfahan or Shiraz was its orientation. The majority of the shops, restaurants and bars were situated in or around Martyrs Square. The square conveniently bordered the walls of the Old City. An enormous citadel (which forms part of the Old City) demarcates the end of the New City and beginning of the Old City.

The other significant difference between Iran and Syria are its people. They originate from different ethnic/racial groups. Iranians are Persian, Syrians are Arab. But whether or not one could clearly define the Arabs as a race is debatable. The streets of Damascus were filled with all manner of people who would describe themselves as Arab. They ranged from dark-skinned males with short curly hair to women with fair skin, blue eyes and long blonde hair. The term Arab is probably more suitable as a generic term describing a social as opposed to a biological group.

For women, the veil is not compulsory as it is in Iran. Many women still chose to wear it, although I probably saw more women unveiled than veiled. The veils that were worn tended to be a simple headscarf. I saw few, if any, Syrian women in the long black robes that many Iranian women wore. Like their male counterparts, women's clothing was very much influenced by Western fashions and I even saw several women wearing skirts. The increase in the public display of female flesh resulted in a proportional increase in that male cultural activity known as 'head-turning'. Indeed, there was plenty of 'head-turning' going on amongst the men of Damascus. And not just 'head-turning' either; I even heard the occasional wolf-whistle and once witnessed a group of young teenage men cruising along in a car honking the horn at two attractive girls. I had changed my mind, Syria was nothing like Iran.

Damascus also had a noticeable number of Western tourists, especially from America. I managed to see more Westerners in one hour than I had throughout the whole of my stay in Iran (which in many ways was a shame because there was so much to see and experience in Iran).

The walk was doing me good. Slowly, but gradually, I was beginning to feel better. I was putting my misfortunes behind me. I was in a new country, seeing a civilisation, a culture, a people that were all new to me.

Having walked past the citadel, I slowly made my way through the market stalls that lie in the shadow of the Umayyad Mosque. Occasionally, I stopped at a stall in order to look at an artefact. On one such occasion I bumped into an English-speaking couple. We struck up a brief conversation, at the end of which they invited me to an evening dinner at their hotel. I was flattered by the invitation, but said that I didn't really have the appropriate clothes for such an occasion. 'Nonsense', they replied, there was no dress code, it was an informal event. I gestured to my clothes (a sweatshirt and jeans) and jokingly remarked, "What ... I can come wearing these"? "Sure", they replied. I took down the details of the hotel and promised that I would try my best to make it. Things were definitely looking up. I could feel it.

I had jokingly enquired as to whether it would be 'okay' for me to attend in the clothes that I was wearing. This in fact was not a joke. Immediately after taking up residency at my new hotel, I asked one of the hotel staff whether they operated a laundry service. They did, so I gave them all my clothes for washing and ironing. All I had until tomorrow morning (when my laundry would be returned to me) was what I was currently wearing. Not that it would have made much difference; all my other clothes were casual as well. The invitation had put a smile back on my face; with a spring in my step I made my way towards the entrance to the Umayyad Mosque.

The Umayyad Mosque is one of the greatest mosques in the world. This was to be a momentous occasion in my life. I had been looking forward to this moment from the day I booked my tickets back in England many months ago. As I neared one of the entrances to the mosque the hairs on the back of my neck stood up. Just before the entrance gate was a sign asking guests to remove their shoes. I slipped off my trainers, picked them up, walked a few feet towards the entrance, lifted my right leg over a small wooden platform that lay at the foot of the gate and then stepped into a big pile of pigeon crap that one of the cleaners of the mosque had kindly piled up by the entrance gate. I could go no further. I had to return to the hotel. I didn't know who to be furious at, the cleaner for stupidly piling up this accumulated pigeon

excrement by the gate entrance, or myself for not being more careful. I walked
past the sign asking me to take off my shoes. Maybe there should have been
an additional sign reading 'Mind the Crap'. What a day!

Back at the hotel, a rummage around the bottom of my backpack unearthed
a clean pair of socks. I washed and cleaned my right foot before either
foolishly or courageously venturing out once more. It was still mid-afternoon.
The dinner invite wasn't until much later that evening. I hadn't even had
breakfast or lunch yet. I decided first to visit an Internet café that I had walked
past on my way back to the hotel and then find a bite to eat.

The Internet café, like those in Iran, wasn't particularly busy, and like
those in Iran, it had no female customers. As in Iran, the average Internet
user appeared to be a young middle-class male.

After e-mailing family and friends and informing them that I had safely
arrived in Syria, I walked around Martyrs Square trying to pick out a
decent and affordable restaurant to eat at. Whilst I was doing this, a young
man approached me and started to speak to me in Arabic. I told him in
English that I spoke no Arabic. Realising his error, he then attempted to
communicate with me in broken English. "You want ma-daam?" he
politely asked. Not again! I said 'no' and nervously walked away from him.
He followed. I walked faster. He managed to catch up with me and again
ask whether I wanted a 'ma-daam'. His persistence was beginning to annoy
me. I again said 'no' and again walked away from him. Again he followed.
I saw a restaurant on the other side of the road. I quickly crossed over and
walked straight through the front doors and into the restaurant. Once
inside, I composed myself and then asked for a table for one. A waiter led
me to an empty table. I sat down and tried to pull myself together. I looked
around; as I had hoped, the man who was following me did not enter after
me. I was safe.

I ordered a meat dish—and like the meat dishes I had eaten in Iran, it
tasted bland. As I was originally from the Indian subcontinent, I had
become accustomed to food with a rich variety of spices. By comparison,
all other food tasted bland. I had heard Lebanese food was good. Lebanon
would be my next port of call and I was looking forward to seeing whether
their cuisine could match that of the Indian subcontinent.

Before leaving to go out that evening, I shaved, showered and put on my
only item of posh-ness, some Armani aftershave that I had brought along

with me. I may not have been able to look very posh, but at least I could smell posh.

It had been a very difficult day. This, I said to myself, would be my reward for all the misfortunes that I had had to endure since my arrival in Syria. My hotel receptionist kindly provided me with a map and directions to my intended destination. I said my goodbyes and told him not to worry as I would be back very late. Outside, it was a bitterly cold evening. I had decided against wearing my jacket, which in retrospect was a very bad decision. It took me half an hour to find the hotel. When I finally turned up at its doors I had almost turned into an icicle.

I looked at the hotel. My lower jaw dropped. It was certainly a deluxe, five-star hotel, frequented only by the rich and famous. Since I do not fall into either of these two categories, one must wonder how a low-life pleb like me would be allowed entry into a grand and exclusive place like this? One must never overlook the fact that I speak 'posh Brummie',[1] or underestimate the power of a 'posh Brummie' accent.

I took a deep breath, walked through the hotel entrance and headed straight for the reception desk. In my poshest posh Brummie, I asked the receptionist for directions to the lift. He pointed to a set of elevator doors located just a few feet from where we were standing, doh! I nodded my head in acknowledgement and thanked him for his kind assistance. I then turned towards the elevator doors, got in and pressed the button that would take me to my floor.

When the elevator doors opened my lower jaw dropped for a second time. I got out and slowly made my way to an expensive-looking set of glass doors immediately adjacent to the lift. The glass doors opened to a large reception and dining area. I didn't go in. I just stood at the entrance, looking and feeling like a modern day Oliver Twist, peering through the looking glass into another, 'other world'. The first thought that ran through my mind perfectly summed up what I saw, a club where billionaire sheikhs meet Western aristocracy. Caucasian men smartly dressed in dinner jackets, Arab men in expensively cut *jalabiyas*, Caucasian women in the most elegant evening dresses, Arab women in equally elegant evening dresses. How did they look? They all looked divine, darling! As for the setting, it was as grand and luxurious as any room in the Ritz or the Dorchester. These high society people slowly sipped from their wine glasses, and engaged in sophisticated chat whilst their cuisine with unpronounceable names (unpronounceable to plebs like me anyway) was prepared; all to the gentle sound of a band playing in the background. These were the beautiful people. They lived in a different world than that occupied by millions of ordinary Syrians. To the average Syrian man and woman on the street, the beautiful people were everything they were not. They were rich, successful, glamorous and above all 'beautiful'. And what about me? Could I also be part of the beautiful people? I looked at myself. I had arrived at this lavish event in a pair of worn-out trainers that I had walked seven thousand miles in, a pair of tatty jeans and a grungy sweatshirt I had been wearing for the last two days (which had a ketchup stain on it from a kebab I had had the day before). I turned around and quietly made my way to the elevator. Posh Brummie was good, but not that good.

The only member of staff left on duty that night greeted my arrival back at the hotel with bemusement. I could not bear to tell him the truth and so I deviously informed him that I had changed my mind about going out (which was the truth in a round about sort of way). The place was quiet, with nobody else about. Rather than go straight to bed, I decided to stay and chat with him for a short while.

The receptionist asked me what my initial impressions of Syria were. Too embarrassed to run through the catalogue of misfortunes that had afflicted me on my first day in Syria, I cowardly focused on highlighting the differences that I had detected between Iranian and Syrian societies. In particular, as a Western observer, I found it bemusing that whilst it was Iran that was the major oil producer, it was Syria that appeared to have a greater abundance of wealth. He quietly listened to what I had to say. When I had finished, he acknowledged that Syria was not a leading oil-producing nation as I had pointed out, but his country was, nevertheless, a much wealthier nation than many Westerners assumed. It excelled in industry and agriculture and this brought in much revenue for his homeland. What Syria suffered from was political and economic corruption and this stagnated both the economy and the aspirations of large sectors of society.

The hotel worker had highlighted a feature of Syrian society that had become apparent to me during my walk around Damascus earlier that day and which poignantly culminated in my disastrous visit to the very expensive and exclusive five-star hotel. One of the side effects of capitalism in third world countries is that class differences can seem so much more lucid and defined than in a 'first-world' nation; the gap between the rich and poor, the haves and the have-nots is much more obvious to the foreign observer. Just a little farther down the road from my hotel was a secondhand book dealer. His books were neatly laid out on the pavement, giving the passer-by the fullest opportunity to browse through what he was offering for sale. I walked past him several times that week. Most of the books were in Arabic. I did notice one book in English, Dickens' *A Tale of Two Cities*. The hotel worker's comments suddenly reminded me of that book. In many ways Damascus was a tale of two cities, with the rich and the poor living in and occupying two very different worlds, leading two entirely different lives.

I believe one of the reasons for the economic strength of the West is the ability of Western states to nurture and utilise the talents of their people. One reason for this must be that a much greater number of people in the West have access to and receive a good education. This gives them the opportunity to develop skills and obtain qualifications that they would otherwise be denied. Another seemingly relevant factor is that the financial and banking institutions of countries such as the United Kingdom and United States are much more open to modern economic policies, free-trade, etc., than those in the Middle East. Financial institutions provide the capital that economic and business ventures need either to 'start up' or gain investment for further growth. Compared to the West, financial institutions in the Middle East seem primitive and underdeveloped, and because of this (at least in comparison to the West), they are much less able to nurture and bring to full fruition the ideas/ventures of so many of their talented and able citizens. It pains me to say this and certainly to see the results of this—capitalist societies invest in enterprise in ways that other systems or ideologies do not. Yes, one of the consequences of this is the possibility that social inequality and inequity will be created in a society. But strangely, capitalism also possesses an egalitarian spirit. It is willing to invest in the ideas of its people, to give those who would otherwise be denied, the capital to turn their dreams into reality. I am sure there are numerous other reasons that account for why the West is better able to nurture and utilise the abilities and talents of its citizens. Countries such as Syria, Iran, or any other third world country face the challenge of developing the most suitable political-economic model for their circumstances. I question whether or not Iran or Syria, or many other Muslim states for that matter, have as of yet been able to do this.

11. THE CONTINUING ADVENTURES
OF MAN'S SPARE RIB
(Damascus)

KNOWN BY MANY names, Old Damascus, Damascus proper, the historic
Damascus, the Damascus of the Apostle Paul and Ibn Tamiyyah; it is indeed
a city to fall in love with. The Old City rests as an ancient labyrinth of small
and winding streets; a place of wonder and enchantment, a gateway to the
Old World—a world where the children of Abraham once ruled. The story
of mankind can be found in the story of Damascus.

Three sites in the Old City stood out for me. First was the Umayyad
Mosque, which I had unsuccessfully attempted to enter. The Umayyads
(705–750) formed Islam's first dynasty; their capital was in Damascus and it
was here that they built this majestic building.

Take two. Making sure that this time my pigeon-crap radar was on full
alert, I successfully managed to navigate my way through the mosque's glorious surroundings. Its architecture was distinct from the dome-shaped,
blue-tiled Persian mosques that I had visited in Iran. Whilst the building
possessed the traditional pillars and arches that form the signature features
of most mosques, there were other parts of its structure that very much
resembled a cathedral, giving the place an Islamic-gothic feel.

The second site worthy of mention is the Sayyida Ruqayya Mosque.
Named after the great granddaughter of the Prophet Muhammad, the
mosque is a recent addition to the Old City and was built by the Iranians.
Small, but breathtakingly beautiful, the building had all the hallmarks of
Persian architecture. Its inside walls were lined with what appeared to be
small fragments of reflective glass, creating a wonderfully surreal effect.

The mausoleum of Salah al-Din (1138–1193) concludes my list of
noteworthy sites. Salah al-Din occupies a somewhat unusual place in the history of the Crusades, in that he is one of the few Muslim figures to receive
a relatively sympathetic obituary from Western historians (most recently in
Ridley Scott's epic, *Kingdom of Heaven*). In 1099 the Christian Crusaders managed to capture the holy city of Jerusalem from the Muslims. But in so doing,
they massacred its inhabitants in one of the worst atrocities ever committed in
the name of Christianity. For many decades the Muslims were powerless in
their attempts to regain control of their third holiest site (after Mecca and

Medina). It was not until 1187 that an army under the control of Salah al-Din managed to expel the Crusaders from the holy land and return Jerusalem to the realm of Islam. This in itself was an achievement that would have guaranteed Salah al-Din a special place in Muslim history. But what distinguished him even further (both in the eyes of the West and in the view of the Muslim world) was that having regained control of the city, far from exacting revenge for the atrocities that had occurred in 1099, Salah al-Din made sure that the Christian and Jewish communities of the conquered lands were allowed to live in relative peace and allowed to practice their religion free from Muslim persecution and torture. As the centuries passed, Salah al-Din became an increasingly mythical figure for many Muslims: he was a noble and brave warrior who not only made Islam great again, but also made sure that it was a benevolent power, one that afforded equity and justice to all its citizens, be they Muslim, Christian or Jew. As I stood in the mausoleum paying my respects to the great man, I thought about 9/11 and wondered what Salah al-Din would have made of the events that occurred on that day. He also lived in a period of history in which there was much tension and unease between the Muslim and Christian communities. In many ways, Salah al-Din's achievements are more relevant today than ever. They teach us one very important lesson: whatever one's grievances, whatever evil has been inflicted on one, the response to that grievance or evil must come within a moral framework. How great therefore, is the contrast between Salah al-Din and Osama Bin Laden.

One afternoon, whilst I was wandering through the bazaars and market places of the Old City I saw several women dressed in the full *hijab*. This was a sight that I had not seen since leaving Iran, and so these women got me thinking about an issue that I had been mulling over since my arrival in the Middle East. In the modern era Western societies and Muslim societies have increasingly used womens' clothing, the clothing of the 'other' as a sort of battering ram to undermine that culture. Specifically, the female couture of the 'other' is used as an indicator and a reflection of the inferior status of women in that society (by virtue of what it symbolises). The observations drawn from this process are then often used to draw wider negative assumptions about that society, i.e., the women in that 'other' culture are exploited/oppressed (the proof of which is in their clothing), and this means that there is an inherent and fundamental social defect in the constitution of that society, and because this social defect is absent in our society, 'our culture' is superior.

For instance, if we look through the rose-tinted spectacles of the West, the *hijab, burkah, purdah* (the West is probably more aware of the range of terms used in different parts of the Muslim world than is the Muslim world itself) is seen as a symbol of the oppression of the Muslim woman and an indicator of her low status within Muslim society. How is it that one can arrive at such a conclusion by virtue of a single piece of fabric? How can one garment come to symbolise so much? Well, one might be able to arrive at such an assumption if, amongst other things, there was a widely held belief that most Muslim women are coerced or socially conditioned to wear the *hijab* and that given a real choice, most Muslim women would prefer to cast it off. Given the current public debate within the United Kingdom, France and other Western countries, there is no shortage of material to support the view that the *hijab* is oppressive.

Assumptions such as these are important in the process of creating a discourse that claims Muslim women are oppressed and of low status. The premise that Muslim women are coerced or socially conditioned to dress in a particular way is seen as a violation of one of the bedrock principles of Western civilisation: the sanctity of the freedom of the individual and the right of every person to pursue and make individual choices free from interference except in those circumstances where harm is being caused. It is taken as a fact that the garment (be it a veil or the full *hijab*) limits individual expression, appears to be uncomfortable and restricting and that it is an obligation for women only. Thus these 'facts' reaffirm the belief that both the individual rights of women are being violated and that these clothing conditions mean that Muslim women are being treated differentially (i.e., unequally) to men.

Regardless of how liberal or tolerant one considers oneself, because most people in the West discursively construct their attitudes and opinions of the *hijab* from a pool of discourses that comprise a negative inference on the wearing of the *hijab*, it becomes almost impossible to construct an attitude that sees the *hijab* in anything but a negative light. And yet in most Muslim societies, most Muslim women who wear various forms of the *hijab* do so voluntarily. And the reason they want to wear the *hijab* arises from a genuine and sincerely held belief that their religion obligates that they emphasise their modesty in the public domain in this way. Their attitudes towards the *hijab* differ because they are constructed from a wholly different set of discourses, a set of discourses that are regarded as sacrosanct and that view the wearing of the garment in a completely different way than people in the West view it. This also explains why so many Muslim women whose families have resided in the West for several generations continue, of their own free will, to wear various forms of the *hijab*; a phenomenon that no doubt baffles many Westerners who might find it difficult to grasp why a Muslim woman would want to continue to sport the *hijab* in the absence of any legal or cultural impediments should they choose not to wear it. The academic Katherine Bullock explored this apparent anomaly. Her research concluded that for many Muslim women who live in the West the *hijab*

> ... acts as an empowering tool of resistance to the consumer capitalist culture's beauty game of the 20th century that has had such a detrimental impact on women's self esteem and physical health. Hijab is also a religiously endorsed dress, and its link to religion gives its wearers a gateway into a faith tradition that elevates self-esteem by reminding people that their worth is not based on appearances, but on their pious deeds. From this perspective, hijab is a symbol of a religion that treats women as persons, rather than as sex objects. This is the exact opposite conclusion to a common feminist conception that hijab is a symbol that Islam views women as a sex object, that she must be covered up because she is thought of reductively as 'female' whose only important attribute is her sexuality that threatens the social order.[1]

I am not trying to suggest that there do not exist some Muslim women who reject the idea of the *hijab* and do see it as oppressive. Neither am I suggesting that Muslim women do not suffer a great many grievances and injustices in the societies in which they live (they do), or that they are unaware of these grievances (they are not). My point is this; the *real* inequalities and injustices women in Muslim societies face are not to be found in a piece of cloth, but are located in areas such as the substandard healthcare, education and welfare facilities that are inadequately afforded them by too many Muslim states.

If the West has a distorted image of the position of Muslim women in Muslim societies, then similar accusations can be levelled against Muslim societies and their perception of the treatment and position of Western women in Western societies. Take for example, my earlier observation when I first arrived in Syria of the extent to which the female sexual form is used in the capitalist marketing and selling of products. Western advertising is not the only facet of Western culture that Muslim societies are exposed to in which images of Western women's clothing hone in on sexual identity and little else. I recalled the magazine stands in which virtually every magazine (barring news journals such as *Time* and *Newsweek*) produced in the West and offered for sale in the Middle East had an image of an attractive white woman, dressed in a way that wholly or partly emphasised her sexuality. What of MTV and the other music channels that I trawled through on the satellite television in my room in that expensive hotel? Many of the women in these videos were likewise dressed and portrayed as sexually provocative creatures. When one starts to think about the subject, Arab and Muslim countries (in fact almost all non-Western countries) are saturated with cultural discourses from the West in which Western women are both dressed and presented in a manner which places emphasis on their sexual identity and little else. To the average Arab on the street these images are everywhere from Hollywood films to music videos, from fashion and lifestyle magazines to commercial advertising. Of course, we in the West, as the authors of these discourses, are likewise exposed to such facets of Western culture, but the impact they have in the Arab and Muslim world is arguably different (because in the absence of alternative discourses or any interaction with Western women, they are exposed to little else but these images of them). With the female sexual form prominent in so many aspects of Western popular culture that they are exposed to, many Muslims can only conclude that the West exploits women and treats them as sexual objects (not surprisingly, it also makes the Caucasian female very alluring to many Arab men). So a beautiful model wearing next-to-nothing and selling a mobile phone is seen as a prime indicator of the ways Western societies exploit women, ways in which Muslim societies simply do not. Furthermore, the multi-billion dollar cosmetics, fashion and diet industries (now being imported to the Middle East) in which women are constantly being persuaded to dress, look and mould their bodies in a particular way, are likewise seen as a damning indictment of the way in which Western societies exploit and mistreat women.

Such cultural images not only provide a highly distorted view of the way women in the West live and dress, but are also based on the flawed assumption that a woman wearing what they perceive to be sexually provocative clothing is necessarily being exploited by men. It doesn't automatically follow that the power-control relationship of exploiter-exploited always flows in this direction. Take my earlier reference to MTV and female pop stars. Few would dispute that many of the women who appear in today's hip-hop videos are being exploited (I don't accept the argument that 'hip-hop videos allow women to express their sexuality'). However, the same argument cannot necessarily be levelled against some of the more successful women pop stars, such as Madonna, Britney or J-Lo. They also use their sexuality in their videos, but it might reasonably be argued that rather than being sexuality exploited by men, the opposite is happening: the reason for their success is partly based on their exploitation of men's sexuality (or more accurately men's sexual impulses).

In conclusion, where the West points a finger at the *hijab* as symbolic of the way in which Muslim countries oppress women, the Muslim world points its finger at Western media, advertising, fashion, cosmetics and diet industries (this list is not exhaustive) as symbolic of the way in which the West exploits women. How ironic, one society is accused of exploiting and oppressing women because of a perception that they are pressured into wearing too much clothing, whilst the other is accused of the very same exploitation and oppression because of a perception that women are pressured into wearing too little clothing.

The real and fundamental difference between Western women and women from the Muslim and non-Western world is not to be found in the type of garments they wear, but centres on the fact that Western women have, on the whole, a greater degree of control over their lives than their non-Western sisters. This appears to have been (amongst many other things) the result of two fundamental changes that have taken place in the latter half of the twentieth century in Europe and North America. The widespread availability and use of effective and affordable contraception is the first fundamental change. The second is the large-scale entry of women into the workforce, which has resulted in a shift from 'economic dependence on another' (usually the father or husband) to one of 'economic independence' or at least 'the ability to become economically independent' should circumstances necessitate. The impact of widely available, affordable and effective contraception is self-explanatory. It gave women a degree of control over their bodies that was unprecedented in human history (it is only in recent years that increasing numbers of non-Western women have had access to affordable and effective contraception). Economic independence or economic freedom is important because in many ways it is the ultimate freedom one can have in a consumer-capitalist society. It empowers one with the ability and freedom to make an infinite range of choices about the type and quality of life one desires. Depending on individual circumstances, being economically dependent has the potential to severely hinder and restrict one's life choices. I only need to look at my own community to see how much these two factors have transformed the lives of second- and third-generation British Asian women and given many of them a greater degree of control over their lives than their mothers or grandmothers could ever have imagined.

Before I am tarred with the same brush that I used against Naipaul and accused of looking at the issue through the spectacles of a neo-Orientalist, there are two provisos that I would like to add. Firstly, the two factors that I have raised are not antithetical to Islam. There is no prohibition on women becoming economically independent and contraception (of various forms) is permitted in Islam. Secondly, and more importantly, the fact that women in the West have a greater degree of control over their lives should not be equated with a greater degree of happiness (far from it). As the American feminist Naomi Wolf comments in her book, *The Beauty Myth*, "More women have more money and power and scope and legal recognition than we have ever had before; but in terms of how we feel about ourselves physically, we may actually be worse off than our unliberated grandmothers."[2]

Wolf provides an explanation as to why she believes this is so:

> The affluent, educated, liberated women of the First World, who can enjoy freedoms unavailable to any women ever before, do not feel as free as they want to. And they can no longer restrict to the subconscious their sense that this lack of freedom has something to do with apparently frivolous issues, things that really should not matter. Many are ashamed to admit that such trivial concerns—to do with physical appearance, bodies, faces, hair, clothes— matter so much. But in spite of shame, guilt, and denial, more and more women are wondering if it isn't that they are entirely neurotic and alone but rather that something important is indeed at stake that has to do with the relationship between female liberation and female beauty.[3]

Wolf appears to be suggesting that social and legal impediments that Western women have overcome and which women in many other parts of the world (including many parts of the Muslim world) are still fighting, have not resulted in true emancipation, but merely a shift from one form of oppression and discrimination to another.

So the next time a Westerner sees a Muslim woman in *hijab*, maybe he or she ought not to pity her plight too much. That woman may in fact be leading a happier, more fulfilled and yes, even a more liberated life than they are. Likewise, the next time an Arab/Muslim sees a Western woman in what they perceive to be sexually revealing clothing, they ought not take it for granted that she is being exploited; as women through the ages have learnt, female sexuality can be very powerful tool, especially against men.

That evening, I decided to visit a special type of public bath, which in the Middle East is referred to as the *hammam*. One might describe it as being similar to a traditional and ancient form of sauna and massage (although after the massage I received the term sauna and actual bodily harm is probably a more apt description).

The bathing area was essentially a large steam room with walls lined with sinks with small necks and large basins full of hot water. The object is to settle down next to a basin, relax and then use a special cup to pour the hot water from the basin over oneself, thereby slowly cleansing the mind and body of impurities. My body may have had a good cleanse but with semi-naked men surrounding me, my mind became—very quickly—cluttered with homophobic thoughts. It wasn't so much that they were semi-naked, it was more the fact that the semi-naked men were washing and cleansing one other. Whether it was rubbing soap into each other, scrubbing each other's bodies down with bits of cloth or slowly pouring cups of hot water over each other, the whole room was at it. For someone completely unaccustomed to this type of male bonding, my extreme unease led me to occupy a space next to an empty basin in a corner of the room, well away from everyone else. I crawled up next to it and remained there, occasionally giving one of my arms permission to venture out into the basin to collect some hot water to wash myself with. On one occasion a very obese man with an enormous wobbly belly waddled towards me, bar of soap in one hand, sponge type cloth in the other, and, as he got closer he raised both his hands, a gesture that I instantly understood as an invitation to participate in this ritualistic male cleansing. I immediately raised my right arm and nodded my head sideways to indicate a firm rejection of his offer. I am sure he was a very nice man, but there was no way I was giving his big jiggling mass a scrub down.

Sitting there in the corner with my eyes fortuitously scanning the steam-filled room, I observed at close hand this ritualistic male cleansing; my mind wandered off and began to think of Michel Foucault's *History of Sexuality* of all things. Observing what I was observing, Foucault's point about sexualities and sexual behaviour being constructs of society seemed to make a lot more sense.

My travels were unearthing subtle but distinct differences in the way in which sexuality is constructed by Western and Arab societies. A peck on the cheek to greet a member of the opposite sex is not at all considered sexual in Western societies, but with gender-segregation deeply entrenched in Arab culture, such behaviour towards the opposite sex might indeed be regarded as sexual if that man or woman is not a blood relation. The construction of sexuality is even more noticeable in male-male relations. In England, public displays of physical contact amongst men, whether it be holding hands in public or kissing one another on the cheek is not only rare, but should one observe such behaviour on the streets of London, Birmingham or Manchester, one would likely come to the conclusion that the two men involved were homosexual (and the chances are that they would be right, because physical contact amongst Anglo-Saxon men is almost non-existent, except at football matches). Within Arab society though, handholding in public by men is commonplace, as is giving another man a peck on the cheek to greet him. And whilst the vision that greeted me in that sauna—men gently washing and cleansing each other—I perceived as a homoerotic environment, it certainly wouldn't be seen as such by the Arab men in that *hammam*. In fact, most of them would probably be extremely offended by the suggestion.

12. THE GOSPEL OF DESCARTES
(Damascus)

MY FIRST TASK on my final full day in Damascus was to purchase a coach ticket to Beirut from the ticket office at Damascus's main bus station. I set off immediately after having breakfast that morning.

With my seat on the bus to Beirut safely booked, I made my way to Damascus University. Unlike my visit to the university in Shiraz, I did not have the luxury of an appointment with a lecturer. Nevertheless, I was hoping that as a Western tourist someone (well, anyone really!), somewhere (anywhere really!) might be interested in speaking to me.

The university campus was very beautiful and like the Umayyad Mosque its architecture had a very European feel to it. I undertook a mini-tour of the campus, then decided to visit the university library (only because I had no idea of what to do or where to go next and the library just happened to be right in front of where I was standing). The library was . . . well . . . very library-like and after a few minutes of walking around this very library-like library I decided to enter an office and seek the assistance of a bewildered middle-aged woman (bewildered as to why I was there!). I explained to this baffled woman that I was looking for the law department. Why I was looking for the law department I did not quite know, but given that I was a lawyer it added plausibility to my story. What my story was, I hadn't quite figured out yet, but I was quietly confident that when I did know, that I would manage to make my question sound legitimate. The woman, now looking a little less bewildered than when I first entered the room, kindly informed me that the law department was at another site and that I needed to catch a taxi to get there. She ripped out a blank piece of paper from a notebook resting on her desk, wrote down the address and handed it to me and explained that I should give this piece of paper to my taxi driver. Since I appeared to be suffering from a traveller's version of writer's bloc, I decided to take my chances and follow the path opened up to me by this impromptu meeting.

The next campus wasn't as beautiful as the one that I had left, but it was packed with hundreds of students hurriedly making their way to lectures and this gave the place a real buzz. I entered one of the main buildings and started to wander along its corridors, at a complete loss as to where I wanted to go or what I was supposed to be doing (looking back at the incident I accept that my actions may have constituted trespass). It didn't take long before I attracted the attention of a member of the university staff. He approached me and asked, initially in Arabic and then in English, whether he could be of assistance. This, I think, was his polite way of saying, "Who the bloomin' hell are you and what the bloomin' hell do you think you're doing here?" I told him that I was a tourist from the United Kingdom and was just looking around this fantastic and wonderful university. To my bloomin' relief, my comment immediately registered a broad smile on the face of the lecturer who held out his hand for me to shake, before going on to inform me that he had studied at Oxford. And then, for reasons that I shall never know, but for which I was eternally grateful, he invited me to his next English language class. I immediately accepted his kind offer.

Whilst making our way to the seminar room, the lecturer told me that he was in fact a professor of comparative literature and criticism and that this term his English language class was studying the Greek tragedy. An interesting but unusual topic to be teaching at an Arab university, I thought, as we made our way into the classroom.

I immediately made my way to the back of the class, with the intention to keep well away from the students. I had no desire to be the subject of attention. On the contrary, they would form the basis of my attention as I observed how English is taught in the Middle East. The only problem with my great idea was that the professor had every intention of making me the subject of attention. Once the class had settled down he introduced me to his students and then invited me to join him at the front. I was going to be assisting his professorship with the presentation of his seminar by reading out extracts from one of the books on their syllabus. This wasn't exactly how I had anticipated matters to progress, but as I didn't have the courage to register an objection, I slowly got up and made my way to the front of the room. I had little to be nervous about. After all, I was a world author-ity on Greek tragedy. Well . . . I was kind of an authority on Greek tragedy. Okay, maybe I wasn't an authority on Greek tragedy or Greek anything, but I did once go and see a Greek play about some bloke called Oedipus who married his mother (that Oedipus had a real complex and really ought to have gone and seen a psychoanalyst to get his condition diagnosed).

In compliance with the instructions that I received from the professor, I read out short extracts from the textbook (written in English), whilst the learned professor extrapolated to his students (and to me) the meaning of what I had just read out. After a while, I actually started to enjoy my role. And of course, what an experience it was for these young Syrian students to listen to the English language being spoken in Brummie (which is how the English language ought to be spoken, none of this 'received pronunciation' rubbish please!).

After the lecture, Professor sahib invited me back to his office, which, as I was about to discover, he shared with a fellow academic (who I believe taught in the social sciences department). His colleague was working studiously and our arrival interrupted him from his work, causing him to sit back in his chair and carefully observe me as the professor introduced me. Introduction over, he smiled and nodded his head as if to both acknowledge my existence and welcome me to his office. Tea[1] was ordered for all and when it arrived, the professor and I settled down to a discussion about the effects of modernity and the European Enlightenment on education and intellectual thought in the Arab world.

The professor felt that in many ways modernity and Europe's Enlightenment had caused an almost permanent rupture within the academic and scholarly community in the Arab world. Ancient academic institutions in Europe, such as the universities of Oxford and Cambridge, he argued, had managed to accommodate the new patterns of intellectual thought that the Enlightenment and modernity brought. So successfully were they able to absorb these ideas that in the end they themselves became major vessels of the Enlightenment/modernity project. Whilst there would be a whole range of responses amongst Middle Eastern intellectuals and scholars to the arrival of the 'Gospel of Descartes', ancient institutions of learning such as al-Azhar in Cairo or Qom in Iran did not wholeheartedly assimilate the Enlightenment/modernity doctrines into their intellectual patterns of thinking. This, he felt, was in part a result of a belief by these mainly religious scholars that the whole Enlightenment project was borne out of Europe's gradual realisation that its early Christian scholars had failed to adequately scrutinise the biblical sources. The Enlightenment project did not apply to Arab scholars because, unlike their Christian counterparts, the early Muslim scholars had always been fully committed to a vigorous scrutiny of their sacred sources. And yet the failure of these institutions to incorporate many of the fundamental ideas and principles of the Enlightenment into their intellectual models of thinking meant that their widespread reputation as great centres of learning would, over time, diminish. So much so, that unlike Oxford and Cambridge in the West, al-Azhar and Qom would, for many secular Middle Eastern intellectuals, eventually cease to be arenas of great academic learning, and instead be regarded simply as centres of religious learning. This was the rupture; between those academics and scholars who believed in and were fully committed to the Enlightenment project and those who were committed to the classical schools of Islamic thought developed in the early centuries after the death of the Prophet Muhammad.

Which side of the fence did Professor sahib stand on? I asked. He sought to distinguish himself from both positions, and argued instead that an increasing number of Arab scholars did not view the debate in such black and white terms (he being one of them). Many fundamental premises that surrounded this debate could be challenged. For instance, he did not view the Enlightenment or modernity as being the sole creation of Europe. For centuries, it had been the Islamic/Arab world that provided the gestation for intellectual culture and ideas that Europe had long forgotten, such as preserving the teachings and culture of the ancient Greeks ironically enough, he commented. At the very least, the genetic make-up of the Enlightenment/modernity contained significant DNA material from the Islamic/Arab world. Therefore, it was also wholly wrong for classical Arab/Muslim scholars to wholeheartedly reject the Enlightenment/modernity—after all, it was their baby as well.

The professor was equally critical of Arab academics that favoured the Enlightenment project and sneered at the backwardness of the classical Islamic scholars and their apparent inability to vigorously and objectively scrutinise the works of the early scholars of Islam with the new tools of empirical scrutiny that Europe had provided. In particular, he was keen to stress that neither the Enlightenment nor modernity were wholly objective or rational doctrines. Arab scholars who were critical of the classical schools of Islamic thought often tended to ignore or overlook the dogma contained within the secular patterns of intellectual thought. Although I did not ask him to elaborate on this point, I assumed he was referring to arguments about the Enlightenment/modernity being Eurocentric doctrines borne out of the socio-political circumstances that Europe was experiencing at the time.

What did I think of the professor's comments? I needed more time to mull over the issues he raised. In the next few days I would be meeting a lecturer who taught at one of the universities in Beirut. I would seek her views on the subject before passing my own humble and rather limited views on the subject.

It was a fascinating conversation and I wished I could have pursued it further, but the professor had a meeting to attend and had to leave us. He wished me well on my travels and I thanked him for taking the time to see me.

I was left in the room with the professor's colleague and a female student who had, during the course of my conversation with the professor, entered the room. She had been attentively listening to the discussion. She was a post-graduate student at the university and very much wished to come to the United Kingdom to continue her education after the completion of her studies in Damascus. The student, I shall call her Aisha, wanted some advice on higher education in the United Kingdom. The professor's colleague had resumed working at his desk and we were now imposing our presence upon him. I suggested we move elsewhere and she agreed.

Aisha asked me to wait whilst she rang her parents to tell them that she would be staying on at the university to speak to me. I obliged. She returned and told me that her father had invited me round for lunch. I gulped. What had I got myself into? Arabs are renowned for their hospitality and so her father's invitation should not have come as a surprise. It would be rude to say no. Furthermore, if I was going to be advising Aisha on the merits of coming to the United Kingdom to study it was understandable that her parents would also be interested in what I had to say. On the other hand, Arab societies are very conservative and during those few seconds that passed before I gave my answer a thousand and one thoughts ran through my mind as to why her father *really* wanted to invite me back to their place. I gulped again before accepting her father's kind invitation.

We caught the bus to her place. The family lived in an apartment complex just outside the town centre. She had lived in Damascus all her life and resided with her parents, two sisters and one brother. When we entered their apartment, Aisha's father was the first person to greet me. I made damn sure that I grabbed his hand, shook it vigorously, looked him straight in the eye and uttered, *assalaamu alaikum* (the traditional Muslim greeting that means 'peace be with you') as loud as I could. The greeting could not be more apt. I was a man who came in peace. Her father smiled, said *walaikum salaam* and invited me in.

Aisha's father had been working for a government department for many years. Her mother was a housewife; her brother was at university, and her two younger sisters were still at school. Their apartment was well-furnished and very tidy. I suppose it would not have been too unreasonable to presume that they were a typical middle-class Syrian family.

Aisha's mother had cooked us a wonderful meal, made all the better by the fact that I had not tasted homemade cooking since I set off on my travels. After the meal was over, I spent the next couple of hours speaking to Aisha and her family (although most of the conversation took place with Aisha, as both her father and her brother spoke very little English). Aisha spoke of the employment difficulties graduates in Syria faced after they left university, which was one reason why she wanted to study abroad.

Her stories about the problems Syrians graduates encountered in securing decent employment seemed to echo many of the problems that Iranian students faced. This crisis in graduate employment does not bode well for the stability of any Middle Eastern country. One might sensibly argue that it is not in any government's interest to educate so many of its people and then leave them disaffected and disillusioned about their future, especially if those increasing numbers of disaffected people start to believe that the prevailing political system is corrupt.

After discussing the merits and de-merits of coming to the United Kingdom to study, we spoke about a number of other issues. One topic above all others monopolised our conversation, Israel. I told her family that I wanted to end my travels by visiting Jerusalem. It would be the high point of my journey to the Middle East, the end destination, the Promised Land. Whether or not the Israelis would think it safe to let me in, given all the 'enemy' countries that I would have travelled through to get to the Israeli border was a completely separate matter and an issue that I would concern myself with at the relevant time. For the moment, I was simply interested in knowing what this young Syrian woman thought about a country which, to put it mildly, was a thorn in the side of Syria.

When I first broached the topic with her, she looked up at me, paused and then slowly uttered, "Israel . . . is . . . our . . . pain". These four words were spoken as if she were speaking on behalf of her people. And in many ways she was, for those four words captured what the average Syrian felt about Israel more accurately than a hundred PhDs on the subject.

Syria, its geography and its borders as they stand today, form only a fraction of a region once called Greater Syria (at one point, its borders extended to areas that now form parts of Jordan, Israel and the Palestinian territories). In addition to playing its part in the wider Arab-Israeli conflict that has afflicted the region since the creation of Israel, Syria also has a personal grievance with its Jewish neighbour. Israel captured Syria's Golan Heights during the 1967 Arab-Israeli War. The Golan Heights tower some three thousand feet over Galilee in Israel. Syrian control of the Golan would give the Syrian army and any Palestinian guerrilla group based in southern Syria an enormous military strategic advantage in any offensive or defensive hostile engagement with Israel. This might also explain why Israel has refused to hand back the territory it captured in 1967.

Whilst such matters naturally concerned Aisha, what concerned her even more than the occupation of the Golan Heights was the influx of Jews that returned to Palestine and the subsequent creation of Israel. She compared the phenomena to an individual who comes to your house and then takes a room without your permission. A short while later he takes another room, then another and another. Soon he occupies the whole house and in the process forces out some of its original occupants. The remaining original occupants can continue to live in the house but they must now abide by the trespasser's rules.

It is almost impossible to capture in words the vehemence with which she argued that Jews did not belong in Occupied Palestine (she never referred to the country as Israel). The majority of Jews who live in Occupied Palestine were the descendants of people who had migrated from various parts of Europe during the course of the last century. These Jewish migrants had made Europe (and other parts of the world) their home for thousands of years. That was where they belonged, she asserted. They may well have suffered anti-Semitism and persecution at the hands of the Europeans, but this had nothing to do with the Arab world. It is Europe that ought to be burdened with the responsibility of compensating the Jews for their grievances, not the Arabs. Why, she argued, should the Palestinians and especially the displaced Palestinians have to pay for the crimes that Europe inflicted upon the Jews? For centuries the West commits unforgivable sins against the Jews, then they feel guilty about it so allow them to migrate, occupy and then rule over a piece of land that is already inhabited by another group of people.

I asked her what her solution to the current conflict would be. Her answer was blunt and to the point. The Jews should return to the countries they migrated from. The land should be given back to the Palestinian people.

Aisha was an intelligent, articulate and charming young lady and on the whole it was very difficult to dislike her. She put her views across very well and there was real conviction behind her arguments. But the more I spoke to her, the more it became apparent that she was very much a product of her environment (as we all are I suppose). And when, on occasions, I challenged the negative stereotypes she expressed about Jewish people, she accused me of being brainwashed by the Jewish-controlled Western media. I have no doubt that there are many Arabs who would have agreed with her stance. On one occasion she pointed out that the numbers of Jews who died in the Holocaust had been grossly exaggerated and that it was all part of a worldwide Jewish conspiracy to maintain global power. To suggest that the figures were inaccurate was one thing, but to suggest that they were deliberately inflated in order to preserve Jewish global dominance was bordering on the absurd. Given her strongly defined views, I knew there was little merit in arguing with her.

I do want to comment on this continuing debate about the number of Jews who died in the German concentration camps and its relevance to how we view or ought to view the Holocaust. Of course I believe that the numbers of Jews who died in those evil gas chambers is important, but it is not (and should not be) the central discourse that makes the Holocaust one of the darkest chapters in human history. Assuming Aisha was right and that we were one day reliably informed that the purported six million figure was in fact wrong and that only three million Jews had died, would that new figure really lessen the horror of what happened in those German concentration camps? Will people suddenly begin to think, "Oh, only three million people died, I think I'm going to be less horrified about the Holocaust now that I know that fact"? Will historians, philosophers of ethics and just plain ordinary people begin to review Hitler's policy on the Jews and consciously tone down the evilness of the Holocaust? People are horrified about the Holocaust (and will remain equally horrified if tomorrow it was discovered the six million figure was inaccurate) because those events that occurred between 1939 and 1945 took the human capacity to commit evil into a territory and place that it had rarely (if ever) been before. It is the inability of normal and decent human beings to comprehend how it was that the human condition could be persuaded of an evil that is so awful that makes the Holocaust so horrific. One could use the 9/11 tragedy to illustrate the same point. Early indications predicted that many more thousands had died than the approximate three thousand persons that perished. But does the realisation of this lower figure in any way result in a dilution of the perceived evilness of what happened on that day? Of course it hasn't.

While I differed with Aisha on issues such as these, there were nevertheless aspects of her arguments against Israel that I found easy to empathise with. Her comment that the Arabs and Palestinians seem to be paying the price for the atrocities committed by the West (and Europe in particular) strongly resonated with my own personally held views. Aisha was absolutely right when she rhetorically asked why the Palestinians should pay for the injustices that Europe had inflicted upon the Jews. The blunt truth is that had the Holocaust not occurred, Israel would not exist today. And if Israel did not exist then the Palestinians would still have a home and the Arab-Israeli conflict would be a mere figment of our imaginations. As a footnote, I might also add that one of the main reasons that Jews migrated from the West to Israel, in the heart of the Middle East, was because they were at risk from Western anti-Semitism.[2] But the latter half of the twentieth century (thankfully) witnessed a dramatic and steep decline in Western anti-Semitism, whilst at the same time there was a disturbing and worrying increase in anti-Semitism in the Middle East, the very region the Jews migrated to in order to escape anti-Semitism (this rise in anti-Semitism is arguably almost exclusively due to the existence of Israel). The reality of the situation may well be that Jewish migration from the West to the Middle East in the twentieth century did not result in a decrease in risk to the safety and security of the average Jew, but an increase in risk and that the average Jew today is probably much safer in the West than in Israel.

One of the most interesting aspects of Aisha's arguments was her 'trespasser' interpretation of how Israel was created. I am sure that most Arabs would agree with her reading of history and that most Jews would not. Whether her reading of history is right or wrong is in many ways not the pivotal issue. What is most crucial is why it is that Arabs and Jews read history so differently. The fundamental divergence in historical interpretation is created because of differing opinions on what rights and privileges each group has over the disputed territory. Or to follow Aisha's analogy, the dispute is over who holds the freehold to the land.

The Jews have always treated Jerusalem as their holy land. The city has always been sacrosanct to them, even when they were in exile from it, or especially when they were in exile from it. Jerusalem is to the Jews what Mecca and Medina are to Muslims. The fact that Jewish people had not been living in sizeable numbers in their holy land for many centuries did not in any way impinge upon the sacrosanct status the city held for them. It would be the equivalent of the holy Muslim cities of Mecca and Medina being occupied by an invading non-Muslim force that expelled the two cities' Muslim populations (which is essentially what happened to the Jews in Jerusalem). As a Muslim, it would not matter to me whether Muslims were barred from these two cities for ten days or ten millennia. These two places are the very heart of Islam and will forever be sacred even if every Muslim were forcefully expelled. One would be hard-pressed to find a Muslim who would not believe that if Muslims were ever expelled from Mecca or Medina they had an absolute and fundamental right to return, irrespective of whoever else was residing in the two cities in the interim period or the length of time they had been residing there. It is the same for Jews and the city of Jerusalem, in that they likewise feel the same absolute and fundamental right to return to their holy city, which they were expelled from. One might therefore argue that 'they' (the Jews) are only feeling what 'we' (the Muslims) would be feeling had we been expelled from Mecca or Medina.

As persuasive as my hypothetical example may appear to some readers, alas there are a number of important differences between my imaginary scenario of Muslims being exiled from Mecca and Medina and Jews being expelled from Jerusalem. Firstly, only one faith community regards Mecca and Medina as its holy city (the Muslims), but at least three faith communities treat Jerusalem as their holy city (Jews, Christians and Muslims). More important than this is the fact that the Palestinian community can claim to have lived on this disputed piece of land for many millennia and they therefore have a justifiable and legitimate claim to also treat this land as their homeland (irrespective of whether the Jews were there before them or not as may be the case). So whilst Mecca and Medina are sacred cities *and* a homeland to one people (the Muslims), Jerusalem (and the surrounding areas) is a sacred city to several faith communities *and* a homeland to at least one other people, the Palestinians. Because Israel/Occupied Palestine is a multi-ethnic and multi-faith land, the Zionist goal of creating a Jewish state and a homeland for Jews can only be achieved by violating the rights of a Palestinian community for which Israel/Occupied Palestine is also their sacred land *and* also their homeland (and who quite understandably have no desire to give up their right to live on their sacred homeland so that it may be set aside as a sacred homeland for Jews). To put it another way, the Jews find themselves in a position where it appears that they can only 'redress' an enormous injustice that was inflicted upon their community by inflicting an equally enormous injustice on another community—the Palestinian community. Simple solutions to this conflict there are not.

13. THE SHAME OF MIDNIGHT'S CHILDREN
(Damascus-Beirut)

THE JOURNEY TO Beirut took about four hours. Syria has borders with Iraq, Turkey, Lebanon, Jordan and Israel/Occupied Palestine. With the exception of the Iraq and Israel/Occupied Palestine, it is relatively easy to travel to the major cities of these bordering nations.[1]

As the coach crossed over the border and entered into Lebanon, I immediately began to notice the change in climate. This is not surprising, given Lebanon's long border on the Mediterranean Sea. The most noticeable difference with Syria though was in the architecture. The buildings had a southern European feel to them; in many ways one could be forgiven for thinking that one was on the Mediterranean coast of a European country.

After my previous escapades in finding a decent hotel, this time I made sure that before I left for Beirut, I knew exactly which hotel I was going to stay at, where it was, how I was going to get there and how much the prostitutes would cost—sorry how much the room would cost. I would be staying at an accommodation that was owned by the American University of Beirut (travellers are welcome providing there is a room available). With the exception of the four-star hotel that I stayed in whilst I was in Tehran, this was by far the best of the hotels I had stayed at. I had a clean and well-furnished bedroom with my own en-suite bathroom. Best of all, my room had satellite TV. In addition to the usual foreign news and music channels I had access to a host of local Lebanese stations.

Before Salman Rushdie went off on his neo-Orientalist tangent (diplomatically-put), he wrote a book called *Midnight's Children*. I think the term 'midnight's children', in the general sense, refers to Indian children born around the time of India's independence from Great Britain in 1947. In the specific sense, the phrase refers to Indian children born at the exact time of India's independence, 00:00 hours on 15 August 1947. On the opening page of the book Rushdie sums up the burden of expectation placed on children born on the midnight hour of India's liberation when, in detailing the birth of the lead character in the novel, Saleem Sinai, he writes,

... at the precise instant of India's arrival at independence, I tumbled forth into the world ... thanks to the occult tyrannies of those blandly saluting clocks I had been mysteriously hand-cuffed to history, my destinies indissolubly chained to that of my country.[2]

Indians had been under colonial rule for so long and had fought for so many decades to free themselves from imperial Britain, that when Britain finally set a date for leaving India, it set off the largest communal dream in history. Free from the shackles of colonial subjugation, the children of post-independent India ('midnight's children') were now free to realise and achieve a potential that for far too long had been repressed by the British. Jawaharlal Nehru, India's first leader, summed up his country's dreams and aspirations when, on the eve of their independence, he made a speech which began as follows:

Long years ago we made a tryst with destiny, and now the time comes when we shall redeem our pledge, not wholly or in full measure, but very substantially. At the stroke of the midnight hour, when the world sleeps, India will awake to life and freedom. A moment comes, which comes but rarely in history, when we step out from the old to the new, when an age ends, and when the soul of a nation, long suppressed, finds utterance.

Big words indeed, but what, you may ask, has any of this got to do with a book on the Middle East? Well, ever since I became familiar with the term 'midnight's children', I have always thought of the Jews as being the original midnight's children. For centuries they lived in exile, banished from Jerusalem. For centuries European Christendom subjected them to persecution. And for centuries they yearned to return to Jerusalem and create their own state. To adopt the language of Nehru, for the Jews, the state of Israel is their 'tryst with destiny'. History, or Jewish history, would dictate that the story of the Jews be 'handcuffed' with the story of Israel. Like the character Saleem Sinai in *Midnight's Children*, their 'destinies would be indissolubly chained to those of their country'. And yet I sometimes wonder whether the 'modern state of Israel' is the 'Israel of history', the Israel that was foretold. Could it be that today's Jews have inadvertently handcuffed themselves to the wrong country, which they have then subsequently christened Israel and that the real Israel, the Israel that was foretold is quietly resting somewhere in the future, patiently awaiting its arrival in the world. Certainly some orthodox Jews who do not believe in the modern state of Israel think so. The reason I mention this in my opening chapter on Lebanon is because, when I think about what Israel has done to the people of this country, I really do wonder whether this is the Israel that so many Jews throughout the centuries of exile had dreamed about. The writer and academic Noam Chomsky describes Israel's invasion of Lebanon in the 1980s in the following way: "If you take the official U.S. government definition of terrorism—the threat or use of violence to achieve political, religious or other ends through intimidation, inducing fear, and so on, directed against civilian populations—Israel's invasion of Lebanon is a textbook example. You couldn't have a clearer example."[3]

For a long time when I thought about Lebanon, I almost always thought of the massacres that occurred at Sabra and Shatila, two Palestinian refugee camps in Lebanon. On the sixteenth and seventeenth of September 1982, Israeli troops allowed Lebanese Christian militia to enter these Palestinian refugee camps. This militia then went on a rampage, massacring hundreds upon hundreds of innocent and unarmed men, women and children. The world was outraged. Quite rightly, many Israelis were outraged and the results of an investigation into the massacres that were set up by the Israeli government resulted in Ariel Sharon's resignation as defence minister. To the Palestinian people and to the Arab/Muslim world at large, he is, with some justification, seen as a man who masterminded some of the worst war crimes since the Second World War. You can then imagine the disgust and horror the Palestinians and Arab/Muslim world felt when the Israeli people elected this man prime minister. Israel's actions in Lebanon during the 1980s and its more recent actions in the summer of 2006, cause one to wonder, is this the kind of Israel that was foretold?

Looking at the issue of post-colonial history from a wider perspective, one might argue that the first generation of children of all nations that achieved independence could be defined as 'midnight's children'. This would include most of the Arab nations, many of whom gained independence during the early- to mid- part of the last century. Their supposed 'tryst with destiny' initially appeared to be a form of pan-Arabism. The ideology seems to be dying a slow death, with Saddam Hussein one of its last champions. In recent years a form of neo pan-Arabism seems to be gaining support in the region. However, it is much too early to predict which direction the next generation of Arab leaders will take the Arab world (partly because one cannot necessarily predict with any degree of accuracy who the next generation of leaders will be). It might be argued that the 'midnight's children' of the Arab lands have similarly failed to live up to the high expectations that were placed upon them post-independence. One might even argue that the burden of expectation on today's Arab/Muslims is much higher than that on the Jews, on the Indians or any other colonised people, because unlike these other subjugated or colonised races, the Arabs once had a great empire, which at its peak covered much of the known world. The Arab people are forever 'handcuffed' to their glorious past, to the legacy of the Prophet Muhammad and to the great Muslim empires and civilisations the early Muslims built. And because of this, the children of the Arab lands will forever be judged and will forever judge themselves by that time and place in history when they were kings.

Of all the Arab nations, Lebanon is by far the most liberal and Westernised. In part, this is because of its cosmopolitan make-up. It has one of the largest Christian communities of any Arab country, with thirty percent of the population Christian. Even amongst the majority Muslim population, there is a significant Sunni and Shiite division (although Shiites form the largest religious group). Add to this mix Palestinian refugees (almost half a million), Kurds and Armenians and the result is either one big happy melting pot or a recipe for ethnic conflict. Unfortunately, until the 1990s ethnic conflict was the norm; even before the Israeli invasion of 2006, the south of the country was a UN buffer zone where sporadic fighting frequently took place between the Israeli army and Muslim paramilitary groups.

Since gaining full independence in 1941, power in Lebanon was monopolised by right-wing Christians whose manner of ruling antagonised large sections of the Muslim population. By 1975 civil war broke out between Christian and Muslim militia. The following year Syria intervened to assist the Muslims. To complicate matters even further in this war of factions, the PLO then decided to set up base in Lebanon (after they were ousted from Jordan). From strategic locations in the south of the country they were able to successfully launch attacks on northern Israel. If that were not enough for the Israelis to contend with, a number of non-Palestinian groups of Shiite origin also eventually based themselves in southern Lebanon. These groups were often sponsored by the new religious elite in Iran and were ideologically committed to the destruction of Israel. They included Amal, Islamic Jihad and of course Hezbollah. The Israelis, who no doubt took a very different reading of events than that taken by Professor Chomsky, sent in forces to defend themselves from these attacks and further attempted to eliminate the PLO. For much of the 1980s the country was a war zone and its capital Beirut was the centre of much conflict between the various factions. Just prior to leaving for the Middle East, I represented a Lebanese asylum seeker. Whilst waiting for his case to be heard we had a lengthy discussion about Lebanon's civil war. He blamed the country's recent turbulent history on foreign influences interfering in

Lebanon. These foreign influences included Syria, Iran, Israel, displaced Palestinians, the United States and the United Nations (the list does go on a bit). He dreamt of a Lebanon free from outside influences, where all its peoples could live together peacefully without other nations and people meddling in its affairs and causing division amongst its people. Somehow I imagine that he was probably not the only Lebanese who'd had this dream.

When the civil war ended in the early 1990s much of Beirut had been bombed out. The country began a massive reconstruction programme to build a new Beirut—a programme that continues to this day (and has no doubt suffered a major setback after Israel's re-invasion in the summer of 2006).

As I walked around Beirut on my first afternoon, the enduring image I had of the city was of fantastic plush new buildings standing alongside derelict, crumbling and shell-ridden concrete monstrosities that were once part of old Beirut. At times I thought I was in west London, other times Milan, and still other times Bosnia. Bosnia meets Bayswater in Beirut.

The quality and design of the newly constructed buildings reflected wealth. I mean real wealth. An obscene number of five-star hotels, banks and other financial institutions cluttered the central district. Beirut is one of the financial hubs of the Middle East, a sort of mini Hong Kong. I don't think I had ever seen so many Mercedes in my life. This city must have one of the highest ratios of Mercs per person in the world.

At the time I visited, much of the construction work was complete and the new Beirut was very impressive. Before the civil war began this city was called the 'Paris of the East'. It was well on its way to regaining that title.

As with virtually any major city in any part of the world, where there is wealth, there is often poverty in equal measures and Beirut was no exception. The poor, the beggars, the underclass, they all shared the same streets as the businessmen, the entrepreneurs, the rich kids draped in designer clothes, driving Beemers and Mercs paid for by wealthy parents. Lebanon, like far too many Arab countries, was a society of the super rich and super poor; a society in which modern day Oliver Twists shared the streets with gentleman Arabs.

The shops that lined the streets of the central district reflected Lebanon's liberal attitude. The most significant cultural difference between Lebanon and its Arab neighbours is the widespread availability of alcohol. Because of the Lebanese Christian population, alcohol is much more freely available here than in most other Arab countries. There were bars, clubs, gambling casinos and even strip joints. The number of women wearing *hijab* was very small and although it was the middle of winter, I saw several women walking around in mini-skirts. Iran this most certainly was not. These streets also told the story of Lebanon's colonial heritage. The influence of European architecture was evident and many of the streets had French-sounding names: Ave de Paris or Ave du Gènèral de Gaulle.

After I had finished my walk, I entered a branch of McDonalds and had what was my first ever Big Mac (the halal version). Honestly, it tasted rather bland. But food aside, the majority of the branch's customers appeared to be of middle-class background (as I was to discover, the other American fast food outlets in Beirut had a similar type of clientele). This is not surprising, since for many poor and working-class Lebanese, a Big Mac and fries would probably constitute a very expensive meal.

There aren't many areas in which the Indian subcontinent is a world leader. I can think of two: cricket and curry. In the same way that the US dollar is the benchmark currency by which all other currencies are measured, for me, Indian cuisine is the 'benchmark curry-ency' by which all other cuisines are measured (okay, okay, I apologise, that was terrible). The only cuisine that seems to achieve parity with 'curry' is Lebanese food. I was therefore looking forward to tasting Lebanese food in Lebanon. It did not disappoint. Even the cheap Lebanese street food was far superior to the American junk food I had consumed.

Within the United Kingdom, curry has become the nation's favourite dish. It is very much part and parcel of modern British life. Indian restaurants span the breadth and depth of the country. Every town in the United Kingdom now has several Indian restaurants. The curry has irreversibly changed the eating habits of one of the oldest countries in Europe. One might describe the phenomena as being a form of 'inverse colonialism'. In the same way the European imperial powers fiercely competed with each other to carve up Africa and other parts of the world, in the United Kingdom, Asian restaurateurs and businessmen fiercely compete with each other to carve up Britain and establish their own Indian restaurant within a locality. The European imperial powers, after obtaining a particular locality, used it to reflect parts of their culture onto the natives and to also economically exploit them, and now Indian restaurateurs do much the same thing. They obtain their locality then use it to reflect aspects of their culture (in this case their eating habits) onto the natives, whilst at the same time economically exploiting them (charging ten pounds for a standard curry which any Asian mum would tell you she could make for two pounds). If I were a sociology teacher I would set my students the following essay question, 'The similarities between European imperial history and the curry trade in the United Kingdom. Discuss.'

Death of the Author

Shall I hear the lament of the nightingale, submissively lending my ear?
Am I the Rose to suffer its cry in silence year after year?
The fire of verse gives me courage and bids me no more to be faint.
With dust in my mouth, I am abject: to God I make my complaint.
Sometimes You favour our rivals then sometimes with us You are free,
I am sorry to say it so boldly. You are no [more] fickle than we.

Complaint to God, Mohammad Iqbal

Since I have referred to Salman Rushdie in the opening paragraphs of this chapter and the title of the chapter is itself the result of the 'fusions, translations and conjoinings' of two of his novels, I should, therefore, deal with the topic of Salman Rushdie and a particular book he wrote.

In modern times nothing has reflected the apparent cultural and ideological gulf between the Muslim world and the West as much as the Satanic Verses affair. The polarisation in attitudes towards Salman Rushdie's fourth novel could not have been greater, the principles and ideals upon which each side staked their position could not have been higher.

To someone who has never read *The Satanic Verses*, one of the most puzzling aspects about the affair must be the vastly opposing interpretations one can reach about the controversial parts of the novel. Where one group reads the contentious passages within the novel as a brilliant intellectual critique of Islam and Muslim scholarship, the other group, reading the same text, interprets it as the redeployment of a cultural tool, Orientalism, designed by the West to rape the traditions, reality and history, of 'other' cultures. Where one group interprets certain passages within the novel as a verbal outpouring of offensive and abusive remarks that ridicule and mock the Prophet Muhammad and the religion of Islam, the other reads the same text as an attempt by Rushdie to deploy wit, satire and irony to reflect the failures in the Prophet Muhammad's egalitarian vision and highlight the inconsistencies and hypocrisies within his lifestyle. *Prima facie*, it is not easy to reconcile these opposing interpretations as emanating from the same text.

For the West, irrespective of the artistic merits of the book, Rushdie's 'right to write' touched upon one of the foundations of Western civilisation, the right of free expression, of freedom of speech and thought. It was not a fanciful or abstract right, a right whose merits could not be measured.

The unprecedented success, influence and continuing dominance of Western civilisation is, in part, built upon Western constitutions protecting and promoting the fundamental rights of their citizens. For the Muslim world, the position is best summed up by Edward Said, who said, just as the controversy was reaching international audiences,

> Why must a Muslim, who could be sympathetically interpreting us, now represent us so roughly, so expertly and so disrespectfully to an audience already primed to excoriate our traditions, reality, history, religion, language, and origin? Why in other words, must a member of our culture join the legions of Orientalists in Orientalizing Islam so radically and unfairly?[4]

For the Muslim world, concern and anger over the book would concentrate on parts of the novel in which Rushdie appeared to mock and ridicule the Prophet Muhammad and in turn the Muslim community, but it extended beyond that. It was almost as if a thousand years and more of Western writing in which the figure of the Prophet and in particular his character had been distorted, maligned and lied about, came to a head with the publication of this book, with an exasperated Muslim world reaching the breaking point and saying, "enough is enough!" It was as if we were collectively uttering aloud, "You (the West) cannot continue to lie about us, you cannot continue to malign us and justify your absolute right to do these things under the banner of 'freedom of speech'—'freedom of expression' does not extend to having the right to peddle untruths, to ridicule and abuse 'other peoples' and 'other communities'." When Ziauddin Sardar and Merryl Wyn Davies equate the novel in the following terms, "it is as though he has personally assaulted and raped every single believing Muslim man and woman",[5] for many Muslims this wasn't an overstatement. The French philosopher Ronald Barthes famously argued that the intentions of the author are meaningless to the interpretation of any given text. On one level Rushdie's *The Satanic Verses* is a prime example of this. On another level, nowhere is this theory more challenged than with the publication of this novel, because sometimes, it was as if the whole debate was specifically about the true intentions of the author and nothing else. To talk about the threat of the 'death of the author' in the context of this book took on a whole new meaning.

Rushdie's two previous novels had earned him numerous literary awards. *The Satanic Verses* earned him a fatwa that took an enormous toll on his personal life. The misfortune that befell him was not so much the result of simply writing an offensive book on Islam. As Said pointed out, in writing *The Satanic Verses*, Salman Rushdie joined a whole legion of writers who had gained membership to the 'Orientalist Club'. Rushdie's misfortune lay in the fact that circumstances conspired against him so that it would be *his* anti-Islamic book that lit the spark that in turn ignited the anger of a Muslim community that had long felt its identity had been abused and distorted and was no longer prepared to sit back and accept it.

Before I comment on the affair, it might be helpful if I laid all my cards on the table, so that the reader is able to gauge the standpoint from which I begin my exploration of the novel and its aftereffects. I do this because too often in this affair, supporters of Salman Rushdie have accused Muslim critics of not being fit to speak on the book since they have not read the text and cannot place it within the context of Rushdie's other work (of course, this has not stopped them from going on to comment that the book is not offensive about the Prophet or Islam even though many of them have never read a book about the Prophet or Islam). Rushdie himself has even pleaded, "It has been bewildering to learn that people, millions upon millions of people, have been willing to judge *The Satanic Verses* and its author, without reading it, without finding out what manner of man this fellow might be ..."[6]

The Satanic Verses is generally regarded as the final book in a trilogy of novels in which Rushdie explores the post-colonial histories of India (*Midnight's Children*), Pakistan (*Shame*) and the Indo-Pakistani diaspora in the United Kingdom (*The Satanic Verses*). Whilst I cannot by any stretch of the imagination claim to be some sort of literary expert on Rushdie, I have read all three novels. From a purely literary point of view, his most signifi-cant novel is *Midnight's Children*. Not only did it win the prestigious *Booker Prize* in 1981, in 1993 it was awarded the Booker of Bookers (the best novel in the twenty-five year history of the Booker Prize).

I do recognise and appreciate the significance and importance of *Midnight's Children* to both Western literature and Indian/post-colonial literature. The novel was established as a literary form in Great Britain in the eighteenth century and went on to firmly establish itself as an integral part of Western culture. Towards the latter part of the twentieth century, for some in the West the novel as a literary form, as a serious art form, had become stale, unambitious and bland. The West is indebted to post-colonial writers such as Rushdie, because, through novels such as *Midnight's Children*, they resurrected this dying art form by introducing new literary techniques and concepts. The Indian author Anita Desai sums up Rushdie's contribution to the novel in the following words:

> Salman Rushdie had turned his back on the Victorian/Indian tradition that had rooted itself so powerfully in colonial soil, and ushered in post-colonial impulses and attitudes—delightedly and insouciantly jumbling genres and

employing post-modern techniques such as discontinuous narrative, cinematic images and metaphors, mirror games and linguistic blasphemies that one was told composed the school of magical realism . . .[7]

The West did not give this brown-faced Indian man the Booker of Bookers for nothing.

Rushdie's contribution to Indian and post-colonial literature is arguably even greater. The rise of the novel as a literary form coincided with the rise of European imperialism and European colonial experience. Western literature and the novel in particular were frequently used by the imperial powers to observe, interpret and classify colonised subjects and colonised societies. However, when the colonised people and their cultures were observed through the prism of the novel, too often false realities were created—false realities which project an image of a rational, enlightened and civilised West and an irrational, ignorant and uncivilised East. The end of colonial rule has seen a generation of bright and talented third world writers and thinkers intelligently and expertly deconstruct the colonial experience recorded in colonial discourses (such as novels from that era), and highlight and increase our awareness and understanding of these 'prisms of false realities'. Some writers, such as Edward Said, did this through academic literature. Others, unapologetically and unashamedly, hijacked the novel itself, turned it around and shone its light back in the face of the West, so that they themselves could see the distorted prisms their literary ancestors had created. Salman Rushdie's *Midnight's Children* is a seminal text within this field of post-colonial literature. Panoramic in its scope, amongst other multiple objectives, the novel attacks the West's attempts under colonial rule to capture the 'essence of India', to bottle it and sell it back home in the form of a cheap novel. As if such an objective was even remotely possible. As any reader of *Midnight's Children* quickly becomes aware, there isn't one India, the vast geographical size of the country coupled with its enormous and varied population generates not one India, but multiple Indias. Any attempt to classify colonial subjects and colonial society into 'one essence' is absurd. As I said, he wasn't awarded the Booker of Bookers for nothing.

Although Rushdie is more famous for his fiction, he has also written many pieces of non-fiction. Throughout the seventies and eighties, when British Asians and British Afro-Caribbeans were subject to the most awful racism from various parts of the state machinery and by some of its white subjects, and they were without a voice to air these grievances, Salman Rushdie was one of those few Asians in the public arena who sought to consistently speak out on issues concerning race relations. For example, in an article in 1982, he vehemently and passionately spoke out about the institutionalised racism and racial violence that blacks and Asians were subjected to from certain elements within the British police force:

> ... British society has never been cleansed of the filth of imperialism. It's still there, breeding lice and vermin, waiting for unscrupulous people to exploit it for their own ends. One of the key concepts of imperialism was that military superiority implied cultural superiority, and this enabled the British to condescend and repress cultures far older than their own; and it still does. For the citizens of the new, imported Empire, for the colonized Asian and blacks of Britain, the police force represents that colonizing army, those regiments of occupation and control.[8]

It would be nearly another two decades before the government publicly acknowledged that institutionalised racism exists in our police force.

Before the Satanic Verses affair, Rushdie's work, both fiction and non-fiction, was acknowledged by other high-profile Muslims. Professor Akbar Ahmed in his book, *Discovering Islam: Making Sense of Muslim History and Society*[9] pays homage to Rushdie's literary skills and at the time even placed him within a South Asian Muslim tradition. Ziauddin Sardar, one of Rushdie's fiercest critics, has recently conceded that before the publication of *The Satanic Verses* he admired Rushdie's work, saying; "I had respect for Rushdie as a spokesperson for the oppressed; I'd enjoyed the exuberance of his 1981 Booker Prize winning novel, *Midnight's Children*."[10]

It is against this backdrop, against this recognition of his prior achievements that I approach *The Satanic Verses* novel. As a footnote, it is worthy of mention that although I present the debates that the novel created as an ideological confrontation between the West and the Muslim world, each with its own homogenous and distinct position at complete odds with the other, this is a gross generalisation (forced upon me by the limitation of exploring the debate within half a chapter). As Paul Brians has correctly noted,

> To many Western readers *The Satanic Verses* appears as a brilliant attack on religious bigotry. To many Muslims, East and West, it appears as a vicious series of insults to many of their most cherished beliefs. There are other positions: liberal and conservative non-Muslims deplore his irreverence and liberal Muslims deplore the fatwa against Rushdie and support his right to publish, or even admire his work; some American and British non-Muslim critics have been critical of him.[11]

But before I proceed to explore the text and the affair, it may be helpful to briefly explain the story of the satanic verses.

The Story of the Satanic Verses

The origins of the story of the satanic verses can be traced back through the annals of Islamic history to sometime shortly after the birth of the religion in the seventh century. Although there are variations in the story, generally it reads as follows. Early on in Muhammad's prophethood, when he was still in his home city of Mecca, he preached his divine message that called for the worship of one god, Al-Lah, and the abolishment of the town's 'idols of worship'—the very idols, gods and goddesses that had made the city wealthy from pilgrims who flocked to the city in droves from all over Arabia. During this period and around the time that his message and his followers had grown large enough to cause real and genuine concern to the old order (e.g., by increasingly dissuading/disrupting the lucrative pilgrim trade), but not large enough to prevent them from being persecuted and tortured by elements from within the 'old order', the worried rulers of Mecca offered the Prophet a compromise deal (some say that in the early days of Islam he was offered many compromise deals). In return for accepting three of their most cherished 'idols of worship', they would; a) recognise his one god, Al-Lah; b) allow him to preach freely in the city and; c) stop the persecution of his followers. The story goes on to tell us that the Prophet Muhammad accepted the deal after he received a revelation from the Angel Gibril (Gabriel) confirming that Mecca's three main goddesses were worthy of worship, even though the 'deal' compromised his central monotheistic message of one God. It is said that the revelation (not surprisingly) caused much confusion and uncertainty amongst his followers who were now asked to accept the fact that even though they had been told by the Prophet from the very first day of his prophethood that there was only one God, this was in fact not strictly accurate as Mecca's three main goddesses also had some claim to divinity and were also worthy of worship. The story concludes by telling us that a short time after this revelation, the angel Gibril appeared before the Prophet Muhammad and informed him that the earlier revelation, in which the alleged verses affirmed the divinity of the three goddesses, were not from him at all, but were actually from Satan himself, who had tricked the Prophet by disguising himself as Gibril (hence the name of the story, the satanic verses). As a result, the Prophet Muhammad ordered these verses be expunged from the Quran. This in turn meant that he reneged on the compromise deal, much to the annoyance of the Meccan rulers.

The majority of Muslim scholars studying the accuracy and authenticity of the story have concluded it to be a fabrication; a small number have not.

Of the major schools of Islamic thought (both Sunni and Shia), none have accepted the story as being true.

The Text

Apart from Muslims themselves, the only other scholars that have seriously studied the life of the Prophet are Western Orientalists. The central question that has vexed them in their study of the Prophet, which their scholars have wrestled over for more than a thousand years, is how to explain the Prophet Muhammad? How can his life and his legacy be explained? By this I mean, if it is not accepted that the Prophet Muhammad's preaching was the result of divine revelation, then what were his underlying motives?

In the West, the historical treatment of the Prophet Muhammad's motives has gone through two distinct phases, pre-modern and modern (although it seems that the West has just embarked upon its third era of Islamic scholarship, post-modern). From a Muslim perspective, the Western interpretation of his message has been altered from essentially that of 'a madman to a con man'. The first concrete impressions of the Prophet Muhammad were popularised through the Crusades, during which Christendom sought to dismiss this desert Arab man's claims to be in receipt of divine revelation as the rantings of a sexually perverted, power hungry, madman.[12] As a result, the Prophet Muhammad of the medieval period was subject to an unprecedented level of ridicule and abuse—abuse that even then found itself seeping into the works of the great literary figures of the day, such as Dante's *The Divine Comedy*. Abuse extended to offensive names specifically invented for the Prophet, such as 'Mahound'. Rushdie in his wisdom sought to name the Muhammad of his *Satanic Verses*, 'Mahound'.

The modern period saw a reinterpretation and a rethinking of the Prophet Muhammad's motives. Western scholars now conceded that a man who was intellectually and politically astute enough to unite the warring tribes of Arabia (something that neither the Persian nor Byzantine powers could manage) and who was able to overturn an 'old order' and replace it with a new one which, only a few years after his death, would manage to conquer much of the known world, was unlikely to be a demented madman who uttered 'crazy talk' as he walked the streets of Mecca. Now equipped with the tools of modernity, they used modern scholarly techniques to objectively study his life. And from the pens of these Orientalist scholars, a new Prophet Muhammad was created. Well . . . kind of.

The newly revised story is that the orphan Prophet was born into an important Meccan family, but one which, by the time he was born, was on the fringes of the power circle in Mecca. He grew up to be a very success-ful and able businessman, respected by the Meccan rulers, even admired; but he was without political power. *And it was political power that the Prophet Muhammad sought.* An astute man, he was able to unite the poor and those of the middle-classes who (like him) were denied access to the corridors of power, and he was able to mould them into a powerful oppositional polit-ical and military force that, with his political acumen, would eventually defeat the 'old order'. How was he able to do this—through the creation of a new message that was called 'Islam'.

In this revised assessment, the Prophet Muhammad is seen as some sort of con man who uses the very effective medium of divine revelation to establish his right to power, and then frequently makes use of it in order to maintain power. Revelation is thus deployed by the Prophet Muhammad as an instrument of power to maintain and extend his authority. In *The Satanic Verses*, the author frequently makes reference to this 'revelations of convenience' argument. For example, one of the passages from the book reads:

> After that Salman began to notice how useful and well timed the angel's revelations tended to be, so that when the faithful were disputing Mahound's views on any subject ... the angel would turn up with an answer, and he always supported Mahound ... It would have been differ-ent, Salman complained to Baal, if Mahound took up his positions after receiving the revelation from Gibreel; but no, he just laid down the law and the angel would confirm it afterwards ... [13]

Another part of the book makes reference to the Prophet Muhammad's polygamous lifestyle:

> 'That girl couldn't stomach it that her husband wanted so many other women,' he said. 'He talked about necessity, political alliances and so on, but she wasn't fooled. Who can blame her? Finally he went into—what else?—one of his trances, and out he came with a message from the archangel. Gibreel had given him full divine support. God's own permission to f★★★ as many women as he liked. [14]

The non-Muslim reader might reasonably argue, 'what is wrong with such a conclusion?' If one does not believe that the Prophet Muhammad was in receipt of divine revelation, then it is a perfectly reasonable conclusion for Western scholars to arrive at. Furthermore, Western and non-Muslim writers are perfectly entitled to corroborate the 'revelations of convenience' argument by making reference to incidents such as the 'satanic verses story', for the incident is a perfect illustration of how the Prophet Muhammad, in his pursuance of power, was prepared to compromise the central tenant of Islam (that of 'one God') in order to gain some level of political legitimacy (the fact that he reneged on the deal when he realised its implications only adds greater probative value to the 'revelations of convenience' doctrine). Muslim sensitivities over Rushdie's reference to established Orientalist/Western critical thinking on the Prophet and Islam simply reinforces the Western belief that Muslims have not yet reached the stage in their intellectual development in which they are prepared to critically review their scriptures. As Professor Paul Brians informs his readers, "Islam has never undergone an equivalent to the European Enlightenment, let alone the development of a 'higher criticism' such as the West has subjected the Bible to for the past two centuries."[15] And later on, "In the secularized West his [Salman Rushdie's] critique seems routine; in much of the Islamic East, it is unspeakable."[16] In conclusion, the West's position may be summed up in the following way: whilst Rushdie may have been insensitive in the manner in which he sometimes deploys his colourful language, he is, nevertheless, perfectly entitled to express his doubts over the legitimacy of the Prophet's message.

Muslim thinkers reading the same text, studying the same words, see entrenched and subsumed within Rushdie's prose a completely different historical and intellectual discourse/tradition. When Rushdie uses the novel as a vessel to forward Orientalist critical thinking they do not see what Professor Paul Brians and his fellow contemporaries see. Beneath the same text, behind the same words, a different history, a different tradition can be seen; one that is rooted in cultural imperialism and a discourse of power that they cannot sit idly by and allow to slowly obliterate their history, their traditions and their identity. As Sardar and Wyn Davies surmise:

> The vast majority of Muslims wish Salman Rushdie no physical harm: but equally, they are not able to forgive him. They would be fools to do so on two counts. If they do not defend their cultural and historic territory, they cannot hope to survive the future without losing their identities ... Moreover, they should not forgive because 'their forgiveness [would have] made possible the deepest and sweetest corruption of all, namely the idea the he [has done] nothing wrong.[17]

Western Orientalist scholarship is premised on the assumption that their conclusions are more reliable than Muslim scholarship because of their use of 'modern scholarly techniques' to objectively study the life of the Prophet. Or, as Paul Brians argued, the West has developed a 'higher criticism' in its intellectual tradition, and this 'higher criticism' is absent in other academic traditions, particularly Muslim scholarship.

However, from the Muslim viewpoint, there are two serious ailments in Orientalist thought. The first, which I have mentioned several times before in other contexts, is that Western scholars/writers have too often studied colonised/third world/ 'other' societies from the viewpoint of their belief in a rational West and an irrational East/ 'other'. In the context of the study of the Prophet, this has manifested itself in the belief that, on the whole, Muslim scholars were incapable of objectively studying the life of the Prophet and much of their scholarship should therefore be rejected. Why? Because Muslim scholarship has made use of inferior methodological techniques and such works were produced by scholars with a highly deferential and subjective attitude towards the Prophet. Such comments understandably anger Muslims. Furthermore, as Sardar and Wyn Davies observantly point out, in dismissing the merits of Muslim intellectual thought, the Western Orientalist tradition seeks to "make a quarter of mankind voiceless appendages to their own history and identity."[18] Having dismissed the ability of Muslims to reliably study their own history, Western scholars seek to replace unreliable Muslim scholarship with reliable Western scholars. Reliable, because Western scholars make use of more modern, more sophisticated and more advanced methodological techniques ('higher criticism' as Paul Brians might argue), and such works are produced by scholars with a more objective and impartial stance towards the Prophet. Such a sweeping generalisation of the worth of one's own tradition and the worthlessness of over a thousand years of Muslim scholarship does itself smack of a form of partiality that more recent Western scholars have begun to acknowledge.

The second ailment, which is largely linked to the first, is a rebuttal argument that responds to Western criticism of Muslim scholarship by arguing that when one analyses Western scholarship on Islam it is anything but objective. On the contrary, Orientalist and neo-Orientalist thinking on Islam is riddled with subjectivity and the methodological techniques adopted by such thinkers are too often set within a normative framework that is designed or loaded to produce results that favour Western assumptions about the Prophet, such as the 'revelations of convenience' theory. The West's almost blind acceptance of the original satanic verses story is a prime example of this. Muhammad Haykal for example, comments that the "story arrested the attention of the western Orientalists who took it as true and repeated it ad nauseam".[19]

I will deal with the topic of Muslim scholarship in greater detail in the next chapter. Turning to the issue of Western scholarship on Islam, there is some substance to the rebuttal arguments forwarded by Muslim scholars concerning the reliability and accuracy of Orientalist scholarship. This in turn means there is some substance to the further allegation that modern Western scholarship on Islam is a 'discourse of power' used to enforce a partial and normative viewpoint on Islamic history. This is because Western scholarship is part of a dominant world culture (which may be broadly defined as Western civilisation) that has colonising tendencies in its interaction with 'other' cultures and as a result it advertently or inadvertently seeks to marginalise Muslim/ 'other' scholarship. Therefore, when Rushdie repeats these Orientalist arguments in his book, Muslim thinkers are absolutely right to highlight the West's aloofness in respect of its intellectual superiority and to tackle head on the less-than-objective position of Western scholarship on Islam. Take for example, the Western acceptance of the original satanic verses story as true. I managed to dig out W. Montgomery Watt's biography of the Prophet from my collection of books; he is arguably the most significant Western scholar of Islam in the twentieth century. Watt believes that the story of the satanic verses is true and the main reason he cites is as follows; "This is a strange and surprising story. The prophet of the most uncompromising monotheistic religion seems to be authorising polytheism. Indeed, the story is so strange that it must be true in essentials."[20] Let me just again remind the reader that the quote is from arguably the most important Western scholar on Islam in the last century. Let me also reiterate that the main reason he cites for the story being true is that, 'it is so strange it must be true'.[21] Watt is not the only one. Maxime Rodinson, a major Western scholar on Islam in the latter part of the twentieth century appears to simply regurgitate Watt's thesis on the Prophet Muhammad when he argues that, the satanic verses story "... may reasonably be accepted as true because the makers of Muslim tradition would never have invented a story with such damaging implications for the revelation as whole"[22] 'Higher criticism!' 'Modern and sophisticated methodological techniques!' If I may be allowed to be pedantic for one moment; I could go through each one of the Orientalist arguments Rushdie repeats in his contentious novel, trace it back to the Orientalist from whom the argument is derived and further analyse the basis upon which that Orientalist scholar accepts the story as being true, and just as in the illustration above, find that I could quite fairly argue that the particular finding is fused with conjecture, speculation and partiality. I don't want to enter into a tit-for-tat debate about whose scholarship and intellectual tradition is better. The only point I wish to make is this; that when one looks at the Muslim backlash against parts of the novel in which Rushdie criticises Islam, that response shouldn't automatically be placed within a discourse that sees Islam/Muslims as being unable to accept 'higher criticism' of its historical discourses as Professor Paul Brians suggests, but a quite separate and legitimate response against a tradition whose study of Islam has itself, more often than not, failed to hold up to the principles of 'higher criticism' and which seeks to impose its rather subjective world view on 'other' cultures and traditions. Sardar and Wyn Davies are right, Muslims or any other non-Western culture should not become voiceless appendages to their own history, nor should they simply remain silent against the distorted Orientalist tradition of the West that Salman Rushdie invokes. Adopting Rushdie's quote on racism in British society, which I mentioned earlier, one might argue that Western society has never been cleansed of the filth of cultural imperialism. It's still here, breeding lice and vermin, waiting for unscrupulous people to exploit it for their own ends. One of the key concepts of cultural imperialism is that politico-economic superiority implies cultural superiority, and this has enabled the West to condescend and repress cultures far older than their own; it still does, through novels such as Salman Rushdie's *The Satanic Verses*.

The Affair

Before I move on to discuss the issues surrounding whether or not Rushdie had set out to abuse/ridicule Islam and if so, whether such acts ought to be protected under the banner of 'freedom of speech', it might be appropriate to begin by cross-referencing Rushdie to see what he himself says his intentions were when he set out to write this book. Rushdie himself has written much on the topic. In an article titled, "In Good Faith", written shortly after the affair, he gives us an insight into his intentions:

> I set out to explore, through the process of fiction, the nature of revelation and the power of faith. The mystical, revelatory experience is quite clearly a genuine one. This statement poses a problem to the non-believer: if we accept that the mystic, the prophet, is sincerely undergoing some sort of transcendent experience, but we cannot believe in the supernatural world, then what is going on?[23]

There were many important events and occurrences in the Prophet's life in which themes such as faith, doubt and revelation could be explored, so why seek to concentrate on the story of the satanic verses? He answers as follows:

> I felt the story humanised the Prophet, and therefore made him more accessible, more easily comprehensible to the modern reader, for whom the presence of doubt in a human mind, and human imperfections in a great man's personality, can only make that mind, that personality, more attractive.[24]

In respect of those parts of the novel in which he appears to be criticising the Prophet, Rushdie states the following:

> *The Satanic Verses* is, I profoundly hope, a work of radical dissent and questioning and reimagining. It is not, however, the book it has been made out to be, that book containing 'nothing but filth and insults and abuse' that has brought people out on to the streets. That book simply does not exist. That is what I want to say to ordinary, decent, fair-minded Muslims, of the sort that I have known all my life . . .[25]

I was in my final year at school when the novel came out. One of my friends had purchased a copy so he could find out for himself what all the fuss was about. When he finished reading the book I asked to borrow it. I remember going to pick it up from his house. It was only when I had arrived at his place that it dawned upon me that I would need to transport this book on the number 8 bus from one heavily Muslim-populated inner city area of Birmingham to another heavily Muslim-populated inner city area of Birmingham. Now carrying a copy of *The Satanic Verses* in liberal Islington or some posh part of Surrey may be an everyday occurrence, to which no one bats an eyelid, but when the controversy surrounding the book was in full flow, carrying such a book in the Small Heath, Sparkhill, Sparkbrook, Washwood Heath, Alum Rock or Lozells areas of Birmingham, risked getting your very own no-questions-asked fatwa. I made sure that I wrapped the book in sixteen plastic carrier bags before nervously taking it home.

Before I set out to write this chapter I re-read *The Satanic Verses* (in fact I re-read *Midnight's Children* and *Shame* for good measure). It had been well over a decade since I last read the novel. But before I read this literary work, I began my research by reading a great deal of what Rushdie has said on this book, about his aims and intentions (some of which I have quoted above) behind such an ambitious project. Rushdie's own comments on his motives for writing the book do not reconcile themselves easily with what some Muslim critics believe Rushdie's real intentions were. Was his book really that bad? When I first read the novel had I been caught up in the hysteria created by my community and had my subsequent conclusions been clouded as a result? I now read the book well over a decade after it had been published, in the privacy of my bedroom, door shut, windows locked, outside world firmly blocked out. What did I think now?

When I read *Midnight's Children* I came across an author who was fully aware of his sense of history and his place as an Indian writer in that history. By this I mean I came across a Salman Rushdie who was fully aware of the Western literary discourses that had attempted to define his people and his community (Indians). I came across a Salman Rushdie who was aware of the distortions and misconceptions these Western observers had made about his society. And although the novel is dark in parts, there is a warmth about it. Through the trials and tribulations of the main character one is left with an impression that the author is someone who genuinely and deeply cares about the well-being of his country, and of the many people of the many faiths and ethnicities that reside within it.

I was left with an almost opposite impression when reading *The Satanic Verses*. As much as I listened to the arguments forwarded by Rushdie in defence of his book, I remained unconvinced. I came across a Salman Rushdie who again was fully versed in the Western literary discourses that had defined the Prophet Muhammad and the early period of Islamic history. However, rather than write a novel that tackles and deals with the distortions and misconceptions that these Orientalists construct about Islam (in the same way that he attacked Western constructions of India and Indians in *Midnight's Children*), rather than write a novel that seeks to deconstruct the alleged pillars of objectivity and impartiality upon which Orientalist understanding of Islam is built, this post-colonial writer wrote the classic colonialist novel. Rushdie uses the novel as a vessel to repeat one Orientalist argument after another. And where the warmth and goodwill of the author comes through in *Midnight's Children*, in *The Satanic Verses* there is a hate and a lack of honesty that pervades the novel. As much as I disagree with him, Rushdie is free to believe and express these Orientalist arguments. But for the reader who is aware of Rushdie's other work, who is aware of his importance beyond *The Satanic Verses*, it is extremely sad and disheartening to see one of the greatest critics of Orientalism metamorphosing into the greatest Orientalist of our time.

If Rushdie had simply confined his novel to regurgitating old Orientalist arguments, then it is unlikely that his novel would have received the attention that it did. But he went further than this. On several occasions in the novel Rushdie takes a traditional Orientalist argument and blends it into his novel. He takes a disputed or an accepted historical fact from the early history of Islam and literally bleeds it into his fictitious story. But he doesn't stop there; Rushdie then quite cleverly weaves even more into the mesh of fact and fiction; namely insults, ridicule, abuse, a verbal kick against the Prophet, his family or one of his companions. As Richard Webster comments: "The overriding impression is that the novelist is making use of the ambiguities and uncertainties of fiction to disguise a deliberate attempt to defile the most precious sanctities of Islam in a language which is simultaneously wounding and obscene."[26]

It is because he does all these things that we are left with a work from which such vastly opposing interpretations can be drawn. It is Rushdie's ability to load a scene with such multiple discourses that allows for such multiple interpretations. Therefore a Muslim reading one segment of the novel will immediately be able to pick up the insult, the abuse. Someone in the West, reading the same segment, will read what they might feel is a valid criticism of Islam. To quote one example, in his book Rushdie challenges Islam's claims to have given women equal rights. He does this by using metaphors to describe how some of the Prophet's very own wives were traded off in marriage (to the Prophet) and as a result treated as political chattels between the Prophet and other tribal leaders in order to secure geopolitical stability. But he also uses these same metaphors to imply that the Prophet's wives were whores and prostitutes. If he used this literary trick once or twice one might ignore it, but he does it several times. It is for this reason that I say there is a lack of honesty in the work, because Rushdie denies he is doing such things. In his defence, a) he makes reference to the Orientalist criticism he is citing in that particular passage, and/or b) says that it is only a piece of fiction, so the reader shouldn't take what he says or implies so literally or seriously. But because he repeats this trick several times, with so many events surrounding the Prophet's life, I simply do not accept his argument. Rushdie knew what he was doing. He may well have wanted to explore the issues he mentions, but he also uses the novel as an opportunity to launch an extensive attack on a figure revered by so many in the world and has the audacity to expect them to just sit back and buy the argument that such comments are part and parcel of his intellectual discourse on the Prophet's life.

It is for these reasons that I believe Muslims were absolutely right in highlighting, in protesting and in voicing their concerns over a writer who used the arena of literary fiction to pile abuse on their faith and founder. And protest they did. News of their cries, their shouts and their book-burning episodes reached international ears. Had the response against Rushdie simply been a series of nationwide protests in the United Kingdom that received international attention, it is unlikely I would be writing about the subject over a decade and a half after the publication of the book. It is because of Khomeini's fatwa against Rushdie that you find yourself reading about the affair. As much as I disagree with what he says, should Rushdie be killed because of what he wrote? The simple and emphatic answer is 'no'. The writer Ziauddin Sardar responded to the death sentence by commenting that, "Ayatollah Khomeini's fatwa not only declared a death sentence for Rushdie, it made me redundant as an intellectual. Implicit in the fatwa is the belief that Muslim thinkers are too feeble to defend their own beliefs".[27] I agree with him. If someone claims to be upholding 'a truth' or 'the truth' and some-one else launches a verbal attack on that 'truth', and the only way in which you feel you can fend off that verbal assault is by killing that person, it shows that either you do not really hold 'the truth' or are incapable of 'defending' it with intellect and reason, but only with barbaric violence. Islam as a religion, Muslims as a people, are more than capable of fending off Rushdie's personal diatribe against them without even considering the need for violence.

The next question is whether the book ought to be banned. This is a much more difficult and more interesting question to answer.

The affair brings into play a number of competing rights that need to be balanced. On the one hand there is the right of free expression. This is the right that Rushdie and his allies rely on. As Silvia Albertazzi said in support of Rushdie, "Freedom of expression is more important than any offence any book might cause". Rushdie himself pitches into the debate by asserting:

> What is freedom of expression? Without the freedom to offend, it ceases to exist. Without the freedom to challenge, even to satirize all orthodoxies, including religious orthodoxies, it ceases to exist. Language and the imagination cannot be imprisoned, or art will die, and with it, a little of what makes us human.[28]

On the other hand, people and groups within a society have an inviolable right to be protected from, and to be able to seek redress against, another group or person who publicly indulge in unnecessary or unwarranted 'false criticism', 'hate speech', or 'defamatory comments without justification'. Even freedom-loving Western societies construct laws that curtail freedom of expression in certain freedom-loving circumstances. This is the right Rushdie's opponents seek to rely on.

In the context of the Rushdie affair, most people in the West (whatever they may personally think of Rushdie or his book), fell on the side of Rushdie's 'right to write', and in doing so appeared to endorse the right of freedom of expression over the other competing rights. Why is this so? Well, most Westerners did not decide which side of the fence they sat on by individually weighing each of the allegedly offensive comments Rushdie makes in the novel and then balancing them against the various competing rights at play. Most people were advertently or inadvertently persuaded in their decision-making not by the substance of what Rushdie said, but the form in which he wrote it. Let me repeat that, it is the form, the novel, in which Rushdie's writing appears, not the actual substance of what he wrote that determined people's responses. This is because in the West, freedom of speech, when expressed in the arena of literature, is not subject to the same set of checks and balances as when it is expressed in other arenas (for example the press or media). Literature is given this special privilege. It is afforded this special status. Why? Professor Paul Brians provides the following explanation:

> In the Twentieth century the novel came to be viewed as primarily oppositional, critical of the culture which produced it. Rather than providing values, it challenges them. Modern novels are praised for their courage in exposing hypocrisy, challenging tradition, exploring forbidden themes. . . . The writer who does not challenge the beliefs and prejudices of the reader is generally viewed by the literary establishment as dull if not cowardly.[29]

In Hanif Kureishi's novel, *The Black Album,* the lead character Shahid defends the case for Rushdie's *Satanic Verses* before a group of Muslim students, and puts the case forward for the novel in similar terms; he advocates that one of the aims of the literature is to: ". . . tell us about ourselves. . . . Surely literature helps us reflect on our nature . . ."[30] " 'a free imagination,' Shahid said 'ranges over many natures. A free imagination, looking into itself illuminates others'."[31]

The novel in the West has a history, it has a biography and it has its own discourse which is rich, normative, noble, and distinct from other print forms. The novel thus acts as a discourse of power over and above anything Rushdie has written that may influence the Westerner's stance on the book. Let me put it another way. One of the lead characters in *The Satanic Verses* is heavily-based on an actual Bollywood movie star. If Rushdie were to take the same unkind statements that he levels against him in the novel and repeat them in the press or media, society and the law would be less sympathetic towards him. People would be more willing to concede that freedom of expression should not protect writers for any lies, untruths, hate speech or defamation they print against others. Another example, this one not so hypothetical, was a movie produced by the Pakistani film industry, in which Rushdie is tracked down and killed by secret agents. When the movie came before the British Board of Film Classification they had to apply the law and ban it on the grounds that its contents were defamatory towards Rushdie (i.e., impinged upon his fundamental rights). Rushdie, placed in a somewhat embarrassing position (given his moral crusade in support of free speech), was left with little alternative but to forgo his right to sue the makers of the movie for defamation (thus allowing the movie to be lawfully distributed within the United Kingdom). The example is a good illustration of the way in which Western societies ensure that freedom of speech is subject to a checks and balances system with other competing fundamental rights.

Rushdie supports the special status literature holds, in which people are more freely allowed to abuse and criticise others without being subject to the same rebuke from society or the same checks and balances from the law. In an article on the subject he argues:

> Carlos Fuentes has called the novel 'a privileged arena'. By this he does not mean that it is the kind of holy space which one must put off one's shoes to enter; it is not an arena to revere; it claims no special rights except the right to be the stage upon which the great debates of society can be conducted ... He then poses the question that I have been asking myself throughout my life as a writer: Can the religious mentality survive outside of religious dogma and hierarchy? Which is to say: Can art be the third principle that mediates between the material and spiritual worlds; might it, by 'swallowing' both worlds, offer us something new—something that might even be called a secular definition of transcendence? I believe it can. I believe it must. And I believe that at its best, it does.[32]

It all sounds very persuasive. Indeed novels *do* provide us with a precious forum to explore the essence of what it is to be human and provide a stage to explore the great debates that human societies generate. I do not dispute this. But to give an individual absolute protection and a licence to unconditionally utter comments that he could not utter in other arenas, which society would forbid him from uttering for very good reasons, such as the fact that such comments legitimately and unfairly harm the fundamental rights of others is wrong. To argue that the protections afforded by other fundamental rights should lie suspended in the arena of literature if they happen to cross paths with the right of free expression; that there should be an amnesty in invoking redress for breaches of these other fundamental rights; that any recognised harm generated through the exercise of the right of free expression is to be considered less worthy of recognition and protection simply because the comment happens to take place in this special arena; to say that literature should be the only arena in society where free expression should be allowed to reign free, unconditionally, without the normal qualifications that Western society places on free expression; to give literature this type of special status which is afforded to no other arena in society, is surely something no reasonable person can support or endorse?

Richard Webster has written extensively on this subject. Consider his response to the suggestion by Rushdie and his supporters that novelists should be allowed to say whatever they want without any form of qualification:

> ... almost without exception, they have endorsed the ideal of 'free speech' without qualification, as though it possessed a single uncomplicated historical origin which is entirely benign. By doing this there can be no doubt that they have defended traditions which are precious and which need to be defended. But they have simultaneously defended a profoundly authoritarian tradition which is full both of intolerance and of religious hatred. . . .
>
> One of the most astonishing and at times frightening features of the debate that has developed around the Rushdie affair has been the willingness of so many literary intellectuals to defend the Western fortress of free speech in unconditional terms without ever pausing to inquire why that fortress was erected in the first place, and which values it was designed to defend. . . .
>
> Something very similar seems to have happened in the way Rushdie's novel has been deployed by Western intellectuals. For there can be no doubt at all that both Rushdie himself and his most energetic supporters are sincere in their belief that they represent the forces of freedom and enlightenment and that they are right to attack cruel and repressive forms of faith. What they have failed to understand, like the Christian monks who preceded them, is that the contemptuous disrespect they have shown for the sanctities of others is itself repressive and destructive. That so many Western commentators have seen such offensiveness as part of a programme of liberation only goes to show how deeply we have ourselves internalised a repressive form of "religious faith".[33]

One of the flaws in Rushdie's argument is that he assumes all those who enter his sacred arena will enter the stage where the great debates of society are conducted. But this is not the only stage a writer is capable of entering when writing fiction. There are other stages. What if the individual writer concerned wants to enter or erect a stage on which he is able to unconditionally engage in a type of hate speech that he (for very good reasons) would be prevented from doing in other arenas (such as the press). As I mentioned earlier, as much as I disagree with the Orientalist arguments Rushdie cites in *The Satanic Verses* and however weak I think those arguments are, I would not forbid him from expressing such views. It would amount to a form of intellectual censorship (however intellectually flawed the argument he puts forward may be). But that is not the same as saying that Rushdie or any other writer can say what he likes about whomever or whatever, whenever and however, without any form of censure—no matter how much he may trample, restrict, or curtail other fundamental rights that the West recognises and would otherwise uphold. As we have discussed earlier, Rushdie doesn't simply use his novel to repeat Orientalist arguments. He also uses the novel as a forum to abuse and to vilify the Prophet and in turn the Muslim community.

In answer to the question that I posed earlier, on whether *The Satanic Verses* should be banned (or at least the offending passages censored), on balance I would say no. Rushdie has been clever in his use of language in that the contentious passages within the novel generate multiple discourses. Some of these, I believe, should not be subject to any form of censorship, however much I might disagree with the comments expressed (the debates that take place in the loosely described intellectual context). Of the remaining discourses the text generates, Western societies should subject the text to the normal checks and balances that free speech is subject to when it conflicts with other fundamental rights (the debates which take place in the loosely described 'gratuitous abuse' context). But as the text is composed of all of these differing discourses, one cannot hold differing positions on the same text. In conclusion, I would rather the book not have been published in its current format, I would rather some of the passages not have seen the light of day, but we cannot erase history and we cannot erase the controversy the novel has provoked. To censor the novel as it stands, after the controversy it has generated, would again give the impression that Muslims are incapable of intellectually tackling the issues the book generates. The novel and the affair therefore must be addressed through reasoned and intelligent debate, not through violence or censure. However, I will end by saying this: Rushdie argues that "language and the imagination cannot be imprisoned, or art will die, and with it, a little of what makes us human." But not everyone's 'language', nor everyone's 'imagination' can be equally expressed. As Rushdie knows all too well, power is not distributed fairly and equally in society. And if the language and imagination of people who are privileged enough to operate in the dominant culture of our times (such as Rushdie) is misused and abused, especially against the subaltern and marginalised, then although it might not result in their precious language, their precious imagination, their precious art being imprisoned or left to die, it does place at serious risk the language, the imagination, and the art of the subaltern, of the marginalised, being imprisoned and being left to die a slow death, and with it, a little of what makes 'them' and 'us' human will also die. Salman Rushdie, once a spokesperson for the oppressed, seems to have forgotten this. As Professor Michael Dummett advised Rushdie, "Much as you may want to, you can never again play that role: You can never again assume the stance of the denouncer of white prejudice. For now, you are one of us. You have become an honorary white."[34] And that, Salman, is the real 'shame of midnight's children'!

14. FINDING HERMES FOOTPRINTS: A CRITIQUE OF PURE DOGMA? (Beirut)

THE WEST'S BEAUTY industry appears to have firmly set its anchor in Lebanon. Western female fashions are beamed directly into Lebanese homes via satellite channels such as MTV, they are plastered across a thousand billboards throughout the country, they decorate the stands of every magazine seller in the land and they adorn the shopping aisles of many of the nation's high street stores. Whilst standing in the queue at the bank one morning I wondered if it was simply its fashions, cosmetics and ideas of beauty that the West was importing to the Arab world. Indeed, I wondered if there wasn't something else that the West might be importing. I wondered whether young Lebanese women suffered the same physical and psychological side effects that many of their Western sisters were inflicted with as consumers and competitors of the West's beauty game. I wondered how many of today's young Lebanese women felt the need to go on unhealthy diets to look thin and beautiful. I wondered how many of them at times felt depressed over their inability to be something they were not. How ironic I thought, when Christopher Columbus and the first Europeans colonised the Americas they brought with them their diseases. Now America is the imperial power and through cultural colonialism is exporting its diseases to the colonised. America's cultural colonialism has been achieved less through supremacy of the 'sea-waves' and more through supremacy of the 'air-waves'. And whilst the original natives of lands such as the Americas caught the European white man's diseases through direct contact, America's colonised subjects never need see or come in contact with an American in their lives. American satellite music and entertainment channels ensure that the new imperial power's diseases can be imported directly into the homes of every Arab family with a satellite dish and an audience with an appetite for American culture.

That afternoon I had a meeting with a professor who taught at one of the American universities in Beirut. I had arranged by telephone to meet up with her at a branch of Starbucks.

As we settled down to our coffees in this latest American company to go global, I began by relaying to her the very thoughts and concerns that had preoccupied my mind that morning, highlighting in particular the impact certain Western satellite channels might be having on the health of young Lebanese women. To my slight surprise she wholeheartedly agreed with my observations and further added that when these American satellite channels were first beamed into Lebanese homes, people were excited about the idea. Today, they are not so sure. Her people were increasingly noticing how young Lebanese women were becoming obsessed and depressed by a need to diet in order to lose weight. She felt that many Lebanese citizens were now beginning to ask serious questions about the damaging effects that exposure to Western popular culture was having upon their society and in particular upon their young women.

The traffic of cultural and social observations wasn't all one way. As our conversation progressed and we moved onto other subjects and topics the professor asked me to comment on an observation that many Arabs had apparently made about Muslims living in the West. She commented that one of the side effects of the 9/11 tragedy was that it had resulted in a rise in prominence of Arab news channels (in particular al-Jazeerah). Many of these Arab language satellite news stations gave exposure to Muslims living in the West. Quite unintentionally, 9/11 had opened a window through which Arabs in the Middle East could view in greater depth the lives, the opinions and the feelings of Muslims living in the West. Previously many Arabs had felt that Muslims who lived in Europe and the West would be more enlightened and less inclined to hold intolerant views on the major political issues of the day. But to their almost collective and universal disbelief, they were discovering that Western Muslims were often the most fanatical and intolerant of all Muslims. What in particular astounded many Arabs was the discovery that Muslims born, bred and educated (some of them highly educated) in countries such as the United Kingdom were following the views of Arab expatriates whose religious/ideological convictions held little or no respect amongst the vast majority of Arabs living in the Middle East. It was an almost surreal experience she commented, to watch people who were political non-entities in their native Arab countries gain an ever-increasing constituency in Western countries such as Great Britain. I held my head down. Whether it was in shame or embarrassment I don't know. I could see where she was coming from and how it was that she arrived at her conclusions. Whilst there was some substance in the point she was making, I nevertheless disagreed with her. The Western media (and now the Arab media, it appeared) has a tendency to give the type of people she was referring to (the Arab expatriates and their British-born supporters) exposure that is not necessarily a reflection of their popularity within the British Muslim community. Such people make good headlines and they reinforce a negative stereotype of Muslims, but this is often to the annoyance of the wider British Muslim community, who feel frustrated that such fringe groups should receive such a disproportionate level of exposure. Little did I know that the behaviour of these groups was also causing Arabs to look at British Muslims in bewilderment and bemusement.

Fortunately (for me), the British Muslim community wasn't alone in being singled out by her for criticism. The events of 9/11 had also resulted in the Arab world becoming familiar with leading political figures such as George W. Bush and Tony Blair. This Arab intellectual wasn't sympathetic towards either politician. She questioned George W. Bush's intelligence, said he was a bad orator and added that many Arabs found the language he deployed in the aftermath of 9/11 offensive (I presume a reference to his 'crusades' speech).

Of Tony Blair she was just as scathing, accusing him of patronising Muslims by appearing on Arab TV and giving them a lecture about Islam and how it was a religion of peace (and she wasn't even a Muslim!). The Prime Minister obviously had motives behind such a move (maybe even noble motives), but it was clear that such words would alienate even further an Arab world that saw American and British foreign policy rife with double standards.

The conversation moved on to the effects of American foreign policy in the Middle East. I felt her views on the subject were very much a reflection of what many Arabs in the region felt. The fact that they were being uttered by a Christian Arab with liberal and secular aspirations for her country only reinforced for me how deep-rooted and widespread dislike of American foreign policy in the region has become. The professor felt that too many Arabs simply did not trust America; that some regarded America as 'evil' was not surprising to her. Such a negative image of the United States was largely the result of two factors. Firstly, a belief that America was not acting as an impartial arbiter in the Arab/Israeli conflict. She argued that many Arabs felt that the United States frequently ignored or failed to adequately recognise the Arab/Palestinian position in this conflict. Secondly, that America's foreign policy decisions in the region were often motivated by self-interest. In particular, their support and implementation of policies that ensure easy access to the oil fields in the region.

Having mentioned the issue of Israel, I decided to ask her opinion on the subject. Did she, for example, believe in the existence of the state? She thought this was an irrelevant question. "The country exists, Israel exists, whether it ought to exist is an irrelevant question", she replied. She did however elaborate on the theme of how the United States fails to appreciate the Arab/Palestinian position, and argue that there exists an indifferent attitude towards the victims of the conflict, especially a failure to properly recognise the atrocities, the hardship and the suffering that Israel has inflicted upon the Palestinian people.

Whilst the professor was vehemently opposed to the policy of suicide bombings and very much hoped for a peaceful resolution to the conflict, she felt there was a perception amongst Arabs in this conflict that the United States views Arab blood as being cheaper than Jewish blood. If an Israeli dies in a suicide attack the whole world hears about it she said, yet innocent Palestinians were dying all the time as a result of the unlawful actions of the Israeli military, but no one in the West hears about the everyday victims of Israel's aggression (which vastly outnumber those who die at the hands of suicide bombers).

The professor also sought to highlight the differing attitudes towards the current leaders of the two states. Arafat was viewed as a terrorist by the United States. But what of Sharon, she asked. They (the Lebanese) knew his character better than most. They were the victims of his brutal policies during the eighties. Sharon had blood on his hands, she asserted. For her, "he was the biggest terrorist of them all".

To some extent I could understand the points the professor made. As I mentioned in an earlier chapter, Israel/Occupied Palestine is a sacred land and a homeland for the Jews. It is also a sacred land and a homeland for Palestinian Christians and Muslims. In this dispute between the Jews and the Palestinians, the United States has not acted as a neutral arbiter. It has sided with the Jews and provided them with arms that have allowed Israel to repress Palestinian claims to the land and have also made it the military superpower in the region. As such, the Arabs are absolutely right to question the neutrality of the United States in this conflict. Occupation of this disputed land is maintained by Israel's overwhelming military power. Any Palestinian opposition to Israeli sovereignty is swiftly dealt with by this overwhelming military power. Young Palestinian boys throwing stones at Israeli tanks might temporarily raise the morale of the Palestinian people, but it does not get them their homeland back, it does not rectify the desperate conditions they live in or lessen the human rights abuses the Israeli military frequently commit against the Palestinian civilian population. When some Arabs/Palestinians rejoice at the death of innocent Israeli civilians who perish at the hands of suicide bombers, their perverse sense of joy may, in part, be derived from a realisation that the Israeli people are finally being subjected to the same pain that Israel's military force has inflicted upon the Palestinians. Palestinian suicide bombers cannot bridge the enormous military gap that now exists between their community and the Jews, but they can ensure that there is at least some sort of parity in the pain and human suffering the two communities are inflicting upon each other.

I asked whether her hopes for a peaceful solution to the conflict were realisable. She wasn't overly confident that a lasting solution would be found in the immediate future. Attitudes that had been hardened by decades of Arab/Israeli conflict needed to change, not only between Jews and Palestinians, but between Jews and Arabs as well. This was no easy feat. For decades Arab governments churned out propaganda that told their people they were at war with Israel, that Israel was an illegal state and needed to be destroyed, that the occupied lands should be returned to their Palestinian brethren. Then suddenly, after decades of this relentless, non-stop, anti-Israel rhetoric, many Arab governments went behind the backs of their people. They spoke to the enemy, negotiated with the enemy, some of them even signed peace treaties with the enemy. Then they told their people that the years of hate were misplaced, that peace and not war should be sought with Israel, that the Jewish state should not be destroyed but should be allowed to coexist peacefully with Arab nations and that the Jews were not evil infidels but part of their Semitic family. Why, she asserted, should it surprise these same leaders if much of their population find it difficult to swallow such a pill. She was right. If the Arab people (not their governments) are ever to make peace with Israel, it would be tantamount to committing the 'mother of all u-turns'.

Before we left I wanted her perspective as an Arab intellectual on the subject of Islam and modernity. Why was it that of the three monotheistic religions (Islam, Christianity and Judaism), it was Islam that appeared to be the most uneasy with modernity? Her reply was controversial but not wholly surprising. I had heard such views before. As a Christian, she was asking Muslims to think the unthinkable. She began by reminding me that it had taken both Christianity and Judaism many centuries before some of their believers started to question and scrutinise the validity and authenticity of their sacred sources. By scrutinising the scriptures in ways that were never done before, they too were questioning the unquestionable. At the time Christendom (and Judaeo-Christianity in the wider sense) formed the social fabric around which European culture and life existed. The dismantling of the most powerful cultural and social force in European society took several centuries. But without this 'dismantling', modernity would never have flourished. She felt that Islam needed to go through its own reformation. The fact that it still hadn't may be a factor as to why it struggles to make peace with modernity, whereas Christianity and Judaism seem to excel under it.

One of the central aspects of the discussion on Islam and modernity is the role of the state. She felt that most Arabs were against a state governed by a religious hierarchy as in Iran or Taliban Afghanistan. The Iranian Revolution had been a failure; most Arabs recognised this and were against subjecting their country to such a form of government. People wanted democracy, not a religious state run by religious clerics. This view did slightly surprise me and I questioned whether most Arabs, if they really yearned for democracy, yearned for the secularised form as it exists in the West. Should democracy be imposed upon the nations of the Arab world, surely Islamic parties would dominate the political landscape I thought (as happened in Algeria before the civil war and as might happen in Iraq). This I felt was one of the reasons why the United States was, for many decades, reluctant to vehemently champion the cause of democracy in the region. They knew perfectly well that should democracy find a footing in the Arab world, it might well propel into power Islamic parties that were opposed to US foreign policy in the region and this in turn could seriously jeopardise American interests in the region (such as easy access to the oil fields). Since I had this conversation with the professor, the toppling of Saddam's regime has seen a fundamental change in US policy on this issue. The United States now wishes to see democracy established in Iraq (and if it works and is successful no doubt they hope that Iraq's successful experiment with democracy has a snowball effect on neighbouring Arab states). It is a risky strategy for the United States to adopt and may well backfire on them. Whilst Iraqi Arabs have historically been more secular than some of their Arab brothers, Islamic parties have grass roots strength in Iraq that a pro-US, secular party could not match. A pro-US secular party I assume would be the preferred 'party of power' for a US administration (not that I am suggesting that the United States would interfere in the internal politics of an Arab country, of course not, perish the thought!).

Ever since that meeting with the professor from Damascus University, I had spent much time thinking over the relationship between Islam and modernity. My meeting at Starbucks seemed to confirm what the Syrian professor had been saying about the intellectual rifts developing in Arab thought, in particular, the relationship between classical Islamic thought and the new methods of empirical study imported from the West and taught and studied at an increasing number of Arab universities. One may make comparisons with the history of European intellectual thought from the fifteenth century onwards; it had witnessed the genesis of a growing and eventually permanent rift between the Church and the new modes of thinking pioneered by philosophers such as Descartes. How ironic that it was about fourteen hundred years after the advent of Christianity that an increasing number of thinkers such as Descartes began to ask Christian Europe to rethink the veracity of its centuries-old models of intellectual thought. It is now a little over fourteen hundred years since the message of the Prophet Muhammad was first heard. Has Islam likewise found itself at the same crossroads where Christendom once stood? If so, will it take the same path as Christendom?

If modernity has indeed pushed the Muslim world towards this ideological crossroads, then one can quite reasonably argue that it really ought not to have found itself in such an unfortunate position. Before the advent of modernity, of the three monotheistic religions of Islam, Christianity and Judaism, it is arguable that one might conclude that it would be Islam (relative to the other two faiths) that would be most at ease with modernity. Unlike the Judaeo-Christian tradition, Islam never had a complex with science (the bedrock of modernity) as another method of attaining knowledge, alongside revelation. Islam's revelation positively encouraged its followers to pursue scientific methods to attain knowledge of the world. This encouragement was posited to both the natural and social sciences (which is why Muslim societies were able to build several great empires and civilisations rich in both artistic and scientific discovery). Furthermore, the Islamic tradition of *ijtihad*[1] created a built-in mechanism that allowed Islamic societies to adapt their norms/traditions to changing socio-cultural conditions (brought on by factors such as technological advancement). It could be argued that this mechanism for socio-cultural evolution, alongside Islam's natural affinity towards the natural and social sciences, ought to have facilitated an easier passage into modernity. One of the great debates within human history must surely be, why has the Muslim world made such an uneasy transition into modernity?

My travels did seem to suggest that the Muslim world is indeed at some sort of ideological crossroads, that a fierce ideological battle is raging within the Islamic world to win the hearts and minds of Muslim people and governments, that this ideological battle appears to be between those who believe the current intellectual, economic and political malaise within the Arab/Muslim world will only be resolved through a reformation of the sacred models of intellectual thought and those who believe the answer in fact lies in a reaffirmation of the classical models of thinking.[2] The outcome of this ideological struggle will have a huge bearing on the direction the Arab/Muslim world takes in the new century and in turn this will have a huge impact on world affairs in the twenty-first century.

The two differing intellectual positions are best epitomised by two Arab thinkers, Sayyid Qutb (reaffirmationist) and Mohammed Abed al-Jabri (reformist). A largely unknown figure in the West, Sayyid Qutb is one of the most influential figures of the twentieth century and an inspiration to a thousand and one Islamic fundamentalist groups. In the opening chapter of his book, *Milestones*, Qutb is very clear as to which direction salvation for the Muslim world lies:

> ... the Messenger of God—peace be upon him—intended to prepare a generation pure in heart, pure in mind, pure in understanding. The training was to be based on the method prescribed by God who gave the Holy Qur'an, purified from the influences of all other sources.
>
> This generation, then, drank solely from this spring and thus attained a unique distinction in history. In later times it happened that other sources mingled with it. Other sources used by later generations included Greek philosophy and logic, ancient Persian legends and their ideas, Jewish scriptures and traditions, Christian theology, and in addition to these, fragments of other religions and civilisations. These mingled with the commentaries on the Qur'an and with scholastic theology, as they were mingled with jurisprudence and its principles. Later generations of this generation obtained their training from this mixed source, hence the like of this generation never arose again.
>
> Thus we can say without any reservations that the main reason for the difference between the first unique and distinguished group of Muslims and later Muslims is that the purity of the first source of Islamic guidance was mixed with various other sources.[3]

Qutb is unequivocal in his message. Muslims have declined as a people because over time they started to mix the pure message of Islam with alternative ideologies. The solution to the difficulties that both Muslims and humanity face is for Muslims to return to the original and pure form of Islam that was practised by the first generation of Muslims.

Mohammed Abed al-Jabri's writings take a very different approach than Qutb's. He calls for a full-scale and fundamental rethinking of Arab-Islamic thought. Abed al-Jabri is critical of the fundamentalist reading of history, arguing that:

> The fundamentalist reading of tradition is an historical one and can only provide one type of understanding of tradition: an understanding of tradition

that is locked inside tradition and absorbed by a tradition that it cannot in return include: it is tradition repeating itself. The reading of religious fundamentalists proceeds from a religious conception of history. This conception treats history as a moment that is expanded into the present, a time that is stretched inside the affective life, a witness to the perpetual struggle and the eternal suffering endured for the sake of affirming one's identity. And since we are told that it is both faith and religious conviction that define this identity, fundamentalism posits the spiritual factor as the sole engine of history. As for other factors, they are considered as secondary, depending upon the spiritual, or disfiguring the "true" course of history.[4]

Abed al-Jabri is clearly questioning writers such as Qutb who do regard the 'spiritual factor' to be the sole engine of history. But if it is not spirituality that is the 'sole engine of history' then what should it be? Like Qutb, Abed al-Jabri is also very clear on this issue; "Reason is a beacon that we must not only light in the middle of darkness but also learn to carry around well into broad daylight." He continues:

> This is the conception of modernity that we ought to define in light of our present. Modernity is above all rationality and democracy. A rational and critical approach to all aspects of our existence—of which tradition emerges as one of the aspects that is most present and most rooted in us—is the only true modernist option. Our concern with tradition is therefore dictated by the necessity to elevate our approach to tradition to the level of modernity, in order to serve modernity and to give it a foundation within our authenticity.[5]

For Abed al-Jabri it is 'rationality' that is the sole engine of history, or at least the sole engine of modernity.

After travelling through several Muslim countries, I can see why an intellectual rift has developed in Arab/Muslim thought, though it saddens me to see it (it ought not to exist) I can see why it exists.

In the centuries immediately after the birth of Islam many of the world's leading natural and social scientists were Muslim. Since the advent of modernity, the majority of the world's *most influential* natural and social scientists have originated from or resided in the West. Muslim scholarly reaction to the knowledge these non-Muslim thinkers have produced is interesting. Developments in knowledge within the natural sciences and in technology have been received without much scholarly scepticism (exceptions exist in areas such as human evolution). But an almost opposite reaction is evoked in relation to certain major developments within the social sciences. Herein lies the source of the rift. The advancements that modernity has brought about in the social sciences have the ability to effect a) the veracity *and* the understanding of the Islamic sacred texts, and b) the veracity of other texts from which Muslims derive their understanding of the early history of Islam. If Muslim scholars and religious clerics from al-Azhar to Medina University were to accept these intellectual trends (and they do not) and accommodate them into the classical schools of Islamic thought, then it would undermine the foundations of more than a thousand years of Muslim scholarly thinking. In the same way that post-modernity has sought to dismantle the whole idea of modernity within Western thought, the fusion of certain modern and/or post-modern ideas (especially the latter which espouse a rejection of grand meta-narratives) into traditional Islamic thought could have a similar dismantling effect. For Muslims, the Quran isn't simply a grand meta-narrative. It is the grand meta-narrative of human history.

The source of this intellectual/ideological debate, while dense, is necessary to a clear understanding of Islam's relation to modernity.

More than anything else, traditional/classical Islamic scholars pride themselves on the authenticity of their sacred texts; this is, in fact, the defining feature of Islamic scholarship, and it is this belief in the certainty of the sacred texts that fuels Muslim scholars like Sayyid Qutb with such an absolute and total confidence that he can dismiss all other religions and ideologies.

The sacred texts within Islam are essentially in two forms. Firstly, there is the Quran. Muslims believe that the Quran is direct revelation from God, transmitted to humans through the Prophet Muhammad and recorded by the Muslim community as it was being revealed to his Messenger. For Muslims, the fact that revelation was captured and preserved as soon as it was relayed to humans prevents the risk of human subjectivity imposing itself onto the 'objective' word of God, as can occur in instances when the process of recording God's word is left to humans *after* the source of that revelation has left the earth (as Muslims believe happened in the case of Christianity).

The second source of the sacred texts is the hadith. If the Quran is the word of God, the hadith represent the manifestation of the word of God into human action. In Islam this is the life and deeds of the Prophet Muhammad. The hadith represent more than just a comprehensive biography of the Prophet of Arabia, they attempt to record his every action, however minute or trivial. Almost every aspect of his private and public life was recorded, from how he ate, washed, dressed, and spoke, to how he conducted the affairs of the city-state he ran in Medina, including how taxes were raised and distributed, how government was run and how military campaigns were to be waged.

The volumes of hadith that are with us today were collated in the early centuries after the death of the founder of Islam, and the majority of the hadith that are regarded by today's Sunni Muslim community as being the most authentic, reliable and accurate are contained largely (although not exclusively) in the collections of two Islamic scholars, Imam al-Bukhari and Imam al-Muslim.

Both Bukhari and Muslim were great social scientists at the heart of a fierce scholarly debate that took place within the Muslim community in the first few centuries after the death of the Prophet Muhammad. This debate concerned which of the hadith that were in popular circulation at the time were true and accurate and which were either fabricated or unreliable. The scholarly debate wasn't a pedantic one either, for in the early decades and centuries after the death of the Prophet Muhammad it appears that many hadith were invented for self-serving purposes. What makes Bukhari and Muslim such great social scientists (and why their work is held in such high esteem by later generations of Muslim scholars) is that their research to locate and find the 'authentic' hadith was based on two fundamental principles: a) a commitment to vigorously search through the hadiths that were in circulation, explore the arenas and avenues where human subjectivity and partiality could have seeped into these hadith, and b) the development of methods that could be used to reliably scrutinise these hadith, thus weeding out the authentic ones from the fabricated or unreliable ones. In practical terms, these scholars ensured that both the chain of narration of a particular hadith that was attributed to the Prophet Muhammad could in fact be reliably traced back to him (and was not manufactured at some later date or place) and the personal character of the narrators themselves was heavily scrutinised to ensure their trustworthiness, accuracy and reliability (both those who witnessed the Prophet uttering the concerned 'saying' or 'act' and the chain of people whom this 'saying' was relayed to).

It is easy to appreciate now why the professor from Damascus argued that the germ cells of the Enlightenment project are to be found in the natural and social scientists of early Islamic history. This may be, but during the Enlightenment, Europe planted these intellectual seeds into its great universities and allowed them to grow and branch out into a spectacular array of academic genres. By the end of the twentieth century the number of social sciences and humanities taught at Western academic institutions had grown to cover almost every aspect of human social endeavour/activity imaginable. This growth in the social sciences could not have occurred without one crucial ingredient, the proliferation in methodological discourse. Methodological discourse is the oxygen that allows the social sciences to live, to breathe and to develop. It is this development in methodological discourse that has caused the 'rupture' in Arab thought.

Arab academics (let's call them 'reformist scholars') that wholeheartedly believe in the Enlightenment project cannot study the history of Islam or the sacred texts of Islam in the same way as classical ('reaffirmationist') scholars do. The reason for this is simple. The advancements that the West has made in the empirical and abstract social sciences, coupled with developments in methodological discourse, have changed the way in which the sacred texts and early Islamic history can be scrutinised. As such, history is not as black and white or as straightforward or simple as classical scholars and their supporters think. For instance, as I mentioned earlier, Bukhari and Muslim undertook painstakingly extensive research to locate and find the 'authentic' hadith. Contemporary classical scholars firmly believe that Bukhari and Muslim were able to successfully achieve these goals. The reformist Arab/Muslim academics do not (or cannot). For them, while the works of scholars like Bukhari and Muslim were great and profound, their work presents only the *beginnings* of a field of study in which they were able to highlight *some* (not all) of the areas where human partiality could have deliberately or inadvertently reflected itself onto what are considered to be divine texts. For example, during the last century the natural and social sciences provided us with a much greater understanding of how the human mind works. The 'reformist' Muslim scholar might argue that such knowledge can be and should be applied to the field of hadith studies, because it asks important and serious questions about the reliability of the human mind as a 'vessel' for recording, storing and relaying an oral transmission. Hadith studies are, after all, devoted to the accuracy and reliability of oral transmissions. So even if we were to accept that the great hadith scholars were able to find an authentic line of narration back to the Prophet, even if we were to accept that they were able to find trusted, honest and reliable narrators, their research can be taken further by then enquiring into how good the human mind *per se*, is, as a vessel for recording, storing and relaying information (and in this case divine information). If research into the workings of the human mind over the last century suggests that our minds are not like tape recorders, in that they cannot necessarily record, store or playback information that is heard with complete precision, then such knowledge is surely important to this issue of human partiality reflecting itself onto what is considered to be divine text.

Let me give a second example. In 1992 Leila Ahmed published her long-awaited study on women in Islam.[6] In it she challenges the commonly held belief that the *burkah* (veil) worn by Muslim women can be traced back to the time of the Prophet (arguing instead that the practice arose after his death). Her work was controversial—but not because of her comments on the veil. Differing opinions on the veil (including the one she expressed) have existed in Islamic societies for centuries. Her work was controversial because of the methodology she used to explore the subject. Ahmed navigated her way through the monumental task of describing the histories of Muslim women by drawing upon a vast array of discourses. Naturally she referred to Islamic literature such as the Quran and the hadith, but she also drew upon the work of archaeologists, anthropologists, historians and social scientists and she surveyed historical documents from her periods of study, everything from literature to civil and legal records that had been preserved.

The methodology that Ahmed adopted (before making known her findings on issues such as the veil) was applauded by reformist scholars but 'criticised' by many classical/reaffirmationist scholars. If a classical Muslim scholar wanted to find out what Islam said about women and the veil, he would refer himself to the Quran, the authentic hadith and the works of one or several of the great scholars of Islam. He certainly wouldn't waste his time reading or researching the works of an infidel historian or anthropologist.

So, for the reformist Islamic scholar, the fact that Ahmed 'casts her net' wide and draws upon so many different sources from so many different social sciences before publishing her findings on the veil make her work more reliable. This is because her findings are corroborated and validated by a large number of different sources. For the classical Islamic scholar, this methodology makes her work less reliable, because she is drawing upon sources that are not considered authentic (i.e., sources other than the Quran or Sunnah). To put it another way, such a researcher is appealing to discourses that are not divine in order to find the answer to what the divine said on a particular issue. The Quran and the hadith address the issue, so why look elsewhere?

It isn't only in the empirical social sciences or in methodological discourse that divisions between reformists and classical scholars have arisen. Most controversially of all, differences also exist in the abstract social sciences (in particular the field of discourse analysis). For example, the Prophet Muhammad received his divine transmission in a human language (seventh-century Arabic). Human language and its ability or inability to reflect with complete precision concepts, ideas, material or abstract facts/objects has been the source of much debate within Western philosophy during the last century. The relationship between human language and a divine transmission and the possible risk of human subjectivity reflecting itself onto the objective word of God is something that classical Muslim scholars ceased discussing centuries ago—and a debate that some reformist scholars wish to open again.

In its attempts to win over the 'hearts and minds' of the Muslim *ummah* one of the hurdles the reformist tradition has to overcome is the negative publicity it will receive as a result of its intellectual heritage. Any reformist model will find it almost impossible to escape the influence of Western civilisation on the development of its own academic discourse—the very civilisation that has both imperially and culturally colonised and oppressed Muslims. Furthermore, reaffirmationists also see the reformist model as a sort of Trojan horse that introduces negative and unwanted cultural side-effects into Muslim society—and by incorporating the Western intellectual tradition into Islamic thought one cannot avoid importing un-Islamic Western values that are alien to Muslim society and far removed from the kind of community that the Prophet of Islam created in seventh-century Arabia. The end result is a continuing form of cultural colonisation by the West.

The reaffirmationist model is itself not without reproach. Its critics argue that although it purports to return the *ummah* to the purity of that first-generation Muslim community, its ideology is not only unable to transcend the socio-cultural circumstances in which it exists; it is itself a product of the very socio-cultural environment that it is reacting against. In other words, far from being that pure, un-tampered, shrink-wrapped Islam, hand-delivered all the way from seventh-century Medina, some of its writers have a zeal that is reminiscent of nineteenth- and early twentieth-century European revolutionary thinkers and movements. It is argued that scholars such as Qutb are in fact just as much influenced by Marx as by the Prophet Muhammad. Aftab A. Malik, commenting on the more extreme discourses relating to resistance within the reaffirmationist model has argued:

> *Jihad* was seen through the lens of an "anti-imperialist struggle" that resisted capitalism that had corrupted humanity. The most violent and radical of these revivalist trends viewed any Muslim that did not rule by God's law as apostates. Since there was no true Islamic government in the world, these revivalists condemned the entire Muslim world and the "infidel" West . . . Only a select few amongst the Muslims were chosen to form a "vanguard" of true believers, whose divine task was to cleanse the world of idolatrous materialism. . . . The idea of vanguard is so alien to the Islamic tradition that it more resembles a concept imported from Europe, through a lineage that stretches back to the Jacobins, through the Bolsheviks and latter-day Marxist guerrillas. . . . The irony is that while showing their putrid hatred for the West, al-Qa'ida and those that have any sympathy for them are actually following an Islam that is fused with "Islamicised" nineteenth-century

European revolutionary writings. The results of merging a warped interpretation of Islam along with ideas that demand blood sacrifice, revolution and anarchy, would have "horrified Muslims in the past."[7]

Though the last few pages may seem somewhat abstract, suitable only for the university campus, this is in fact an extremely important issue; one which Arab/Muslim societies just simply have to get right. Knowledge forms the building blocks of every great civilisation. As many Arab nations will find out at some point during this century or the next, when the oil runs out, knowledge will be the fuel that propels their societies forward. And if these concepts are not clearly understood, their societies will be left behind in the dust clouds of competitors who disappear without a trace.

15. SOCIAL(IST) UNREST ON ANIMAL FARM
(Beirut)

BEFORE I MOVED on to Jordan, I had penned into my diary that my last day in Lebanon would be spent relaxing on the beach. The significance and importance of this particular day in my travels could not be underestimated. This day had been planned months in advance. I had dreamt about 'this day' on every night of my travels. For a Brummie, such a day does not occur very often (unless you move out of Birmingham). It was the day I took a break from all the walking and talking and thinking and mulling and allowed myself time-out for quiet enjoyment and relaxation.

Before I trekked off to the beach to enjoy the sun, the sea and the sand, I had one prior engagement to fulfil. The professor that I had met at Starbucks had invited me to her university department. I had duly accepted her kind offer.

The professor shared her room with two other colleagues. I didn't stay long. We had a brief conversation about the British Asian author Hanif Kureishi (I can't recall how we arrived at discussing him). She confessed to being a fan of his. So much so, that his first novel, *The Buddah of Suburbia*, was on her students course syllabus.

I must have stayed about twenty to thirty minutes; I thanked her for taking the time out to see me. She had given me much food for thought (as one could gather from reading this last chapter).

I left the department and began the thirty-minute walk to the beach. I was about twenty minutes into my walk when it happened, and when I realised that the 'law of sod' had followed me all the way from England and had mischievously performed a rain dance whilst I was speaking to the professor in her office. Just as I entered the final straight, just as I could make out the beach, just as my wonderful daydream of me relaxing on the sandy beach with a picturesque vision of the beautiful big blue Mediterranean Sea, the heavens opened. Within two minutes I was drenched and soaked to the bone. I didn't turn back and head for the comfort of my hotel room, as I ought to have done. Stubbornly, I continued walking towards the beach. I was determined to see the sea.

When I arrived I stood silently by a bench that overlooked the beach and a sea that separated three continents. She looked very angry. Over and over again her waves crashed onto Beirut's landmark site, Pigeon Rocks, almost as if she was punishing them for some wrongdoing. Ten minutes later and a little more soaked, I made my way back to the hotel.

I spent the afternoon detained in a coffee shop, sheltering from the rain and enjoying the comforts of a coffee, cheesecake and a book. This was more like Birmingham. This was more like home. Never mind, I thought to myself. I planned to spend the last two days of my travels at the even more beautiful beach resort of Aqaba in Jordan. My bad luck today would only make my time there even more enjoyable.[1]

When the rain died down I made my way back to the hotel, rested and then got ready to go out for the evening.

The plan was to dine out at a restaurant run by a friend of a friend. Before leaving I asked the only member of staff on duty for directions. He was unable to assist me. I left the hotel premises to seek help elsewhere.

Outside, it was still wet and miserable, with very few people venturing out onto the streets. There was a restaurant across the road from the hotel and it seemed to be the only place where I could detect the existence of life. Embarrassingly, I decided to go into a restaurant and ask for directions for another restaurant.

A waiter confirmed my worst fears when he told me that the restaurant was some distance away and to get there I either needed to catch a cab (which would be very expensive) or take a bus (which would take ages). The apathy in my body language must have been very obvious because he suggested I try eating out here. Although he appreciated that his views weren't impartial, he assured me that their chefs were very good. He was just about to finish his shift and as was normal for him he had his evening meal here before going home. I could even join him if I liked. I looked outside. It had started to rain again. It wasn't really much of a choice. I accepted his kind offer and decided to stay.

The waiter turned out to be a PhD student, studying physics at the American University of Beirut. His work at the restaurant funded his studies. He attended one of the most prestigious universities in the Middle East, but even that wasn't enough to alleviate his fear of being jobless after he obtained his doctorate. He took from his pocket a packet of cigarettes, waved it in front of me and uttered, "this is all I have to look forward to", before taking out a cigarette and lighting up. His apathy was all too clear to see.

By the time our food arrived we had already begun discussing class divisions within Lebanese society. He agreed with my observation that Lebanon was a country divided into the 'super rich' and 'super poor'. Like the professor that I had met, he cautioned me against drawing any conclusions on the wealth of the country based on the extravagant displays of 'bling' that I had seen parading the central districts of Beirut. If I had time (which I didn't) he urged me to travel to other parts of the country where I would be able to observe the 'real Lebanon'. The 'real Lebanon' was occupied exclusively by the super-poor. In the 'real Lebanon', the lucky ones were those who were able to secure slave labour jobs, sufficient only to support a poverty-line existence. It was at times like this that I reminded myself how lucky I am.

In his inaugural address President Kennedy remarked, 'ask not what your country can do for you—ask what you can do for your country'. I wonder whether Kennedy might have reviewed his position had he travelled to the Middle East in the present circumstances and seen how many of its young people struggled to put themselves through college and university, only to find out that once they had graduated there were very few decent employment opportunities open to them. These people had done something for their country. They had contributed to the creation of a highly skilled and highly educated workforce. In such circumstances surely they were entitled to ask what their country had done for them. I am reminded of the final lines to a famous poem by Samuel Taylor Coleridge, "work without hope draws nectar into a sieve, and hope without an object cannot live".

Something else that Lebanon's youth had 'done for their country' was fight in its recent war. I asked him about this. To my slight surprise (and scepticism) he said that although he was a child at the time, he had fought in Lebanon's war against Israel ('a war against Israel' is how he described the conflict). At an age when most children were learning to put together jigsaw puzzles, he and his friends were learning to put together AK47 rifles. Whether he was exaggerating I do not know. Something I did know and which I was left in no doubt about was the vehemence with which he hated Israel. On one occasion he finished off a sentence by saying that he was immensely proud to be Lebanese and would have had no qualms about dying for his country against the aggressor nation (Israel).

Since he had brought up the topic of Israel, I asked him about it. He spoke uninterrupted and at length on the issue. To summarise his arguments, he believed that Israel was an 'illegal state' whose existence had created tension and instability within the Middle East for over five decades and he believed that the conflict had held back and was continuing to hold back the economies of many Arab nations, especially the non-oil producing states. If it had not been for Israel, the Arab world might not lag so far behind the United States and Europe. Israel's presence in Lebanon during the war and the continuing tension that still exists along the border between the two countries was having a particularly devastating effect on the economy of Lebanon. Before the war, tourism, an important part of Lebanon's economy, had thrived. The war may have ended more than a decade ago, but Israel's continuing incursions into the south of the country gave the outside world an impression that the country was not safe to visit. Because of this, tourist numbers were still very low, especially from the West. But it wasn't simply the tourist industry that was being affected. The instability in the south of the country was sapping other parts of the economy by deterring many foreign companies from investing in Lebanon. This lack of foreign investment had a knock-on effect on people like him, because it reduced the number of decent graduate jobs open to the educated young. Many were leaving the country to seek better opportunities abroad, thus damaging the economy even further.

The conversation moved on. He told me he enjoyed reading English novels. His favourite novel in the English language was George Orwell's *Animal Farm*; a story about a group of farmyard animals who, fed up at the ill treatment by their human owner, plot a takeover of the farm and start to run it along a socialist vision. That vision is never realised because soon after the takeover, the pigs seize power and eventually start ill-treating and exploiting the other farmyard animals in the same way that the human owner had. The book is supposed to be a critique of the Soviet Union and a commentary on how power corrupts the human condition. He didn't have to tell me why this novel meant so much to him. I kind of figured it out myself and my suspicions were confirmed when he started to draw parallels between the novel and the plight of the Arab people, who he felt were being treated unjustly by their rulers (like the animals in the farmyard). He wished for a successful revolution so that these unjust rulers would be ousted, and a fairer and more equal society could be created (again like the farmyard animals). But he feared that should the Arabs be successful in overthrowing their leaders, they would most probably end up squabbling and fighting between themselves, with one group eventually rising to power and oppressing the rest of society, just like its predecessor.

As I sat there, listening intently to this outspoken young man, I began to wonder about his ideological beliefs. I asked him whether he believed in socialist ideals. He said that he wished for the creation of a fairer society where people were treated equally (I took that as a 'yes'). From the way he spoke he didn't come across as particularly religious. I wasn't even sure of his religious background, but given his comment on a 'fairer society' I decided to play devil's advocate by suggesting to him that given that Islam was committed to the creation of a fair and equal society, did he believe that it, or another religion, should have a strong voice in the Lebanese political system? 'No' he answered firmly. Like the professor, he felt political Islam was dead. People were fed up with it. Again, reiterating what the professor at Starbucks had concluded, he believed that most Arabs did not want their societies to be run along theocratic lines, in which the religious elite had a strong say over how the country was run (as was the case in countries such as Iran and Saudi Arabia). I argued the point that I had failed to make to the professor, by suggesting that if the Arab people had a choice (such as in a democracy), surely they would place in power Islamic parties. So whether it was through a theocratic system or a democratic one, it seemed that if the 'will of the Arab people' was to be recognised, then political Islam—far from being dead—was still alive and kicking. He listened patiently to what I had to say and then nodded his head in acknowledgement. What I was saying was probably true he replied, but this was only because there wasn't another ideology alternative to Islam that was held in the same esteem by the Arab masses. Not only this, but he felt it would be near on impossible to plant a foreign ideology on Arab soil that could over time successfully compete with Islam. I noticed he didn't appear to be overly happy when making this point. His appearance resembled a man resigned to the fact that this was just the way things were in the Arab world.

After the above remark, to my surprise, he interrupted me halfway through a comment that I was making about the death of Marxist ideas in the Arab world. "Marxism is not dead" he retorted. "It was", I replied. The collapse of communist regimes the world over towards the end of the last century was pretty strong evidence to me that Marxism (and its socialist siblings) as a major political ideology was dead. He didn't agree. Societies progress through cycles, he pointed out. There will be points in that cycle when certain political ideologies will be popular and others not, but further down that cycle one will find that the unpopular political ideologies had reinvented themselves and become popular again. We were simply at a point in the political cycle in which Marxist/socialist ideologies were unpopular.

One of the reasons he believed that the communist states had collapsed was because socialist leaders across the world had imported this abstract Euro-centric doctrine and implanted it into their societies without making the necessary adjustments in the ideology to allow it to flourish. Lenin recognised this defect in Marxist ideology. Before I could reply with the obvious question that arose from this comment, he read my mind and answered that Lenin's error lay in the fact that he made the wrong adjustments. Capitalist globalisation was creating much inequity within the world. It would only be a matter of time before Marxism was popular again. I listened, but remained somewhat unconvinced.

Our discussion moved onto Britain and her historical role in the region—another topic that he was passionate about. He hated the British and the legacy they had left behind. This was the first time that I had experienced open hostility towards Britain. I wasn't naïve enough to think it didn't exist. If anything, I was surprised that this was the first time that I was hearing someone so openly berating Britain's imperial legacy. He highlighted everything from the Balfour Declaration (which signaled Britain's commitment to create a homeland for the Jews in Palestine) to the exploitative way in which the British divided up the Arab nations before granting them independence.

By the time we concluded our meal and were ready to leave, we had been speaking for several hours. I had entered this establishment in order to ask for directions, but ended up staying well into the evening. I may not necessarily have agreed with some of the views expressed by my eating partner, but I did find his company refreshing and hoped that when he finished his studies he could go on to bigger and better things.

16. CAUGHT BETWEEN THE PIT AND THE PENDULUM: THE NEW RELIGIOUS INQUISITION
(Beirut–Damascus–Amman)

> Every time they see me, fear me—I'm the epitome, a public enemy.
> *Don't believe the hype,* Public Enemy

I HAD RESIGNED myself to the fact that the journey from Beirut to Amman, Jordan was going to be long, arduous and boring. It was complicated by the simple fact that there was no direct coach service running from the two Arab capitals. I would need to travel via Damascus to get there and the journey would take the best part of a day.

The coach to Damascus left early one morning from a rather unimpressive bus station in Beirut. Four and a half hours later I arrived in the Syrian capital. From Damascus I booked myself onto the coach to Amman. The journey to the Jordanian capital was about four to five hours.

On our arrival at the Syria–Jordan border crossing, several Jordanian officials boarded our coach and requested that we hand over our travel documents for inspection. We were then asked to vacate the coach with our luggage and take it to one of the several designated checking desks so that a Jordanian customs official could sift through the contents.

It was whilst I was in the process of dumping my backpack onto one of the enormous checking desks that an official approached me and asked me to accompany him. His tone of voice concerned me. Something didn't quite feel right, but in the circumstances there was little else I could do but follow him.

He led me into a small office and introduced me to two senior-looking officials who were seated behind a large table, these officials asked the first man to leave the room, which he did, firmly closing the door behind as he left. I was seriously getting concerned. I could sense something was not right. Acting as cool as I could I asked if all was well? All apparently was not well and I was about to find out why.

The officials requested that I seat myself on a small wooden chair adjoining the other side of their table. I coolly walked over and sat myself down. The officers were now seated directly opposite me. They both looked at me. I had been brought here for a reason.

Over the next twenty minutes the officers subjected me to a good cop/bad cop type interrogation. They were mainly interested in finding out what exactly it was that I had got up to in the countries that I had just visited. Which cities had I travelled to? What did I do when I got to these places? Who had I met? What did we discuss and where did we go?

My passport had made its way into the possession of the two officials. It revealed that I had travelled to Pakistan. So in addition to the countries that I had just visited, I was also asked a whole barrage of questions about my 1994 trip to Pakistan. Again, the officers were interested in knowing why I went there. What had I done? Had I visited Peshawar (which is not too far from the Afghan border)? Had I travelled to Afghanistan itself (I think you've probably guessed by now what they were trying to get at)? Pakistan is the country that I was born in, I had family there. I only pointed this out to the officers about twenty-seven times. My visit to Saudi Arabia also attracted similar questions (could I have done any more to fit the profile of an al-Qa'ida suspect?).

At the time it seemed extremely odd (but not now), but I was also asked a number of questions on which mosques I had been to in the United Kingdom and whether I had met a number of people they listed for me. I didn't recognise any of the names they put forward, except a man by the name of Abu Hamza. I paused before answering when his name was mentioned. I had heard of the name and would even recognise a photograph of him (he's the one with a metal hook for one of his hands and christened by the 'aren't-we-so-witty' British tabloid press as 'Captain Hook'). Should I confess to this, or simply deny any knowledge as I had done with the other people? I decided honesty was the best policy and explained to them that whilst I had never met the man, I had heard of him. They seemed content and asked no further questions on the matter.

Having established all that they wanted to know about my past, they then moved onto the future and in particular what I planned to do in Jordan.

My passport was lying on the desk. The junior of the two officials picked it up and slowly flicked through it until he got to the page stamped with my Jordanian visa. "You come to Jordan on tourist visa, why you come here?" Given that he had just read out aloud that I had been granted a tourist visa, I thought it was obvious why I was entering the country.

"Tourism" I replied. They both looked at me with suspicion. I smiled a fake smile. This same officer then asked me this same question over and over again. On each occasion the question was rephrased slightly so as to give the impression that it was a different question. But it was the same bloomin' question, over and over again. "What your purpose in Jordan?" "Why you come to Jordan?" "What your reason in Jordan?" "Why you in Jordan?" "You in Jordan? "Yes". Why?" This same question was repeatedly met with the same answer, "tourism".

I began to get restless. They began to get restless. They were making no headway and they knew it. We all knew it. It was at this point that the human capacity to completely screw up things just when they seem to be going well kicked in. Hmm! I thought to myself, these officers' English isn't very good and when one thinks about it, the pronunciation of the word "tourism' isn't too dissimilar from the pronunciation of the word "terrorism' (especially in a Brummie accent). And as much as I tried to repress it, a mischievous voice within me kept saying, "go on, say it, say it, say the word 'terrorism', they won't notice the difference between the two words". And as difficult as it was to refrain from succumbing to this reckless temptation, I did somehow manage to repress the wicked thought.

Content that their searching examination had unearthed no terrorist motives, the officers' masks dropped and with beaming faces and open arms they both bellowed out towards me, "Welcome to Jordan, have a nice day".

Before I left, the senior of the two officers informed me that I had to register first thing tomorrow morning at the nearest police station to the hotel I was staying at. I suppose I could understand why he made the request, but I felt like I was being treated like a criminal.

I returned to my waiting coach and we set off for Amman. By the time I booked into my hotel it was past 10 p.m. It had indeed been a long and arduous day as I had anticipated. But boring? Probably not.

Before going to bed that evening my mind ran through the events of that day. I cannot say for certain that had 9/11 not occurred I would not have been interrogated (I doubt it though). What I can say with a fair degree of certainty is that the type of questions I was being asked was very much reflective of the post-9/11 climate that these officers were operating in. I can also conclude with a fair degree of certainty that had I not been a Muslim I would not have been called in for interrogation.

Anti-terrorist legislation, immigration profiling, detention without trial, greater surveillance of Muslim groups, curtailment of freedom of expression, increased cross border security intelligence, tougher asylum legislation, stricter border controls and being verbally savaged by two Arab officials. This is the life of a modern-day Muslim. It may still be too early to make the following conclusion, but is the West about to embark upon another religious inquisition? Different in form and method, but nevertheless a movement underpinned by prejudices against a particular religious group and a failure to recognise that these prejudices can and are causing harm to innocent people. Whether history records it as such may ultimately depend upon whether over time the above policies implemented in the aftermath of the 9/11 tragedy are seen as an 'adequate reaction' or an 'over reaction' to the threat Muslim terrorists pose to the security of the West.

It would be unfair not to mention the fact that there are many in the West who do recognise the inequity and injustice that government policies aimed at curbing terrorism could have on the civil liberties of Muslim citizens living in the West. The real dilemma for Western governments in the post-9/11 era is how they strike the right balance between the values of freedom of expression and the civil liberties that they hold so dearly and the need to maintain national security in a climate where there exists a heightened risk of terrorist attack. It is no easy feat. Freedom of expression within the Western tradition includes the right to be openly critical of the society one lives in, including its culture and its values. But by tolerating an individual's right to have a deep hatred of the society he lives in, they increase the risk of some individuals being drawn to groups that pose a real threat to the national security of the country. Getting the balance right is far from easy.

17. FLOAT LIKE A BUTTERFLY STUNG BY A BEE
(Amman)

JORDAN'S BIRTH INTO the modern world is strange and remarkable. That this small and fragile fledgling state has managed to survive in one of the most turbulent and war-ridden regions on earth is even more strange and remarkable. Despite all the adversities it has faced in its short life, Jordan continues to exist and in many ways the region is the better for it.

The country's genesis can be traced back to the fall of the Ottoman Empire. Based in Turkey, the Ottomans ruled the Arab world up until the First World War. Their empire finally came to an end in 1923 when it imploded from within. The Turkish secular leader Kemal Ataturk successfully overthrew the Ottoman regime and established his vision of a secular Turkish state expunged of all Islamic influences. He managed to drain Islam from the public life and confine it to the private sphere, to separate state and religion—he believed this was necessary if the Muslims were to ever catch up with the European imperial powers, who long before the turn of the twentieth century had overtaken the Ottomans (the last great Islamic empire) in technological advancement and in political, economic and military prowess. Religion was made the scapegoat, the reason Muslims were failing, and so it was thought that the Muslims had to do what the Christians had done, that is to divide state and religion.

When the end came in 1923, the Ottomans had all but lost their power and influence in the Middle East to the British and French. These two colonial superpowers were successfully able to exploit Arab national sentiments that had been fermenting in the region during the last days of the Ottoman dynasty. At the outbreak of the Great War, the British offered Arab leaders independent Arab states in return for their support in the war. The Arabs agreed. Their Ottoman rulers chose to side with the Germans.

If it seems that the Turks were foolish for aligning themselves with the Germans, then the wisdom of Arab leaders who aligned themselves with the Allied forces likewise needs to be questioned. For at war's end, Britain reneged on its agreement with the Arabs, implementing instead the Anglo-French Sykes-Picot mandate that carved up the Fertile Crescent into four states; Lebanon and Syria, which were to be controlled by the

French; and Iraq and Palestine, which were to be controlled by the British. A few years later (1922 to be precise) the British created a fifth state in the region when it divided Palestine into two, creating a new country with the rather unusual name of Transjordan.

Transjordan had a rather short existence. During the Arab-Israeli War of 1948 (which led to the creation of the state of Israel) the country managed to obtain East Jerusalem and the West Bank while the Jews captured much of the remaining land, leaving the Palestinians essentially without a homeland. The country's then ruler, King Abdullah, shortened his nation's name to the much better-sounding 'Jordan'. In 1951 he was assassinated. Two years later his teenage grandson Hussein ascended to the throne at the tender age of seventeen. Few expected the child king to survive in the politically dangerous world he inhabited, where assassinations, overthrows and coup d'etats were commonplace. But survive he did, overcoming several assassination attempts, an internal war with his Palestinian population and two wars with Israel (one of which, the Six Day War of 1967, resulted in the loss of east Jerusalem and the West Bank to the Israelis). He ruled the country until his death in 1999.

For many in the West, King Hussein was and arguably still is the moderate face of the Arab world. After his death, his son Abdullah took over the throne and rules to this day. He appears to have adopted the same ideological mandate as his father, cautiously navigating his country through the unstable and murky waters of Middle Eastern politics and the Arab-Israeli conflict.

When I awoke that morning in Amman, my first thought was that I should report at the local police station before doing anything else that day. The very last thing I wanted was trouble for not registering with the Jordanian authorities. I also wanted to get the next phase of the inevitable interrogation that I would endure over and done with so that I could enjoy the rest of my stay in Jordan.

The nearest police station just happened to be on the same street as my hotel. After breakfast I made the short trip to the police station. The weather was bitterly cold and for the first time on my trip I put on warm clothing before venturing out.

From the outside, the station looked rather shabby and run down. I took a deep breath and entered its premises. After yesterday's experience I was praying that there would not be a repeat performance.

Inside, I spoke to a junior officer and explained to him why I was there. He listened carefully before escorting me to what I assumed was the chief police officer's room. If yesterday's experience taught me anything, it was that I perfectly fitted the profile of an al-Qa'ida foot soldier; young single male Muslim, who had been on a holy pilgrimage to Mecca during the nineties (indicating that I had fundamentalist tendencies), had allegedly visited al-Qa'ida bases in Afghanistan (as signified by my Pakistani visa) and had just travelled through a whole host of nations accused of backing international terrorism. The police forces of Arab countries are not known for treating suspected enemies of the state with TLC and so my mind with great courtesy and timing played out various scenes of torture, as I followed the junior officer to my impending doom.

Having arrived at our intended destination, the escorting officer took from me my passport and asked me to wait outside the chief officer's room whilst he explained to his senior the reasons for my presence at the station. I waited patiently, knowing the end was nigh.

My fears proved to be totally and completely unfounded. After a short wait, the chief officer opened his door, came out, uttered the Islamic greeting, shook my hand and promptly invited me in.

Once I had seated myself inside his office, he ordered my escort to bring us tea. We introduced ourselves. He welcomed me to Jordan and added that he prayed that I had a pleasant stay here. The contrast with yesterday could not have been greater.

I stayed in that room for the best part of the morning, discussing with the officer a whole array of issues concerning Jordan and the wider Arab world. It was apparent from very early on in my conversation with him that he was a conservative who valued the traditional customs of the Arab people and feared that the increasing influence of the West on Jordanian society was eroding these traditional customs. On several occasions the officer would pause and then utter with genuine sadness how his people had abandoned Islam, how the West was their new god, their new qibla.[1] It was because the Arabs had abandoned Islam that they were weak and unable to rid their region of the United States and Israel.

He mentioned Israel a number of times and, surprise surprise, he had nothing but ill-will towards the country. "We hate Israel", he said loudly, 'we', signifying the whole of the Jordanian nation. He asserted with equal vigour his explanation for why they hated Israel. Jordanian people hated the Jews because they had arrived from all over Europe and had taken away land that Arab Palestinians had been residing on, he said. It was as straightforward and simple as that.

When he spoke of Jewish people, most of us in the West (including myself), would probably have regarded the officer's comments as being anti-Semitic. His cartoon-like caricatures were almost laughable, were it not for the fact that such discourses provide fertile soil for hatred and distrust against Jews to flourish. I was also acutely aware that his perception of Jewish people as inherently devious in nature and leaders of a worldwide conspiracy for global domination weren't simply his own views. ('If only we were so powerful', some Jews might say.) There were many in the Arab and wider Muslim world who would agree with his views about the inherently mischievous nature of the Jewish race. His comments reinforced the extent to which the wider world has underestimated the enormity of the problem in the Middle East. Securing political agreements that establish equity for all parties in the conflict is the easy part, changing people's hearts and confronting ancient prejudices (from both sides) is where the real battle lies. It is possible that one day Arabs and Jews will live in true peace and harmony, but that day (if it ever exists) is a long, long way away.

I mentioned to the Arab officer that it was very much my wish to travel to Jerusalem. However, events at the Jordanian border had led me to become increasingly fearful of how the Israelis might treat me once they saw the contents of my passport. He conceded that my concerns were indeed genuine and strongly urged me not to travel to Israel, for my own safety. To say that this senior police officer put the fear of god into me was an understatement. The Israelis could not be trusted he said. After 9/11 they had become increasingly paranoid and if I chose to travel to their country then my life and liberty would be in danger. The contents of my passport would petrify them. They would never allow someone like me to enter their country and would immediately think that I was entering it for some devious terrorist purpose. "But I have nothing to hide", I stressed to the officer in some vain hope that he might change his mind. That did not matter, he said. If, after searching my belongings they found nothing on me they were sure to plant something so as to prevent me from entering their country. Plant something! Plant something! The comment was absurd. Surely! It was a ridiculous remark to make. I reasoned with myself, "It was an absurd remark". I repeated the thought several times. Too late. The seeds of doubt and fear had been planted and taken root. However absurd the comments, there was a bizarre kind of rationale behind his theory. My heart sank. Maybe it was not such a good idea to go to Jerusalem. Maybe under the circumstances my safety was at risk.

Had this information come from the average Arab on the street with strong anti-Israeli views I might not have taken it as seriously. But this information was being relayed to me by a senior police officer, a man of authority, a man to whom respect must be afforded. I left that police station a deeply depressed man.

Remarkable as it may seem, the officer's bullish advice on travelling to the Holy Land was not be the enduring memory of that morning. No! That privilege was to be afforded to an extraordinary comment he let slip regarding police attitudes towards overtly practising Muslims in his country. The admission came towards the end of our conversation. We had been speaking generally about the threat that Arab terrorist groups posed to Arab governments in the post-9/11 world. Halfway through this discussion he looked to the floor and started to shake his head, as if he felt thoroughly ashamed about something. I looked confused. Was he about to confess to something? I think he was. And he did. Young Muslim men who were observed going to the mosque on an excessive basis raised suspicions amongst the authorities, who questioned their ideological commitment to the state. Some might be taken in for questioning to ascertain whether they were indeed attending the mosque purely for the purposes of praying, or whether their excessive religious behaviour had led to the development of harmful motives towards the state. He looked at me and uttered with genuine remorse and sadness that this was how low Arabs had sunk, that men who were committed to their religion were being treated like criminals.

In the last chapter I argued that in the post-9/11 climate Western governments were asked to make hard choices. It seemed Arab governments also have had to make hard decisions in order to protect the national security of their countries. I could appreciate why this senior officer, a sincere Muslim, was so concerned about what state officials were being asked to do. In Arab societies, the most devious had now come to resemble so closely the most pious that the two were almost indistinguishable. How does the state distinguish between a good man and an evil man when the two look almost identical?

The officer also spoke at some length about Osama Bin Laden. Resting his hand on my arm he asked me who had created Bin Laden. "The West", he told me before I could answer. It was the United States that had fed and nurtured him and his like. It was the United States that provided people like Bin Laden with military hardware and training in their holy war against the communist infidels. There was some truth in what the officer was saying. The last and most decisive battle in the Cold War between the United States and the Soviet Union had taken place in Afghanistan. But the war was not fought by America—the Muslim *mujahadeen* who flocked from all over the world to oust the communists from Afghan soil fought on their behalf. People like Osama Bin Laden. People who would eventually go on to become future Taliban and al-Qa'ida members. How ironic that the individuals and personalities who fought to win the last battle of the Cold

War for the Americans would go onto become the very people who initiated the first battle in America's new war, the War on Terror.

The officer condemned the acts that were committed against the States on 9/11, but stressed that he understood why some people were driven to commit such atrocities. In a telling remark he confessed that he supported Bin Laden's motives, but condemned his method (his motive, he believed, was to drive the United States out of Arab lands). The worst-kept secret in Arab society he reminded me (if I needed reminding) was that there were many Arabs who were secretly happy about 9/11 because they believed that the United States was finally getting a taste of its own medicine.

It was fascinating listening to the officer and how he grappled with the phenomenon that was Bin Laden. Al-Qa'ida's actions appear to be centred around a policy that is highly critical of the way the United States has intervened and implemented its foreign policy in Muslim lands. Most Arab leaders are unable/unwilling/too afraid to articulate a highly critical response to US policy in the Middle East (Iran, Syria and Saddam's Iraq being the exceptions). Such a lethargic response is all well and good if the majority of one's subjects agree with the approach taken. But what if they don't? What if increasing numbers of these people, who live under various types of dictatorships, become increasingly incensed at their ruler's failure to properly and effectively articulate grievances about the inequities of US policies in the region. Such an unhealthy state of affairs can only increase the risk of some sections of the populace gravitating towards groups such as al-Qa'ida.

During my now ritualistic first day walkabout, a local shopkeeper asked me what I thought of Jordan. I smiled and told him that I liked Jordan. Jordan, I told him, reminded me of a butterfly. He knew my observation was meant as a compliment, but couldn't quite understand the analogy. I explained to him that his country shared many characteristics with a butterfly. It was small and innocent like a butterfly. It was also incredibly beautiful and fragile, also like a butterfly.

For all the natural and historical beauty that is contained within its borders, central Amman (known as 'the downtown') is, surprisingly, somewhat lacking in architectural beauty. Like many other Middle Eastern cities, it is a sprawling mass of unattractive buildings bursting to the seams with commerce, people and noisy traffic. But unlike other Arab cities, there is an absence of heavily armed police on the streets. And, oh how wonderful this was. It felt as if the people were allowed to breathe. Downtown Amman was alive and buzzing.

I'm sure ... no I'm convinced that the absence of heavily-armed police is a major factor as to why Amman's central district generated an extra layer of energy and buzz that was absent in the other cities that I had visited. It was fantastic!

Jordan must be one of the few countries in the world where refugees outnumber the native population. Palestinians who fled the Arab-Israeli wars are found in abundance in the country. Their presence puts Jordan in an awkward position. On the one hand the Jordanian government quite rightly feels it has a strong moral obligation to assist its displaced brethren by providing them with a sanctuary. On the other hand, it is not an oil-rich country and the enormous influx of Palestinians that have seeped into the country over the last few decades have stretched their resources to their limits. In addition to Palestinian refugees, many Palestinians who reside in Israel and Occupied Palestine are allowed to make the arduous journey across the border to work in Jordan. And we think our country is being flooded by immigrants!

I may be wrong, but there appears to be much less censorship and less state interference in Jordan than in neighbouring Syria. One such indication was the enormous array of national papers, perhaps suggesting a freer press. As in Syria and Lebanon (and unlike in Iran), the newsstands were filled with magazines of beautiful Arab women, or more accurately, beautiful Arab women and Osama Bin Laden. I don't think even Mr Bin Laden himself could have predicted that one of the side effects of his actions against the United States would be that he would become a 'cover boy', the face that launched a million Arab magazines. His image shifts shed-loads of copies and don't Arab publishers know it. The other most famous Arab face was that of Saddam Hussein. Posters of the man were being sold alongside Michael Jackson and other Western and Arab pop stars. Seeing images of Bin Laden and Saddam being openly sold in the market places and bazaars of Amman only further reinforced my earlier observation that current Arab governments may not be acting as an effective voice box to air Arab peoples' concerns over US policy in the region.

The best thing about Amman is its people—they are its star commodity. There is a sense of goodwill towards foreigners that appears to be endemic amongst most Jordanians; this, along with the high-octane energy that the downtown generates, make Amman a wonderful city to visit.

Much of that first afternoon and early evening was spent exploring the city. In the evening I went to a part of Amman called Shmeisani, where I had my first ever KFC (again it tasted bland). Before leaving for Shmeisani I had returned to my hotel to rest briefly. At the door of the hotel I bumped into one of the hotel employees. He immediately stopped me and introduced me to the person he was with, a Palestinian man who worked in Jordan. The hotel worker was aware of the dilemma I was in with regard to travelling to Jerusalem and thought it might assist me to speak to someone who frequently made the journey to and from Israel. After the officer's comments, I very much needed a second opinion. And a second opinion I was given. It could not have been more different than the earlier advice I had received. I had nothing to fear, the Palestinian man stressed. Yes the Israelis were sure to ask me questions, but it would be nothing more than that. He laughed at the suggestion that they might plant something on me or ill-treat me for no reason. "Trust me, trust me", he kept repeating. Oh how much I wanted to trust him. I was desperate to go to Jerusalem. The officer had dashed my dreams of visiting the Promised Land, but this Palestinian worker revived my hopes. I reasoned with myself: This Palestinian man regularly made the trip across the border; I ought to accord more weight to his opinion than the officer's. But then again this Palestinian man's travel documents probably didn't sing to the tune of an al-Qa'ida foot soldier. I decided there and then that I would visit the British Embassy the next morning and ask for their advice. They would be the final arbiter on the issue. If they told me it was safe to enter the country then I would do so. The matter would be left in their hands.

18. BALLAD OF A THIN MAN'S SON (Amman)

Have you come here to play Jesus, to the lepers in your head?

One, U2

THE WAIT AT the British Embassy took ages. I was getting impatient. Things weren't helped by the fact that when I entered the embassy premises the reception area was already full of people. I would have beaten most of them to the queue had it not been for the fact that my dopey taxi driver misunderstood a request to be taken to the British Embassy as a request to be taken to the Ambassador Hotel. I might not have minded, but the first three questions I asked the driver when I entered his cab were, "Do you understand English?", "do you know where the British Embassy is?" and "are you sure?" He answered yes to all three questions when the truth of the matter was that he understood very little English. It had taken the assistance of a kind passerby to explain to him that I wanted to go to the British Embassy. Even then he had no idea where it was and we had to seek the further assistance of several more passersby before we eventually reached the offices of the British Embassy.

When my turn finally arrived I spoke to a very nice young lady. To my relief her advice was similar to that of the Palestinian worker, in that she warned me that I would probably be asked many questions at the Israeli border and subjected to what she referred to as "Israeli nonsense" (which she defined as being asked a whole host of irrelevant questions that have nothing to do with what you're doing in their country), but it would be nothing more than this. I need not fear she said; there was no history or record of the Israelis torturing and persecuting British citizens in the manner so vividly described to me by some of the people that I had spoken to. I should therefore ignore what the ordinary Arab on the street thought. Their advice was based less on actual fact and more on street gossip. The worst that could happen to me would be that they would interview me and then refuse to let me into their country. Her comments seemed to corroborate word for word what the Palestinian worker had told me. Providing I was careful and vigilant, I would be fine. My trip to the Promised Land was back on. I thanked her for her advice before leaving the embassy in a much happier and contented state than I had arrived. My next destination was the law department of one of the several universities that based themselves in and around Amman.

I caught a bus from downtown to take me to the university campus on the outskirts of the city. Seated next to me was a young male student who said that he was studying for an engineering degree. Like so many of the other students that I had spoken to on my travels, he likewise was interested in travelling to Europe to further his education. He asked me for some advice on this. The short journey to the university meant I didn't have enough time to properly discuss the matter with him so I asked if he was willing to meet up with me that evening. He was. We agreed to meet at Pizza Hut in Shmeisani at 8 p.m.

After arriving at the university, I hurriedly made my way to the law department. Because of the uncertain nature of my travels I had once again been unable to fix an exact time and place to meet up with my contact. Like the academics that I had met up with in Shiraz and Beirut, my contact knew I was coming, he just didn't know when.

I need not have worried. I found the professor in his office and he remembered our correspondence very well. He welcomed me to the university and invited me into his study. The bad news was that he did not have enough time that afternoon to see me—he had to attend an extremely important meeting and could not excuse himself. The good news was that he would find another member of the faculty who would be willing to speak to me. He then escorted me to what I believed was the faculty common room.

Seated in the common room was a plump, middle-aged man. We were introduced to one another. He was a lecturer in international law. The kind professor relayed my embarrassing predicament to him. After hearing his colleague's request he laughed out loudly and invited me to take a seat next to him. I thanked him for taking the time out to see me.

Before my contact left us he assured me I was in good company and that I would probably find his colleague a much more interesting proposition to talk to than himself. He was right. My mind was already mentally salivating at the prospect of interviewing a lecturer in international law. You have to understand, for nerdy boring types like me, he was dynamite material. Kapoow! Boy, was I was right! This man did not disappoint.

One of the difficulties that I had on my travels was trying to get the academics that I was speaking with to open up and speak freely about the state and the regimes that they lived under. Their reluctance is understandable and if I were in their position I would probably respond in a similar way. However, this lecturer was a real exception to the rule. From the moment we started to speak he showed no reluctance or hesitation in answering any of the questions I fired at him.

Born of Palestinian parentage in Jerusalem, he was one of the displaced Palestinians who lived in Jordan. Jordan, in fact, had been his home now for many decades. I wondered if after all these years he still felt any affinity with his homeland. Stupid question. I was immediately reprimanded. Palestine was his home and would always be his home. Again, and not surprisingly, he referred to the land he came from as Palestine, not Israel. The academics that I had spoken to on my travels may well have been reluctant to talk openly about the state they lived in, but similar accusations could never be levelled against any of them when it came to talking about Israel. During the course of our conversation this man was no less restrained in his criticism of the state of Israel, frequently referring to it as a fascist state (amongst a few other colourful adjectives that I had best not repeat).

I asked him about his religious background. He said he did not follow any religion. I wondered, but did not bother asking, whether he had any strong secular beliefs. It did not matter that I did not ask such questions, what he was and what he believed in became increasingly obvious the more he spoke. He was a man who passionately and strongly believed in a demo-cratic state in which all citizens were treated equally and all had a basic set of human rights that the state could not violate. Several times he asked whether I was aware that the United Nations had several human rights treaties. I nodded on each occasion. He gave the impression of someone who was ideologically committed to the concept of a 'liberal democracy'. When he spoke of the 'rights of man', he did so in such idealist and utopian terms that it was obvious that he was both an academic and from a country in which there was no liberal democracy. Listening to him I got the impres-sion he firmly believed that so many of the hardships and inequities that the ordinary Arab endured could be eliminated if they were provided with a set of inviolable rights, coupled with a right to choose their leader.

I pointed out to him that if true democracy were implanted in Jordan it might bring into power Islamic parties that wished to curb some of his inviolable rights. After all, their definition of man's inviolable rights might differ from someone like himself, who was not of the Islamic faith and who appeared to ascribe to secular ideals born out of the European Enlightenment. Was he not worried by this prospect? He immediately brushed aside my observation, "if that is the will of the people, then so be it", he replied. I was not convinced, how could he possibly be happy living under a regime that might potentially inhibit or restrict rights that he considered inviolable. I put the question to him again. This time he conceded he would have difficulties living under such a regime, but it was nevertheless a fairer form of government than the present one because it would be a government chosen by the people, as opposed to one forced upon them by the British.

His ideological commitment to democracy coupled with this apparent dig at the ruling regime seemed to reflect an underlying unease he had with the current government. I wasn't wrong. Over the next thirty to forty minutes he provided a critique of the Jordanian monarchy as damning as I had ever heard. I won't endeavour to list all his comments on the alleged failings of the ruling monarchy, except to say there were a number of aspects of the ruling regime that he found especially unjust. Political corruption, which he believed was endemic in the political institutions of his country, seemed to be a reoccurring theme with him. There were far too many members of the ruling class that were more concerned with lining their own pockets than to stimulating growth in the economy or helping the working-classes of Jordan. As an academic lecturer he saw firsthand the frustrations of able and talented students being plunged into a job market low in decent jobs but high on nepotism. Matters were aggravated by the fact that their rulers were distant from the people. Look at King Abdullah he told me, "he can't even speak proper Arabic . . . and he's supposed to be the leader of an Arab people . . . Could a British Prime Minister get into power without speaking English?" 'I guess not', I replied, whilst at the same time wondering whether his monarch's Arabic was as bad as he was making out.[1]

Playing devil's advocate, I asked him whether democracy could indeed resolve the difficulties of the Arab people. Look at my country of birth, Pakistan, I said. It has had/will have again/will probably lose again, its 'democratic government'. What good has it done for the people of Pakistan? The political system is still corrupt to its core, the people trust their democratically-elected leaders even less than their military dictators and they likewise accuse these democratically-elected leaders of ignoring the masses and lining their own pockets. Their suspicions aren't born out of fantasy; there is much justification for their despair. If anything, the country is, at the moment, performing much better under a military regime than the democratic regimes that preceded it. If he is right and political corruption is entrenched in Jordan, what makes him think a different system of government, even a democratic system of government, will eliminate corruption. He agreed. Yes, democracy might not necessarily put an end to corruption, but "look at India" he pointed out to me. It has had a democratically-elected government since becoming independent in 1947.

Yes democracy in India is not perfect; yes there are failings in the system, and yes it still has a long way to go to ensure all its citizens are granted equal rights and opportunities. But at least we can visibly see it sailing towards a more prosperous society, unlike Pakistan and Jordan. India is fast on its way to becoming a first-world nation, whilst Pakistan seems to be lagging further and further behind.

As he was finishing this last remark he noticed that my attention had become drawn to a picture of the Jordanian royal couple hung up on the wall behind him. "That does not mean anything", he remarked. I pointed out to him that if the regime was as bad as he was making it out to be, then why did I see pictures of the young couple and of the king's late father almost everywhere I went. It is those who are most critical of the regime that have the greatest royal paraphernalia surrounding them, he replied. I should not be fooled by this 'window dressing' he warned me, people's intentions behind putting up royal portraits might have more to do with them hiding their true feelings from the authorities than expressing them.

After trying to convince me that Jordan was an undemocratic state that failed to implement many of the human rights we enjoy in the West, the lecturer then moved on to a discussion of America's collusion in propping up undemocratic states such as his own.

America proclaims itself to be the champion of the 'free world' he asserted, especially since the events of 9/11. Bush keeps telling us that the War on Terrorism is supposed to be on behalf of 'freedom-loving people', or the 'civilised world'. The epicentre of this War on Terrorism, this 'crusade' against the 'evildoers' is in the Arab/Muslim world. The United States seeks the assistance of Arab/Muslim people in its struggle against those who wish to challenge 'liberal democratic' values. 'You watch' he pointed out to me in an animated way, one by one the Arab governments will fall into line with what America wants. Why? Because without US support and backing these Arab regimes would find it almost impossible to survive. These ruling regimes will, in the end, bend over backwards to offer assistance to the leader of the 'free world', the 'democratic world', 'the West', where freedom of expression and the human rights of every citizen are cherished. But I want these values for my country as well, he said pounding his chest, "'democracy', 'freedom of expression' and 'human rights', we want them as well . . . and they must be of a type and quality you have in the West". "But I can't have them," he asserted. "Do you know why?" he asked me. "If we openly speak out or even fight for these values we risk losing our liberty, possibly our lives. Isn't that the irony, the hypocrisy of it all", he suggested to me—that the United States is the leader of the democratic world, but it supports and maintains regimes that repress and even persecute peoples and groups that are struggling and fighting for the very values it subscribes to and says it is fighting for.

The room fell silent for a few seconds. Then, without any prompting, he picked up the conversation, switching to the topic of Bin Laden and his relevance to everything he had been talking about. He asked me who had created Bin Laden. I shrugged my shoulders. "The West created Bin Laden", he shouted. (Now where had I heard that before?) "It is because the United States props up regimes that are undemocratic, that do not allow for the free flow of ideas and opinions to openly flourish in society—this is what gives crazy people like Bin Laden a constituency", he yelled out vehemently. In the aftermath of 9/11 he thought that the United States had finally appreciated the folly of its ways, that they would reappraise their policy in the region. But in the months since 9/11 everything that he had heard and seen from the Bush administration seemed to suggest there was to be little revision of their policy. "There will be more American suffering", he warned. "They don't quite realise how much they are making us suffer. When they do", he said, "then maybe they will start practicing what they preach and give an old man like me the very values they have, that I want and which they are playing a part in denying me of".

This part of the conversation with the lecturer continued to reverberate around my mind throughout the whole of the bus trip back to the hotel. I still thought that both King Abdullah and his late father were at heart decent people who genuinely wished the best for their people. Yet when the lecturer articulated his arguments in the way that he did, especially how the United States supported a regime that suppressed true democracy, I found it very difficult to argue against much of what he said about the double standards inherent in American foreign policy. When I returned to the United Kingdom, I looked up on the Internet what the 2004 US State Department country assessment report (published in February 2005) on Jordan states. The US government's *own* report on Jordan draws the following conclusion on its human rights record:

> Although the Government respected human rights in some areas, its overall record continued to reflect many problems. Reported continuing abuses included police abuse and mistreatment of detainees, allegations of torture, arbitrary arrest and detention, lack of transparent investigations and of accountability within the security services resulting in a climate of impunity, denial of due process of law stemming from the expanded authority of the State Security Court and interference in the judicial

process, infringements on citizens' privacy rights, harassment of members of opposition political parties, and significant restrictions on freedom of speech, press, assembly, and association. Citizens did not have the right to change their government. Citizens may participate in the political system through their elected representatives to Parliament; however, the King has discretionary authority to appoint and dismiss the Prime Minister, members of the cabinet and upper house of Parliament, to dissolve Parliament, and to establish public policy. The Government imposed some limits on freedom of religion, and there was official and societal discrimination against adherents of unrecognized religions.[2]

How different is the US government's *own* conclusion on the Jordanian government from what the lecturer in international law was telling me? Let me rephrase the question: is there a *material* difference in their conclusions?

In many ways America is history's greatest contradiction. If one were to compile a chart of the nations that throughout history have done the most to promote, both directly and indirectly, the individual human and social rights of people of all backgrounds, races, colours, creeds and religions (both within its borders and beyond), then the United States would probably come top. Now that may be a very difficult fact for all those who hate America—honestly, it is even at times a difficult fact for me to stomach, but it is true. However, if we were to likewise draw up a chart of the nations that throughout history have done the most to participate (both directly and indirectly) in the violation of individual human and social rights (both within its borders and beyond), then America would similarly top the chart (or at least be very near the top). This may again be a very difficult fact for America and its supporters to accept, but it, too, is true. During its history, the United States has participated in the most awful mistreatment of some of it own people (specifically the hundreds of millions of African-Americans that have resided and continue to reside on its soil). Throughout its history it has also consistently provided financial and military aid to foreign regimes that it has consciously known (or chosen to recklessly ignore) are corrupt, despotic or that brutally repress and violate the very human rights it cherishes and considers sacrosanct. (This was especially true during the height of the Cold War when, in its all out pursuit to stop the communist threat, the United States frequently assisted and co-operated with some of the most despotic rulers in the third world, Saddam Hussein being one of them.) I don't wish to repeat many of the arguments that I have already raised in chapter 6, but in today's new world order, we only need to look at the Arab world as a case study to highlight the continuing blatant hypocrisy in US policy.

Whether or not a US administration will ever acknowledge it, its foreign policy decisions have never been projected exclusively through the sacred prism of human rights and democracy. Pragmatism, not ideology, takes precedence in the world of geopolitical struggles. The harsh realities of international politics mean there are a whole array of factors, issues and events that effect the formulation of a particular policy. Sometimes . . . sometimes, assisting regimes that promote democracy and human rights will be *a* factor that is thrown into the policy-making bowl. For the most part though, America's primary motivation in the formulation of its foreign policy is the same as every other global superpower that preceded it— *self-interest.* Like all the great powers before it, the United States will not allow itself to take up a position that is detrimental to its interests and if taking up that position benefits it, all the better. There has been a consistent failure by successive US administrations to acknowledge or concede that in preserving their own interests, they sometimes harm the legitimate interests and aspirations of other people—people like the professor of international law that I had met that afternoon.

Thus, America straddles this enormous contradiction that in turn creates a situation in which it and its allies are able to look through one set of rose-tinted spectacles and convincingly tell the story of a country that has done more to promote democracy and the rights and freedoms of individuals than any other nation on earth, while the enemies *and* victims of the United States look through another set of spectacles and this time convincingly tell the story of a nation that has, in its pursuit of power and prosperity, supported regimes and dictators that are unjust and repressive. Unfortunately for the United States, in places such as the Middle East, increasing numbers of people are viewing them through that second set of spectacles.

It is within this contradiction that Bin Laden and 9/11 must be viewed. George W. Bush and his administration only see America through that first set of rose-tinted spectacles. They assume that Bin Laden and the al-Qa'ida network also see America through this same set of spectacles, but do not like what they see—they find 'freedom' and 'democracy' abhorrent values that must be defeated. This is a major flaw in the Bush administration's reading of the reasons behind the attacks on 9/11 and the ever-increasing worldwide attacks on American and Western interests. I have no doubt that members of al-Qa'ida dislike American culture and values. I have no doubt that they think the United States is a decadent and morally bankrupt society, that its people have too many freedoms. But it is one thing to suggest they hate 'us' and 'our' values and quite another to suggest they hate us and our values and that is the reason why they hijacked planes filled with civilians and flew them into buildings filled with civilians. That is not the reason behind the attacks on 9/11. Members of the al-Qa'ida network did not sit around in their private meetings saying to themselves, "I hate American values, I hate freedom, I hate democracy, I hate the rule of law, *and* I hate these things so much that I am going to venture onto American soil and kill American civilians for it". As I have said, I have no doubt that they almost certainly abhor many aspects of American culture, but it is fundamentally incorrect to assume that the motives behind 9/11 were based on an abhorrence for things like freedom and democracy. When the al-Qa'ida network planned these attacks they were motivated by what they saw through that second set of spectacles, the one in which it is clear that America actively participates in propping up regimes that implement policies that are designed to benefit US interests and that these 'policy decisions' are often detrimental to the interests of the citizens of these countries. The majority of the 9/11 hijackers were of Saudi origin. Issues such as the House of Saud's decision to allow American soldiers to remain on sacred Muslim land, even after the end of the first Gulf War, is more likely to have fuelled the anger behind the 9/11 attacks than the fact that the US government gives its citizens too many freedoms for their liking or allows it citizens to elect their leaders. To allow US presence on sacred Muslim soil as an emergency measure at a time of war was one thing, but what can be the purpose behind the United States maintaining a presence there after the war had ended? Was it the result of a desire to increase liberal democratic values in Saudi Arabia? Were the dozen or more Saudis involved in the 9/11 attacks motivated by a fear that the United States might persuade the House of Saud to give its citizens democratic institutions and a greater freedom of expression? Or is it just possible that their anger was based (amongst other things) around the fact that US presence on sacred Muslim soil beyond the end of the first Gulf War had less to do with the United States actively promoting liberal democratic values to Saudi citizens and more to do with the fact that the United States felt it needed to retain a military presence in order to protect and preserve vital US strategic interests in the region from people like Saddam. Surprise surprise, as soon as Saddam was toppled, the United States left Saudi Arabia. Did they leave because they felt the indoctrination of Saudi citizens to liberal democratic values had been completed? Or was it simply because the risk to their strategic interests, which necessitated their prolonged presence, had now been removed?

Let us just look at a couple of statements from the al-Qa'ida network to assess the reasons *they give* as to why it is that they hate the United States and why they wish to wage a war against the superpower. The first quote is an extract from the infamous fatwa that Osama Bin Laden issued in 1998 ordering Muslims to kill Americans:

> The Arabian Peninsula has never—since God made it flat, created its desert, and encircled it with seas—been stormed by any forces like the crusader armies spreading in it like locusts, eating its riches and wiping out plantations . . .

> No one argues today about three facts:

> First, for over seven years the United States has been occupying the lands of Islam in the holiest of places, the Arabian Peninsula, plundering its riches, dictating to its rulers, humiliating its people, terrorizing its neighbours, and turning its bases in the peninsula into a spearhead through which to fight the neighbouring Muslim peoples . . .

> Second, despite the great devastation inflicted on the Iraqi people by the crusader-Zionist alliance, and despite the huge number of those killed, which has exceeded one million; despite all this, the Americans are once again trying to repeat the horrific massacres, as though they are not content with the protracted blockade imposed after the ferocious war or the fragmentation and devastation . . .

> Third, if the Americans' aims behind these wars are religious and economic, the aim is also to serve the Jews' petty state and divert attention from its occupation of Jerusalem and murder of Muslims there. . . .

> On that basis, and in compliance with God's order, we issue the following fatwa to all Muslims:

> The ruling to kill the Americans and their allies—civilians and military—is an individual duty for every Muslim who can do it in any country in which it is possible to do it, in order to liberate the al-Aqsa Mosque and the holy mosque (Mecca) from their grip, and in order for their armies to move out of all the lands of Islam, defeated and unable to threaten any Muslim.[3]

The fatwa is very clear as to why Americans must be killed. It does not show any revulsion towards Americans because they are 'freedom-loving people' or suggest that this fact is so disgusting and so abhorrent to Bin Laden and the al-Qa'ida network that one must kill US military personnel and civilians for it. Bin Laden and the al-Qa'ida network are clearly basing their hatred of the United States on what they see through that second set of spectacles. It is the American/Israeli occupation and presence on Muslim soil that motivates them. It is a fact that this entrenched presence is to preserve US economic interests in the region and that is what motivates them. It is a fact that this presence is detrimental to the Muslim citizens of these lands and that is what motivates them. It is a fact that American presence in the region is causing the death of countless innocent Muslims and that motivates them. It is for these reasons that Bin Laden and the al-Qa'ida network felt so angered by the United States that they issued this pre-9/11 fatwa to kill Americans and its allies.

A few weeks after 9/11 Bin Laden issued a press release. The lengthy statement begins with the following words:

> Here is America struck by God Almighty in one of its vital organs, so that its greatest buildings are destroyed. Grace and gratitude to God ... and thanks be to God that what America is tasting now is only a copy of what we have tasted.
>
> Our Islamic nation has been tasting the same for more than 80 years, humiliation and disgrace, its sons killed and their blood spilled, its sanctities desecrated ...
>
> A million innocent children are dying at this time as we speak, killed in Iraq without any guilt. We hear no denunciation, we hear no edict from the hereditary rulers. In these days, Israeli tanks rampage across Palestine ... and many other parts of the land of Islam, and we do not hear anyone raising his voice or reacting. But when the sword fell upon America after 80 years, hypocrisy raised its head up high bemoaning those killers who toyed with the blood, honour and sanctities of Muslims.[4]

The press release ended with the following words:

> The wind of faith is blowing and the wind of change is blowing to remove evil from the Peninsula of Muhammad, peace be upon him.
>
> As to America, I say to it and its people a few words: I swear to God that America will not live in peace before peace reigns in Palestine, and before all the armies of infidels depart the land of Muhammad, peace be upon him.[5]

If we compare the pre-9/11 statement with the post-9/11 statement many of the same issues are raised. Once again, there is no mention of the fact that al-Qa'ida finds values such as 'the rule of law' so abhorrent that it is necessary to verge onto American soil and kill Americans for it. The press release justifies the reasons for the attack by appealing to the 'eye for an eye' dictum of morality. Once again, the organisation premises its war against the United States on factors such as US presence in the region—presence that it believes amounts to an 'unlawful occupation' that results in the death of innocent Muslims.

Bruce Lawrence, who has analysed Bin Laden's speeches over the past decade,[6] says of Bin Laden's motivation:

> Bin Laden's principle innovation has been to organize terrorists' actions thousands of miles away from the territories he is seeking to liberate. But this, he insists, is itself only retaliation for innumerable prior acts of aggression by the West in the Muslim world, thousands of miles away from Christian homelands. For 200 years now the umma (Islamic global community, or supernation), has been under attack, from the first French invasion of Egypt in the last years of the 18th century and the seizure of the Maghreb in the 19th century, the British grab for Egypt and the Italian for Libya, the carve up of the whole Middle East by Britain and France at the end of World War One, the sponsorship of Jewish colonization of Palestine, the suborning of nominally independent rulers in the Arabian Peninsula, down to contemporary American control of the entire region.
>
> Is this an exaggerated description of the unbalanced relationship between the West and the Muslim world? There are no Arab military bases in Texas or California, no Arab contract mercenaries stationed in Britain or France, no Arab fleets in the Gulf of Mexico, no Arab-sponsored schemes of forcible settlement in the Mid-West. All the lines of intrusion and violence historically run in one direction.[7]

If the Bush administration ever hopes to win its War on Terror, then it must begin by assessing why it is that it is being targeted by the al-Qa'ida network and why it is that increasing numbers of Arabs and Muslims dislike them. As things stand, the Bush administration doesn't even appear to know the reasons why they were attacked on 9/11. The al-Qa'ida network is making clear why it hates the United States. And it isn't just al-Qa'ida members that hate America. Many Arabs dislike the United States because they fear that the United States is increasingly influencing Arab regimes, that this influence is primarily designed to protect US strategic interests in the region, that too many Arab regimes are implementing policies which are partially or wholly designed to protect and promote US strategic interests (such as the US military presence on sacred Muslim soil) and that in implementing these US influenced policies, Arab regimes are placing the interests of the United States above the interests of their own people. Until the US government looks through that second set of spectacles, it will never successfully win its self-proclaimed War on Terror. Until there is a realistic and honest appraisal of the harm its own policies are causing the people of the nations that gave birth to its enemies in the War on Terror, it will never win this war. I am reminded of the famous poem, *To the white people of America*, by the African-American, anti-slavery poet, Joshua McCarter Simpson; "See the white man sway his sceptre, in one hand he holds the rod—In the other hand the Scripture—And says that he's a man of god."

19. TWO TRIBES: HOW DOES A ROSE GROW FROM CONCRETE? (al-Quds)

> Did you hear about the rose that grew from a crack in the concrete?
> Proving nature's law is wrong it learned to walk without having feet.
> Funny it seems, but by keeping its dreams, it learned to breathe fresh air.
> Long live the rose that grew from concrete when no one else ever cared.
>
> *The rose that grew from Concrete*, Tupac Shakur

I GOT UP at an obscenely early hour of the morning in order to get ready and make my way to the bus station, from where I would catch a coach to the King Hussein border crossing bridge. At the bridge I would need to board one of the special buses that take people across onto the Israeli side of the border. Once on the other side, I would then need to catch another bus in order to travel to Jerusalem. Because of the large number of stops and checks, a journey that ought to take no time at all, would in fact take several hours to complete. I wasn't sure whether or not I'd be allowed into Israel, what with all the al-Qa'ida inferences they could draw from my passport and the horror stories that I had been hearing. I was half expecting the Israelis to turn me away. But I had to try. I had come this far. Israel/Palestine was the natural ending place for my journey and for this book.

To say that Amman was cold that morning would be an understatement. It had been snowing overnight, the temperature had dropped below zero and there was a chilling wind outside that made my fingers and toes go numb.

The minibus was full of all manner of people: men, women, the young, the old, workers, and tourists. We arrived at the King Hussein Bridge and joined up with a whole host of other buses and coaches. The people wishing to cross the border were separated into two groups. Palestinians were placed into one group, the remaining travellers into another. This second group was composed mainly of Jewish tourists, international backpackers and several American priests. One of the priests noticed I was on my own and very kindly invited me to join him and his wife.

Although it did not feel like it, we were actually in the fast track group. There would be much less interrogation and fewer checks for us to endure.

The Palestinians on the other hand, went through an incredibly rigorous set of strictly enforced security controls and measures before being allowed to travel to Israel or the Palestinian territories. The journey to their homeland would be significantly longer than ours. My initial reaction was horror: in the twenty-first century people were being segregated according to their race and one particular group, the Palestinians, was being treated differently. Israel vigorously defends its position by arguing that such procedures are necessary to maintain security (from the constant and real threat of suicide bombings that the country endures) and maintains that most countries would react in a similar manner if they were faced with a likewise threat. This is probably true, but if I were a Palestinian I cannot even begin to imagine the rage that would burn inside of me if I knew that I would be separated, held back and then thoroughly searched, possibly interrogated, before being allowed to enter my home country. This is the everyday reality of being a Palestinian. This is the humiliation that Palestinians must endure; their liberty and freedom controlled and dictated by their enemies, the Israelis. It is no wonder why many Palestinians find it difficult to empathise with Israel's safety concerns when so many of them are suffering and dying because of Israel's occupation of their land. Until we in the West make sense of their pain, we will never make sense of the crazed actions of some of their people.

There is an awful catch-22 to this all. Israel feels it has to occupy the Palestinian territories; that it has to set up these extensive checkpoints; that it has to exert this level of control over Palestinian lives in order to stop the suicide bombings and attacks on its citizens. They would rather not do this—they are fully aware of the aggravation it causes Palestinians. But they have no option. If they withdraw, the suicide bombings increase. The security of their citizens is more important to them than the effects of that occupation on Palestinian lives. But it is this very occupation of Palestinian land, this Israeli control over Palestinian lives that increases the risk of sui-cide bombings. The Palestinians feel that support for suicide bombers might not be so high if only the Israelis withdrew from the Palestinian territories. As the late Sheikh Ahmed Yassin, the former leader of Hamas, summed up, "Let them stop killing our children and we'll stop killing theirs". When by mutual agreement Israel does withdraw from the occupied territories and the suicide bombers do cease their paramilitary operations, the peace, the cease-fire is so weak and so fragile that it takes just one incident, one event, one individual to do something for the whole thing to ignite and bring the two groups right back to where they were, the occupation and the suicide bombings.

Before boarding the bus I briefly spoke to the Jordanian official who had checked my passport. I asked him whether it was likely that I would suffer problems at the Israeli side of the border. He didn't think so and waved me through.

The King Hussein Bridge that joins Jordan to Israel ought not to take that long to cross. If one were travelling at a moderate speed and without stopping one could probably cross the bridge in a matter of a few minutes. However, with all its checkpoints the short crossing lasted over an hour. I passed the time by speaking to the priest and his wife, who I discovered had been living and working in the Palestinian territories for some time.

When we finally arrived at the Israeli side of the border everybody got off, collected their luggage and made their way to a plush checking-in terminal that resembled the inside of an airport. I joined the queue of travellers that had alighted from our bus. From standing at the back of the queue I could just about make out a young female Israeli official at the front checking-in desk who appeared to be inspecting people's passports and asking them one or two questions before allowing them to move onto the next stage of the registration process. The queue was moving very quickly and the young female official was taking no more than a few seconds with each person. I thought—I hoped that maybe I had been unnecessarily paranoid about what would happen to me.

When I got to the front of the queue I smiled at the young official. She smiled back at me, took my passport and politely asked why I was travelling to Israel. I smiled and said *tourism* (this time I was not even tempted, in any shape or form, to mispronounce this word). She smiled back; I smiled back. Hey this was easy! Then she looked at my passport. O dear me! The smile vanished from her face. She asked me to move to one side. I asked if everything was okay. She didn't answer except to repeat that I should move to one side and that I should not touch my luggage. Another official arrived and took my luggage away. One of the things that I had been warned against was allowing the Israelis to take the luggage out of sight. All manner of frightening scenarios were fed into my innocent and easily impressionable mind as to the things they would plant in my luggage should I part company with it. But there was little I could do. If I objected to my luggage being taken away from me then that would have definitely raised suspicions. I quietly made my way to the seating area that I had been directed to. There I waited, worriedly thinking about what was about to follow.

Ten to fifteen minutes later, a young Israeli official (who looked to be in his mid- to late-twenties) came over to where I was seated and escorted me to a secluded section of the terminal. Once there, he began to interrogate me. All manner of questions were fired at me. Questions such as, where I was born? Where had I lived? Where had I studied? And so on. I was being asked to provide a sort of mini-autobiography of my life to date. I tried to be as helpful as possible by providing full and detailed replies to the questions asked. This I thought would add to the credibility of my answers. Not so. On more than one occasion the official stopped me and asked that I simply limit my answer to the question asked. After he had all the information he wanted on my background he then asked why, if I wished to travel to Israel, did I not start my journey in Israel and then make my way through Jordan, Syria, Lebanon and Iran? The answer to this question was easy. If I had started my travels in Israel, then I would not have gotten beyond Jordan, as neither Syria nor Iran let in travellers who have visited Israel, I replied.[1]

Once he finished interviewing me, I was body-searched using a metal device (no explosives found), before being asked to wait again. Over the next hour and a half I was interviewed on two further occasions, by different sets of people and at different locations in the building. The questions were of a similar nature as those asked in the first interview. All the questions asked were simple and straightforward, in a formal and distant manner; none of the interviewers showed any emotion. At no time were they aggressive or rude and at no time did I feel the questions were designed to trap me. Their style was the complete opposite of the two officers who had interviewed me at the Jordanian border. These people were professionally trained in such matters. Finally, I was taken to a small room where I saw my backpack laid out on a table. Standing on the other side of the table were two officials, both of whom were wearing rubber gloves. One of the officials asked whether the contents of the bag were mine.

The way in which this question was asked gave me the impression they had already examined the bag and found something dodgy. I nervously asked whether they had found anything that concerned them. They repeated the question. I paused. If something had been planted in my bag and I answered 'yes', I was trapped. My bag had been out of my sight for a couple of hours. I had no idea what they had or had not done to it. The room stood silent as they waited for my answer.

After a long pause I nervously replied 'yes'. They then asked whether I was carrying any item for any other person. 'No', I answered after a similarly long pause. Finally, they asked whether I had any guns or explosives in the bag. 'No', again came the answer. I didn't need to pause before answering that question. The deed had been done. If a trap had been set then I had fallen into it. One of the officials began to slowly open my bag. I looked on attentively—more than nervous—petrified and convinced that I had been set up. How many times has this scene been played out on TV, when the exact same questions are put to an innocent party and when the bag is finally opened something dodgy is found? Hundreds of times we've seen this. I prayed it would not be my reality.

With my bag finally open, the official proceeded at a nerve-janglingly slow pace to take out the first set of items. These were two smaller bags that I kept all my toiletries in (I had taken about four thousand toiletries and half a medicine cabinet with me). One by one each of these items was removed and carefully checked. The item then had a liquid substance applied to it. It was then put through some sort of machine (I assume the liquid substance would have showed up traces of explosives if I had handled such substances). When we got to about the fifteenth or sixteenth item in the toiletry bag, I began to calm down. It appeared that nothing had been tampered with, that all was okay. With my toiletries examined, the official removed the remaining contents of my bag and likewise subjected them to the same procedure.

Whilst this was going on, one of the female officials who had interviewed me earlier on came into the room. Several pieces of paper that were found in my luggage were handed over to her. She took the documents and began to read them. The woman I spoke to at the British Embassy had given the pieces of paper to me. It was basically the Foreign Office's official advice to British travellers visiting Israel. She asked me to explain the origins of the paper, not realising they were from the British Embassy. This was my opportunity. I explained to her that I recognised that having travelled through the countries I had, it was obvious I would be of concern to the Israeli authorities when I turned up on their doorstep. I thought it best that I attend the British Embassy in Amman to clarify the conflicting advice that I had been receiving along my travels. Along with this piece of paper, they had also informed me that upon my arrival I would probably be questioned, but it would be nothing more than this. The British Embassy official reassured me that contrary to what I was being told by the 'Arab on the street' I would not be subject to any torture (I particularly highlighted this point two or three times). It worked. She dismissed the Arab 'word on the street' as rubbish and said she was grateful for my understanding of their position, adding that they also had a job to do and it would be naïve and foolish of them to just let me walk into their country without asking any questions.

Once all the contents of my luggage had been examined I was asked to place everything back into my backpack and wait in the seating area outside the room. Before leaving, one of the officials asked for my flight tickets and passport, which I duly handed over.

I waited for about twenty minutes before the same official who took my documents returned to hand them back and to tell me that I was free to go. I was free to go! That was it? No apology, no thank you for your assistance, no acknowledgement for my patience. It was a good thing that I was exhausted and simply relieved to be let in the country. Otherwise, I would have approached this official, looked him straight in the eye, thought up some amazing witty put-down and then . . . well . . . then been too chicken to utter it. That's what I would have done, if I'd had any nerve left! that would've showed him who's boss. Mess with me, hey!

By the time my interrogation was finished the passengers on my coach (including the American priests) had long gone. I asked around for the next coach or bus service to Jerusalem and was told that a Palestinian-owned minibus would be leaving shortly. I made my way to the clapped out minibus and negotiated a reasonable fare to Jerusalem. I could have caught a private taxi, but the fares they were quoting were extortionate and as one rude taxi driver pointed out to me, "this service is for rich Americans, not for people like you". People like me! It was an incredibly rude and offensive remark to make—okay, it was completely true, but rude nevertheless. I had gone from being an Iranian millionaire to an Israeli pleb, all in a matter of a few weeks.

The minibus did not leave immediately. When I boarded, it was only half full. There was no way the driver was going to leave until all his empty seats had been taken up. He may not have had an MBA from Harvard Business School, but even he knew that in order for one to maximise profits, one had to fully utilise one's resources. For this dictum of capitalism to be realised, we had the privilege of waiting for almost an hour. Then we were off.

The minibus shuttled along, cutting through the striking desert terrain on a motorway infrastructure comparable to first-world countries. We didn't head straight towards Jerusalem. As we neared the city the driver started to drop people off. I cannot say for sure whether the places the driver stopped at formed part of Israel or the Palestinian territories. What I do know, was that this minibus drove off a first-world motorway, with its first-world motorcars and first-world taxis, carrying its first-world passengers to their first-world hotels in a first-world part of Israel and drove straight into a world so squalid and so decrepit that I cannot even begin to put it into words. To describe it even as third world would be flattering. The countries that I had travelled through, many of them were third world, but this, this was several leagues below that. The roads, if you could call them roads, were broken, uneven, full of holes and could barely be made out. The houses, if you could call them houses, were derelict, squalid and unfit for human habitation. On many of the street corners there was rotting refuse several metres high. Palestinian children were playing around this decomposing refuse in dirty and ripped clothing. At the time I wished I had a film camera with me. The world needed to see this. The West and America in particular needed to see this, because what I saw and what I am describing to you is the soil in which suicide bombers grow.

I wanted to stay in the east part of Jerusalem (the Palestinian quarter). I wanted my story, this book, to end in their company. East Jerusalem (certainly the part bordering the Old City) was much improved compared to the shantytowns that I had just driven through. But I knew even before I visited Jewish Jerusalem, that east Jerusalem was still, on the whole, very much impoverished compared to west Jerusalem (the mainly Jewish part).

The hotel I was due to stay at shared the same name as a very posh London hotel. But that was the only thing they had in common. If the London hotel was five-star then this hotel was minus five-star. As I stood in the hotel lobby waiting for the manager to arrive, it became so cold that I had to put my gloves back on.

"We have central heating", the hotel manager said in response to my enquiry. "Good", I said. "But it is broken", he said. "Not good", I said. "We can fix it", he said. "When?" I said. "Next week the man will come", he said. "Not good" I said.

I had to have heat. The weather was getting colder and would stay like this for the next few days. I simply could not stay at this hotel. I thanked the manager for his help but said that I would need to look elsewhere for a room. He pleaded with me to stay, saying that he would get an electric heater put in my room. I paused and looked out the lobby window. It had begun to snow. Did I really want to go looking for another hotel in this weather? I looked back at the manager. He seemed desperate for my custom. "Okay" I said. I agreed to take the room on the strict condition that the electric heater be put into my room immediately. He smiled and shook my hand. "It's a deal", he said. "Good", I said.

Seven to eight hours had passed from the time I left my hotel room in Amman to the time I booked into my new hotel room in Jerusalem. I was exhausted and tired. But my fatigue was tempered by an over-riding and uncontrollable sense of excitement. Ever since I was a child I had dreamt of visiting the Dome of the Rock and al-Aqsa Mosque. That dream was about to come true. As soon as I gained entry into my room, I immediately had a change of clothes and got something to eat. Fully recharged, I was now ready to go forth into Jerusalem's Old City in search of the golden dome.

Outside, the snow was now falling more heavily. The streets were rapidly emptying and few people chose to venture out in such extreme weather conditions. The whole situation felt very surreal. I would never have imagined that when I finally visited the Dome of the Rock it would be covered in snow. The ever-worsening weather may have deterred the locals from venturing out, but not me. I was five minutes away, yes that's right, five minutes away from arriving at the third holiest site in Islam. Nothing, not a hurricane, a cyclone or nuclear fallout could stop me from reaching that site within five minutes.

Forty-five minutes later, with my body metamorphosing into a snowman and my nose and left ear about to fall off from frost bite, I still could not find one of the several gates that allowed me access to the Dome of the Rock complex. Jerusalem's Old City is like an ancient labyrinth—just when you think you're nearly there, when you can physically make out the golden dome from above city walls and you know your end destination is just metres away from where you're standing, you suddenly take a wrong turn and find yourself facing a deadend wall. I decided to seek assistance from a couple of armed Israeli soldiers who had the unenviable task of being on duty in such bad weather conditions. Bad move, "wad do you want? Hah! Wad do you want? Raaaaah!" I quickly scuttled away before they had the chance to bite my head off, seeking solace in one of the few tourist shops that was still open in the bad weather. The shopkeeper's face lit up when I entered. 'O dear' I thought, he thinks I've come in to buy something. Boy! did he try his best to sell me something. In the end, I told him that I didn't have any Israeli currency with me as I had just arrived in the country. But after I had cashed-in my traveller's cheques first thing tomorrow morning, I would visit his shop. He reluctantly agreed to ease off, on the strict condition that I keep my word. I promised I would (I didn't promise I would buy anything, but I did promise to return to his shop). He gave me directions from which even I couldn't get lost. I thanked him and then wandered off down the street, comfortable in the knowledge that one of the gates to the Dome of the Rock site was just around the first corner.

At the gate to the Dome of the Rock complex stood an old man and as I neared the gate he approached me and asked whether I was a Muslim. I said that I was. He then asked that I recite a couple of specified Islamic prayers for him. This I did without questioning him. He smiled, welcomed me with the Islamic greeting, *assalaamu alaikum* and then hurriedly ushered me through the gate. Moments later the rationale behind the old man's actions hit me. Since the intifada, non-Muslims were not allowed inside the Dome of the Rock section of the Old City. This is an extreme shame. The Dome of the Rock is the defining feature of Jerusalem. For a tourist to visit Jerusalem and not be allowed to visit the Dome of the Rock is an enormous travesty.

Once inside the complex, I first visited al-Aqsa Mosque, which is a minute's walk away from the Dome of the Rock itself. From the outside, al-Aqsa Mosque doesn't look architecturally beautiful. But on the inside, it can hold its own against any of the great mosques of the world. I stayed there for about thirty minutes before leaving for the Dome of the Rock.

By now, the weather had gotten progressively worse. Outside, the snow was falling heavily and apart from a few Palestinian children having a snowball fight on the steps of the Dome of the Rock, the whole complex was relatively empty. My surreal vision of visiting the Dome of the Rock in a picturesque snowy setting was coming true.

The door to the Dome of the Rock was manned by a security official. Inside, a few people were making their way out. Once they had left, there remained only myself, the security guard and a lady who was sitting on her own and deeply engaged in prayer.

The Dome of the Rock looks awesome from the outside, but the inside is arguably even more spectacular and breathtaking. The artistic beauty of the Islamic calligraphy that lines the inner walls and ceiling of the building surpassed anything that I had seen on my travels so far. On any objective standard, it was art in its highest form. Let there be no doubt though, both the majestic outer golden dome and the aesthetic beauty of the inner calligraphed walls serve one purpose, to encapsulate and cover the centrepiece of the mosque, the floodlit 'rock' which both occupies and dominates the central area of the mosque. This 'rock' is sacred to Muslims because it is believed that the Prophet Muhammad ascended to heaven from it. I spent several minutes walking around the mosque, inspired, dumbfounded and in awe of the majestic inner beauty of one of the most controversial buildings in history.

Thirty minutes later, I made my way towards the entrance to see whether the weather had changed. It had, it had gotten worse. A snowstorm was in full flow. It appeared that I would be stuck in the Dome of the Rock for some time.

At the side of one of the corners of the 'rock' was a staircase that led to a small cave which lies underneath the 'rock' itself. With time on my hands I decided to make my way down there. The small cave was carpeted, with a raised section at the far end corner. But apart from this, the room is bare and unfurnished. I seated myself on the raised section, closed my eyes and allowed myself a brief moment to take in the enormity of where I was. When I opened my eyes the lighting in the small room had gone off and there was no light coming from the top of the staircase either. It appeared that we had suffered a power failure. The lights came on briefly, then went out again. I remained seated in the small and now darkened cave, imagining that the snowstorm and the power failure was some sort of divinely inspired act to keep me in the Dome of the Rock for as long as possible.

I was fully aware of how lucky I was to be sitting here. On my last evening before I left Amman, I had kept my appointment with the student that I met on the bus. He also was from Palestine. His family was part of the large displacement of Palestinians that had flooded into Jordan. It was not a surprise that his attitude towards Israel was extremely uncompli-mentary. At one point during our conversation I began discussing with him the viability of the two-state solution (one state for the Jews, one state for the Palestinians). He immediately condemned the suggestion. There will only be one state in the disputed region, he argued, and that will be the Palestinian state. What would happen to the offspring of the millions of Jews who had immigrated to Israel at some point during the last century and made Israel their home, I asked? They should all go back to Europe or America or wherever they came from, that was their real home, he responded. I spent several minutes arguing over the practical viability of this suggestion, all to no avail. He was convinced that the option was viable and morally just. Although his family was from Jerusalem, neither he nor his family was allowed to enter or return to the city, even to visit. He rhetorically asked what greater right did I have to enter Jerusalem than he did. Al-Quds (Jerusalem) is my home he told me, and yet the Israelis have barred me from entering the city. But people like 'you' he retorted ('tourists' I think he meant), who have absolutely no connection with the city are allowed to visit with no questions being asked. He was right. Jerusalem was his hometown. Not only did he have a greater right to enter the city than me, he had a greater right to return and resettle in Jerusalem than many Jews that Israel has allowed and continues to allow to settle in Jerusalem and the surrounding territories.

20. SYMPATHY FOR THE DEVIL: CLASH OF THE UN-CIVILISATIONS
(Jerusalem)

'I SAY ISRAEL . . . you say Palestine . . . I say Jerusalem . . . you say al-Quds . . . Israel, Palestine . . . Jerusalem, al-Quds . . . let's blow the whole place up'. This morbid take on a popular American song was running through my mind as I left the hotel to explore the ancient city on my first full day. I made sure I wrapped up warmly before leaving. No snowstorm had been forecast, but the weather was still wet and cold. I had finally made it to the Promised Land, I thought to myself. Not that the place much resembled a Promised Land. There was much tension in the atmosphere. There was much unease about the place. Jewish soldiers do not blend very easily into the Palestinian neighbourhoods of east Jerusalem. Palestinian civilians do not blend very easily into the Jewish neighborhoods of west Jerusalem. In the west of the city the air is filled with Jewish paranoia, in the east of the city the air is filled with Palestinian anger. This is a nation of two tribes, each hell-bent on inflicting maximum pain on the other, each hell-bent on deploying ever more novel methods in which to deliver this maximum pain. Berlin was divided, but even then there was little personal hostility between West Berliners and East Berliners (as was evidenced when the Berlin Wall came down). The Israelis are building a similar type of wall to separate the Jews from the Palestinians. The measure is designed to provide security for the Jews of Israel. I doubt it will work. Unless and until the Palestinian people are given a homeland and an independent state (which they are happy with), I doubt any measure short of the total genocide of the Palestinian people will ever keep Israel safe from Palestinian aggression.

Palestinian aggression (be it interpreted as proactive or reactive) was the subject that dominated my thoughts throughout the day. It was a topic that I had often thought about during my travels. The most controversial form of Palestinian aggression is suicide bombing, a phenomena that is so alien to most Westerners that it is virtually impossible to relate or empathise with a people who feel their situation is so hopeless, their plight so desperate, that the only way to remedy the injustices being inflicted upon them is to strap themselves with explosives and blow up other human beings. Suicide bombings are currently the most popular form of activity of a genre that we in the West define as terrorism. To Westerners, the issue of terrorism equally appears to be almost impossible to understand, for how is it that humans can be manufactured (I assume there isn't a gene for terrorist behaviour) to behave in a way that is so contrary to what it means to be human. The events of 9/11 and the resulting War on Terror have elevated the subject of terrorism to new spheres. What 9/11 and the War on Terror have also done is firmly fixate a link between terrorism and Muslims in the minds of many people in the West. Jerusalem was a good place to mull over this issue. And mull over the issue I did.

There is an underlying morality to terrorism, irrespective of whether one wishes to blow up buildings, blow up other human beings or even fly planes into tall towers. Deeply embedded within any terrorist's psyche must be the enormous sense of moral purpose behind the act he is about to embark upon. For the terrorist, the terrorist act is a deeply moral act.

It is not the terrorist himself, but the wider society that labels and defines an individual as a terrorist and his act as terrorism. Why? Because in most instances the act is designed to kill innocent civilians and/or destroy property, or threaten to do these things. Terrorism is pure evil, easily identifiable by looking no further than the act and its intended or desired consequences. It is as simple and straightforward as that, isn't it? Isn't it?

Let's take a look at three of the most notorious terrorist groups of the last century, the Palestinian Liberation Organisation (PLO), the African National Congress (ANC) and the Irish Republican Army (IRA). Apart from the fact that all of these groups have, in varying degrees, renounced terrorism (or not as may be the case, depending on your position), are we able to draw any further parallels between the organisations themselves, and the types of societies they were born into? Possibly.

The first obvious similarity is that all three organisations originate in lands that are inhabited or occupied by at least two identifiable groups, but ruled by only one of these identifiable groups. In Israel the Jews rule, the Palestinians don't. In apartheid South Africa, the white South Africans ruled, the black South Africans didn't. Finally, in Northern Ireland the British rule, the Irish Catholics/Republicans don't.

The second similarity is that in all three countries the ruling group is militarily much stronger than the non-ruling group/s. In Israel, the Jews have a vastly superior military machine than the Palestinians. White South Africans, whilst smaller in number to their black counterparts, were nevertheless in control of the military apparatus of the country and thus able to maintain power for many years. Lastly, the British military, like the Israeli military, is infinitely more powerful than the Catholic/Republican residents of Northern Ireland. We can draw one further important conclusion from this enormous disparity in military prowess, 'the inability of the non-ruling group to engage in direct military warfare with the ruling group'. The Israeli army versus the PLO, the South African army verseus the ANC, the British army versus the IRA, the difference in military power between the national armies and the paramilitary groups of these three countries is so great and so wide that if any of the paramilitary organisations were to engage in direct, face-to-face warfare with the national army of the ruling groups they would be easily beaten. Not only is this fact obvious to the outsider and to the ruling group, it is also obvious to the paramilitary organisation of the non-ruling group. It would be a folly of enormous magnitude for either the PLO or the IRA (or perhaps what should now be called the 'real IRA') to take on the Israeli or British army in face-to-face combat (the ANC now of course rules South Africa).

The third similarity is the almost immeasurable sense of injustice and inequity the non-ruling group feels at being ruled by people who *they feel* have no greater right than they do to inhabit/occupy and/or rule over the land they reside in (or ought to reside in, in the case of displaced Palestinians). On the contrary, the common belief amongst many of these non-ruling people, the Palestinians, the black South Africans and Irish Republicans, is that immigrant Jews (and their children), white South Africans and the British have a lesser right to live on, occupy, or rule over the land they inhabit. This sense of outrage and injustice isn't necessarily confined to the condition of being ruled and controlled by the ruling group. The manner in which they are being ruled and controlled may also play a crucial role in constructing a perception of injustice and inequity. For example, in apartheid South Africa, laws that segregated the races and resulted in white people having greater access to the benefits and privileges of the country they lived in were seen as racist and discriminatory towards blacks, Asians and other non-white communities in South African society. Israel's Law of Return, which gives any Jew in any part of the world the right to immigrate to Israel and be given Israeli citizenship, similarly courts much controversy. On land which is occupied by Christians, Muslims and Jews, for the state to implement an immigration policy which singles out one racial group (that of the ruling group) for preferential treatment by allowing them automatic entry and citizenship in the country purely and simply on the basis of their race is likewise seen as racist and discriminatory. You'd be hard pressed to convince any Arab or Palestinian that a wealthy American Jewish family whose ancestors have resided in the West for thousands of years has a greater right to live in Israel/Palestine than a Palestinian family living in an Arab refugee camp having been displaced from the area in the 1967 War.

To recap, what the PLO, IRA and ANC have in common is that they are all born into societies in which: a) a militarily powerful group (the ruling group) occupies and/or rules a land that is also occupied by a militarily weak group (the non-ruling group); b) there exists a perception by the non-ruling group that the ruling group has no higher right to occupy/rule over the land they reside on; c) a further perception by the non-ruling group that at least some of the laws the ruling group has passed operate in a way that is unjust and unequal and; d) the non-ruling group/s, whilst being incensed and outraged by these injustices, are nevertheless incapable of rectifying the perceived evil/injustice through non-violent means or violent means that put the fighting forces of each group in face-to-face combat (as I mentioned earlier, the paramilitary groups would get splattered should such an option be pursued). In these instances the non-ruling group has two options, either to accept the injustices they live under or to find alternative means to fight these injustices.

The PLO, IRA and ANC conduct their operations in the way that they do because of *the inability of the non-ruling group to eliminate a perceived grave and continuing injustice being committed against them through either peaceful dialogue or direct military warfare.* If the *grave and continuing injustice* that is being committed against them by the ruling group cannot be eliminated through direct military warfare, then to some in the non-ruling group it becomes morally justifiable to adopt other methods to eliminate the injustice. Thus, in the case of the IRA, the targeting of economic sites in London becomes morally justifiable to combat the *grave and continuing injustice* that cannot be combated through direct military engagement or peaceful dialogue (although peaceful dialogue as a means to removing the perceived injustice thankfully seems to have gained increased support over the last decade). Whatever *injustice* such paramilitary actions may cause the people of Britain, it pales into insignificance when measured against the injustices the British have inflicted on the Irish people (the argument would go). Similarly, hijacking civilian planes and holding their passengers (which belong to the ruling group) for ransom unless a demand is met also, in some small way, is a method of tackling the *grave and continuing injustice* that the non-ruling group endures and is thus morally justifiable. And should some of the hijacked passengers die in such an operation, well that is sad, but this is a war (which they started) and anyway, 'our' innocent civilians are dying all the time at the hands of the ruling group's military and security forces (the argument would go).

If we suppose Nazi Germany won the Second World War, destroying the British military forces and achieving a complete occupation of the United Kingdom; and suppose that after the war, a gleeful Mr Hitler, ruling from Berlin, imposed his evil Nazi rule on the nation. No doubt the British people living under this Nazi rule would feel that the fascist occupation and rule of their country was wicked and evil (and they'd be right!). Suppose, in such a scenario, they were incapable of eliminating this *continuing grave evil* either through peaceful dialogue or direct military engagement (because the British armed forces had been virtually destroyed and what remained was no match for the powerful Nazi war machine). Suppose, in such circumstances, a British paramilitary organisation born out of the remnants of the destroyed British military forces decided it was going to remove the evildoers from our green and pleasant land through military operations that targeted the economy of Nazi Germany. This included conducting operations such as planting a bomb in the financial centre of Berlin. But before the bomb went off, a message would be released that the targeted area needed to be abandoned because an explosion was about to take place. How many British people, occupied and ruled by this evil Nazi rule, would be sympathetic to such tactics to get rid of the evildoers *in circumstances where no other military or diplomatic option was viably open to them*? Quite a lot I would imagine, and honestly, if I were living in Britain in such circumstances and conditions I could envisage myself being sympathetic to such a tactic to remove the evil Nazis from our land.

I'm also fairly sure that if many British people were sympathetic to such a course of action, it would be rationalised in ways that made the conduct morally justifiable. As the saying goes, 'one person's terrorist is another person's freedom fighter'.

The above example is extreme, but it helps illustrate the point that when a non-ruling group is unable to eliminate a 'perceived grave injustice or evil' through peaceful dialogue or direct military warfare, then 'indirect military warfare' sometimes is the only remaining viable option. Indirect military warfare was essentially what the ANC, PLO and IRA were engaged in.

Human societies have, through the ages, developed moral or ethical codes by which wars are to be fought (for example the treatment of POWs or the need to keep civilian casualties to a minimum). It may seem strange to some that an activity that involves killing human beings should operate within a moral framework. After all, killing another human being is arguably the most immoral act of all. But if one accepts that sometimes there is no option but to eliminate evil through the engagement of war (or direct military warfare), then it must be right that such conduct operate within a moral framework. It cannot be right that the whole process of war be left to an 'anything goes' morality. One only needs to look at the recent Balkans war or read 'the Nazi's guide to fighting' to see why war, more than any other human activity, needs to be fought within moral boundaries.

The morality or ethics through which modern military warfare is to be conducted has been well discussed over the centuries by academics, philosophers, politicians and holy men. But what of indirect military warfare? If one does not believe in indirect military warfare under any circumstances, or if one believes the act that someone else is committing isn't evil at all (such as the right of Israel to exist in the circumstances that it does, or British rule in Northern Ireland), then to discuss the moral framework through which such conduct must be committed becomes futile. But if one is able to accept that in some circumstances one's only option to eliminate a real evil is through indirect military warfare (such as the hypothetical example of a Nazi-occupied Great Britain), then the issue of such conduct being placed within a moral framework becomes highly relevant. It sounds absurd (even to me) to talk about behaviour that many define as 'terrorism' being conducted within a moral framework, but these are questions that freedom fighters, terrorists, call them what you may, have to address and do address. Some terrorists/freedom fighters target only military sites. Others target important civilian buildings but ensure reasonable time is given for the civilian occupants of that building to vacate before their detonation goes off. In these two examples, there is an underlying morality at work; both operations are conducted in a manner that is designed to either eliminate or reduce the potential loss of civilian life. Other terrorists/freedom fighters however, conduct operations not with the mindful aim of limiting the loss of civilian life, but actually with the express purpose of killing as many civilians as possible. How does the terrorist/freedom fighter justify this to himself? Is the 'eye for an eye' tenant of morality possibly at work here? Or is it that they believe that such action constitutes the most effective 'method' to achieve their 'moral end' (and so is morally justified because it acts to bring about the 'end goal', the 'greater good')? Or is it a combination of both?

It isn't just the terrorist/freedom fighter who is faced with the task of rationalising his indirect military operations in a way that persuades him that they are morally justifiable; outsiders also have to take a stand on the issue and decide whether the actions of the individual or group concerned are those of a terrorist (and therefore bad and morally reprehensible) or a freedom fighter (and therefore courageous and morally justifiable). Of the three twentieth-century groups that I have discussed, the world did not come to a unanimous decision as to whether their activities fell into the category of 'terrorism' or 'freedom fighting'. This is because unfortunately, the labelling of an act as 'terrorism' isn't simply dependant upon the 'act' itself and its desired/intended consequences. Sometimes other factors are thrown into the equation that effect whether or not an act is judged to be 'terrorism'.

One important factor may be the extent and depth to which other people are able to empathise with the perceived moral injustice against which the terrorist/freedom fighter claims to be reacting against, and this depends upon their relationship with either the terrorist/freedom fighter or his victim. Factors such as whether or not one shares a similar religious or cultural heritage, or racial or ethnic background with either the terrorist/freedom fighter or his victim very often (and often unconsciously) play a significant role in determining one's judgement of the terrorist/freedom fighter's action. The Irish American community and the British mainland community's differing reaction towards Sinn Fein and the IRA during the eighties is a good example of how the above factors play a role (and to some extent still play a role) in determining the difference between a paramilitary organisation and the label terrorist. The same can of course be applied to an organisation such as the PLO; many Muslims (including Muslim states) are far more sympathetic to its paramilitary objectives than are Jews or others living in the West.

East Jerusalem feels like a city under siege. Armed Israeli personnel are everywhere. That their presence is resented is too obvious a fact to mention. Social interaction between the Israeli security forces on patrol and Palestinians going about their everyday business is nonexistent. Where circumstances necessitate interaction (as happened several times during my stay in the city), I saw Israeli officials and Palestinians exchanging abuses. On one occasion a Palestinian man had illegally parked his van near an Israeli police/army station. Within a matter of seconds a group of Israeli officers converged upon him, all of them shouting at the man to move his vehicle. To my surprise the Palestinian man did not accede to their request. Not initially anyway. Instead he clasped his hands together, held them up and appeared to be asking the Israeli officers for time. From what I could gather, he was waiting to pick up a delivery from a nearby shop, but could not park his vehicle directly outside that shop as other vehicles were already parked there. Whether his actions were those of a brave or a foolish man

I know not, they did however, incur the wrath of the Israeli security forces. A small crowd (including me) had gathered to witness the unfolding drama. The more the Palestinian man appeared to stall for time, the more angry and impatient the Israeli officials got. Standing to my left were two Palestinian boys, each no more than ten years in age. Both appeared to find the whole thing rather amusing (no doubt they were used to witnessing such matters). So amused were they about the whole situation that they decided it would be rather funny if they could wind up the now red-faced Israeli officers by mimicking their behaviour. In parrot fashion they began to repeat everything the officers were shouting at the Palestinian man. The officers were not amused. They turned and looked in our direction and gave the two boys the evil eye. I walked forward two paces to ensure there was no confusion between the coward and the fools. We continued to watch Jerusalem's own version of reality TV. Israel's version of Big Brother really was 'Big Brother'. To my relief, the Palestinian man eventually relented and agreed to move the vehicle and when the altercation was over the crowd disappeared. New York City eat your heart out, this was 'zero tolerance' super-deluxe style.

This 'city under siege' mentality was also well-reflected in a conversation I had at breakfast one morning with one of the hotel workers, a young man in his late teens/early twenties. He lived outside Jerusalem (in the Palestinian territories) and commuted to the city every day. Officially, the Israelis only allowed him entry into Jerusalem to study at one of the universities in the city. Unofficially, he told me he worked part-time at the hotel. I say part-time, but his long working hours seemed to suggest he was employed full-time and studying full-time. He had no choice, he said. This was the only way he could afford to pay for his education. Part of his income also went to supplement his parent's small income. I asked what would happen if he ever got caught. He shook his head nervously and said the consequences were too horrific to bear thinking about. The Israelis might well refuse to allow him to travel to Jerusalem altogether and that would be the end of his education and any prospect of decent employment (as well as the loss of crucial income for his family).

The Old City clearly stands out from the rest of Jerusalem. Like the Old City in Damascus, it is divided into various quarters (the Jewish, Christian and Muslim quarters dominate). Also like the Old City in Damascus, there are parts of this historical place that feel like they have been frozen in time, a living and breathing museum of a crucial part of human history. Yet there are also parts of the Old City that have quite clearly been given a coating of late twentieth-century commercialism, a concession to the demands of modern tourism. Not that there were many tourists to be seen.

Jerusalem's Old City is the jewel in Israel's crown. It remains one of the most sought-after places on earth. The conflict that rages on today is little different from the conflict that has raged on in this region for centuries. An alien visiting us from another planet might ask, with good cause, what all the fuss is about. What is so special about this place? After all, the land produces no valuable natural commodity such as oil. Leave aside valuable commodities, in this desert land the scarcity of fertile soil means that even staple commodities such as wheat or barley do not flourish easily. Leave aside even staple commodities, the single most crucial commodity to the existence of human life, water, is nowhere to be seen. On one reading, there is nothing about this place that would explain why men have continuously fought over it. Yet this assessment of Jerusalem's value ignores one small fact: that many of the chapters of the history of humanity were written here. Without Christianity, Islam or Judaism, humanity would have taken a very different course. Jerusalem's contribution to the story of mankind is not quite over yet. As I walked the streets of Jerusalem that week, it was very clear that a number of chapters remain unwritten, and will need to be played out.

The New City in Jerusalem is located to the west of the Old City. Its shops, streets, buildings, in fact the whole atmosphere and feel of the place is comparable to that of a Mediterranean European city. If parts of east Jerusalem are third world, then parts of west Jerusalem are definitely first world. As I walked the streets it did not escape my attention that the town centre of the New City was frequented by an incredibly low number of Palestinians. Just as Jewish civilians were few and far between in many parts of east Jerusalem, the same could be said of the Palestinians in many parts of west Jerusalem.

One afternoon, I stopped at a restaurant for a coffee and chocolate cheesecake. I had always thought that the conflict between Jews and Palestinians over this disputed land was exacerbated by religious and ethnic tensions, but seeing the perfectly laid-out tables with their knives and forks and neatly folded napkins perfectly captured the extent to which class is increasingly becoming another factor that widens another cultural gap between these two communities (and thus the prejudices of class snobbery may also be finding their way onto the already long list of prejudices that each group holds of the other). I could live in west Jerusalem or other Jewish neighbourhoods of Israel and never meet or come into contact with a Palestinian (and vice-versa). In the long run how can such racial/ethnic segregation be healthy for a society? What does history teach us about societies that are racially segregated?

The enormous and increasing disparity in wealth and living conditions between the Jews and the Palestinians saddened me. What saddened me the most though, was the enormous and increasing disparity in life opportunities between Jews and Palestinians. In a little over fifty years the Jews of Israel have built their nation from scratch to an almost first-world nation status (and this was done without the assistance of oil). This is in many ways a remarkable achievement. Part of this successful nation-building project has been the creation of a distinct and proud Israeli identity. This Israeli identity is premised on one important factor, Jewishness. Jewishness is the defining feature of Israel. It is why the country was created. Yet this whole nation-building project marginalises non-Jewish communities that do not wish the national identity of their homeland to be premised on a Jewish heritage. Israel wants to be a democracy with equal rights for all. Israel also wants to be a Jewish homeland. But it cannot be both. If I were a non-Jewish citizen of Israel how could I possibly feel a sense of belonging, a sense of attachment, a sense of loyalty to the country I was born in when that country premises itself on something I can never be? By making Jewishness the defining feature of the state, the non-Jewish citizen is forever marginalised. Why would the non-Jewish citizen not, in such circumstances, be entitled to say or feel that he lives in a racist state?

The two-state solution is in Israel's interest. It allows Israel to maintain an equilibrium between its two contradictory principles: a) Israel is a democracy with equal rights for all, and b) Israel is a Jewish homeland. The equilibrium is maintained because Jews outnumber Palestinians. If Israel's borders were to extend to include the Palestinian-dominated West Bank and Gaza, then Israel would be obliged to take in a large number of Arab-Palestinians as citizens (unless they were ethnically cleansed from the land). I have heard some suggest that in such a scenario this intake of Arab-Palestinian citizens, coupled with the fact that the birthrate amongst Arab-Palestinians is much higher than that of Jews will mean that in the not-too-distant future, Palestinians might outnumber Jews. If that were to happen then the equilibrium would be at risk. The very existence of the state of Israel would be in the balance.

Having seen with my own eyes the living conditions of Israel's non-Jewish communities, I went to bed every night that week a deeply, deeply saddened man. My last thought before falling asleep on many occasions was that I didn't think Israel was a Jewish state. A Jewish state, a truly Jewish state, would never treat its minorities the way that Israel treats her minorities.

21. SOMEWHERE OVER THE RAINBOW: THE END OF HISTORY?
(The Promised Land)

What is it thou livest for?
  They ask me
As I recall the weary days of my past,
  My eyes close and slowly I drift back home,
Back to my people,
  To the ways of my ancestors,
The forefathers before us.
  I watch, a stranger, amidst my people,
Watching my family together
  Laughing and carefree,
The land, when we could call it our own;
  The fields were as foliage dark
As fertile as the mother's womb,
  We lived gifted by the heavens,
In eternal peace and love.
  Wherefore our children roamed,
Free and with spirits wild,
  Amidst the trees we played,
At ease with ourselves and nature.
  The spirits watched over us,
Spirits of the dead ones,
  Spirits of the discarded ones,
And so we lived unto our land
  Free and young,
Until the day,
  When dawned the destructive revelation,
Whereupon they came,
  The other men,
We welcomed them with love,
  Yet from us they took our land,
Our home,
  The land of our ancestors.
And so the peace within which we lived was gone,
  Destroyed and discarded, lost and forgotten.

And so as easily as they came
    They brought with them the fatalities of war, blood and death.
Our children age, learning the ways of death,
    Watching their mothers tortured, raped and suffering,
Watching their father's burn;
    Living young ones, a life worse than death.
And with them we learnt to dream the dreams of murderers,
    To lust after revenge,
To claim back our rightful land
    Yet we are labeled as evil,
As extremists,
    As destructive terrorists.
Yet all we crave is our home,
    The return of our land . . .
                  'I live for peace,' I reply . . .
                    The Forgotten Ones, Raabi'ah

THE DAY BEFORE I began writing the first draft of this final chapter, I came across a poem that appeared in an old copy of a British Muslim newspaper.[1] The verse appears to have been written by a Palestinian woman. The author is expressing her personal feelings of hope and despair at the plight of her people. In doing so, she beautifully manages to capture the many discourses through which so many Palestinians discursively construct their sense of history and identity.

In her poem the past is idealised. Before the Aliyahs, that is, before the Jews returned to Palestine, she tells us that her ancestors lived in an idyllic, almost utopian society: "We lived gifted by the heavens, in eternal peace and love". It is as if the nightmare of the present has distorted the past, creating a vision, a dream of a land so pure, so innocent, so perfect, that it must have been blessed by some deity.

It isn't simply the 'land that was gifted by the heavens'; the character of the Palestinians who lived in these times also appears to have been a 'gift from the heavens', especially in their warmth and generosity towards the returning Jews. Again, she tells us, "Whereupon they came, the other men, we welcomed them with love, yet from us they took our land, our home, the land of our ancestors". Were the Palestinians as welcoming and as naïve as the author is suggesting? Or does the truth lie somewhere nearer the following proposition: that whilst indeed some hospitality was shown to some immigrant Jews by some Palestinians, as the influx of Jews throughout the late nineteenth- and early twentieth-century grew, it began to cause much unease amongst the local Arab populace who, far from being naïve to the aspirations of the Zionist movements of the time, were only too well aware of what was unfolding before their very eyes (hence their unease and agitation).

The author does however, manage to wonderfully capture with both a sense of honesty and despair the effect the creation of Israel has had on the children of Palestine, "Our children age, learning the ways of death ... Living young ones, a life worse than death. And with them we learnt to dream the dreams of murderers", she says. And it is for this harsh but honest appraisal of the effects of occupation on Palestinian people that I quote her.

Over the next few days before I returned to Amman, I further explored the Old and New cities of Jerusalem, visiting the Muslim, Christian and Jewish quarters of the Old City and delving into the Muslim and Jewish areas of the New City. The conflict between Palestinians and Jews has all but stopped the flow of Western tourists visiting Jerusalem. Many of the shops in the Old City had been boarded up. Whether this was on a temporary or a permanent basis I do not know, except that the closures were almost definitely the result of the tourism drought Jerusalem is experiencing. So bad was custom that some parts of the Old City resembled a ghost town. Everyone was suffering—Jewish, Muslim and Christian shopkeepers all suffered from a common problem.

On more than one occasion I provisionally booked myself onto one of the officially guided tours of the Old City. Due to lack of numbers they were always cancelled. This, I was told, had now become the norm.

An old Jewish man who was wandering the streets of the Old City one afternoon approached me and offered to be my guide. He said that he was an official guide approved by the Israeli tourist board. It did not take a genius to figure out that this was not true, and that more likely, he had approached me because he was desperate for the money. I agreed to his offer of showing me the sites of the Old City in return for a modest sum.

He had just finished taking me around the Jewish quarter, and was in the process of providing a pleasant and informative commentary, when he remarked that whilst he could tell from my accent that I came from England, he could not tell which part of India I originated from. I told him that I was originally from Pakistan. At this he stopped walking, paused and then uttered, "Oh, you're a Muslim?" Yes, I answered back, knowing immediately that this was going to be a problem. He then told me that the tour was complete and walked away, never again to be seen. In that one small and insignificant moment I realised how wide the gulf between Muslim and Jew had become for some in this city.

I did return to see the Palestinian shopkeeper who had given me directions to the al-Aqsa Mosque when I had gotten lost on my first day in the city. I did not intend on purchasing anything, but was returning simply to fulfill the 'promise of return' that I had made to the shopkeeper. His face lit up when he saw me approaching. His shop was empty. As soon as I entered the premises he again began using all his powers of persuasion to tempt me to buy something. His persistence wore me down and I eventually relented and purchased some gifts for my sisters.

Before I had a chance to leave the old man's shop it started to rain heavily. The shopkeeper kindly offered me coffee and said that I could stay in his shop until the rain died down. Given the awful state of the weather outside I readily accepted his generous offer. Not for the first time on my travels, Arab hospitality had come to my rescue. Far too many in the West are aware of the terrorism of a few Arabs, but unaware of the hospitality of the many.

I stayed in the shop for about half an hour, during which I discussed with him the effects of living under Israeli rule. He spoke incoherently and frequently changed from topic to topic without fully completing the point he was making. I suppose it was, in part, my fault for broaching such a vast topic. One particular theme did come up three or four times and this was his suspicion that the Jews wanted to buy up as much of the Old City as possible. Or to put it another way, I think he was suggesting that Jews were using the levers of capitalism to ethnically cleanse the Old City of Palestinians. It was a serious allegation to make. Whether his belief was founded in paranoia or his fears had some grounding I really had no idea, but on more than one occasion he said that wealthy Jews were offering Palestinian shopkeepers in the Old City ridiculous sums of money for their property. Some had betrayed 'our people' by selling to them he said, but he would never do that. It is difficult to describe in words the way in which he spoke about this issue (and not simply because he was incomprehensible). I got the impression that it were almost as if Jewish attempts to buy out as much of the Old City as possible and Palestinian resistance against this was a form of 'jihad' for him. Again, on more than one occasion he justified his refusal to sell his property to a Jew on the basis that he would have to answer to Allah on the Day of Judgement if he were to commit this unforgivable sin. It was almost as if he felt the Palestinians of the Old City were the guardians of a Muslim soul that resided in it, and that this soul was not to be sold for any amount of money, however tempting. "Allah is watching me", he said wagging his finger at me and further added, "I will never betray my people".

The other major theme we discussed was taxes. It will probably come as no great surprise that he was unhappy about paying taxes. To my surprise, he went to the back of his shop and returned with a small box full of paper slips, which he said were receipts that indicated he had paid his taxes. Taxes I said, cautiously framing my answer knowing that this was a sensitive subject, were a necessary evil in any society. Almost every small business in any country in any part of the world would probably share the same sentiments as his. "Nobody likes paying taxes", I gently told him. He agreed, but went on to say that the Israeli government's spending was not fairly proportioned between Arab Palestinians and Jews. Again I had no idea whether he was telling me the truth. One might even argue that as an Arab he would say that, although on my walkabouts around Jerusalem I had certainly noticed that the public infrastructure of Jewish west Jerusalem was markedly better than Palestinian east Jerusalem. The shopkeeper wasn't simply upset at the broken streets and pavements of the Palestinian neighbourhoods, which he argued the Israeli authorities never seemed to repair. His grievances were wider and extended to areas such as the poor educational facilities that were available to his children. As I sat next him, listening intently to what he had to say, I had to remind myself that he was arguably a lot better off than many of the Palestinians who lived in the West Bank or Gaza or beyond, in the refugee camps of southern Lebanon. He concluded our conversation by holding my hand tightly and saying that all he wished was for his children to have a better future than his. It had taken me nearly half an hour to make any sense of what this man was saying, but I finally understood what he was trying to tell me. As I walked away from his shop I finally realised something that many of the inhabitants of this disputed land might not know, that whatever their differences and whatever their disputes, ultimately, they shared the same goal, the same dream—that their children should live and grow up in a safe environment and have better opportunities in life than they themselves had.

This shopkeeper wasn't the only Palestinian that I spoke to during my stay in Jerusalem. There were others like him, all telling similar stories. Before I came to Jerusalem the image I had of the Palestinian people was of fighters, soldiers and people wanting to reclaim a lost homeland. People who, as the author of the poem had said had, "learnt to dream the dream of murderers". In the few days that I stayed in Jerusalem I seldom, if ever, saw this image. Maybe it was because I spent my whole time in Jerusalem, where the lives of Palestinians are markedly better than those in the occupied territories. If I had travelled to the occupied territories, maybe I would have met up with Palestinians who had indeed, "learnt to dream the dream of murderers". Maybe it was the heavy Israeli military presence on the streets that very effectively repressed open Palestinian dissention. Maybe it was both. What I did see in the Palestinian people (both those who came to Jerusalem to work and those who resided in the city) was despair, apathy and an eternal pessimism. What I saw were not gung-ho fighters, but a broken people, people who no longer had the energy or willpower to fight an enemy that not only had become too strong for them, but one that increasingly sought to control their every movement. The author of the poem was right in one further observation; this is land in which Palestinians were once able to roam free, like the "spirits wild", but no longer. The sight both deeply saddened and angered me. If the PhD student that I met in Beirut could see Orwell's *Animal Farm* in his society, then I could see Orwell's *1984* in this society.

Too often our TV screens haunt us with the evil effects of suicide bombers—the blown-up buildings, the dismembered bodies, the rushing ambulances, the crying relatives, the denouncing politicians. Israelis and much of the Western world cannot comprehend such acts as anything other than evil. This is our picture of the Arab-Israeli conflict. The Arab/Muslim viewer sees another picture. Arab TV shows their viewers the effects of occupation on a people whose land has unjustly been taken from them, and the effects of the Israeli military enforcing this occupation, where dissention is so ruthlessly suppressed that on an almost daily basis the Israeli army creates orphans, widows and mothers with lost children amongst the Palestinian population. What Arab viewers get to see is the soil from which suicide bombers grow. Likewise, Arabs and the wider Muslim world cannot comprehend the Israeli occupation of Palestinian land as anything other than evil. And in the same way that the West sees Middle Eastern countries that fund the groups that support the suicide bombers that kill Jewish civilians as evil, the Arab/Muslim world sees the Western nations (and in particular, the United States) that provide military aid to the Israeli army whose occupation of Palestinian land results in vicious human rights violations against ordinary Palestinians as evil. As with the second Gulf War, one conflict, many versions.

I returned to Jordan before the week was over. My flight to the United Kingdom (via Frankfurt) left from the Amman airport. On my entry into Jordan I was again interviewed, this time by a thoroughly pleasant official who, after establishing that I was no security risk, was more interested in knowing what it was like to live in England than whether or not I was a terrorist.

If you've read the endnote in one of my earlier chapters, you'll be aware that on my return to Jordan I had planned to spend the last few days of my travels in the southern Jordanian seaside resort of Aqaba. Having travelled through five countries, having spoken and met all manner of people and having gathered a wealth of material for this book, I was both physically and mentally tired. Aqaba would have been the perfect tonic for my fatigue. But I never made it to Aqaba. The weather in Amman had worsened on my return. So much so, that the heavy winter snowfall had resulted in the closure of the motorways. Instead, I spent the last few days travelling in and around Amman, visiting its many cultural and tourist sites, everything from the Dead Sea to the place where Prophet Moses possibly, may have been buried.

On the weekend I caught my flight home. As much as I had enjoyed my time in the Middle East, I was glad to be going home. My travels had at times reaffirmed and at times changed my perceptions of the Arab world, of Israel and of the West's influence in the Middle East.

Concluding Remarks

Israel

Ideologically, I have concerns about the modern state of Israel.[2] By this, I mean, that I believe it is wrong for one faith or ethnic community to rise and assert their control of land that has, for several millennia, been multi-faith and multi-ethnic. It is wrong for one faith or ethnic community to define this multi-faith, multi-ethnic land as a separate and distinct homeland solely for their own community. It is wrong because it discriminates against the other long settled faith and ethnic communities of this holy land. Israel/Occupied Palestine is a homeland and a holy land for Christians, Muslims and Jews and has been for many centuries. All of these communities have an equal right to live on that land and all of these communities have the right to be treated equally. Israel (even a secular Israel) cannot adhere to this doctrine of equality if its very purpose, its very existence, is to provide a homeland for Jews. Quite simply, the whole concept of a separate homeland for one ethnic community on land long settled with the communities of several faiths and several ethnicities is wrong.

I have concerns about the modern state of Israel because the circumstances in which it was created caused an enormous injustice to the residing Christian and Muslim Palestinian communities; an injustice that to this day has never been rectified or even acknowledged by Israel. It is the 'original sin' of our modern times. It is the 'original sin' of the modern Arab-Israeli conflict. It is the sin upon which all other sins, Palestinian and Jewish, stem. I absolutely acknowledge that a great injustice was done to the Jews when they were banished from their holy land and forced into a state of Diaspora several thousand years ago. I absolutely acknowledge that in having suffered the most awful persecution in Europe century after century, their wish to create a separate homeland where they would be free from anti-Semitism is a completely natural and understandable desire. But the Israel that was created in the twentieth century could only and was only achieved by causing an enormous injustice to the residing Palestinian community (the 'original sin of ancient times' was absolved, but only by committing the 'original sin of modern times'). To create a separate homeland for Jews on territory that was already a homeland for another community is wrong. Deliberately and inadvertently (or both), the creation of Israel caused the displacement of hundreds of thousands of ordinary Palestinians from their homes. Palestinians that Israel has never allowed to return; Palestinians, the majority of whom had never committed an evil or wrong against Israel. Yet Israel committed and continues to commit an enormous injustice against them in robbing them of their homeland. Of the Palestinians that remained in Israel, quite understandably, many have no desire or wish to see their homeland be designated as a homeland for the Jews of the world,[3] a homeland with a distinctive Jewish identity that can only alienate and marginalise them. Using the 'we won the war, so the land is ours', argument only works if you adhere to the 'might is right' school of thought. Might isn't always right, the victor isn't always on the side of virtuosity. Might wasn't right when the Jews were banished from Jerusalem all those thousands of years ago and might wasn't right when the modern state of Israel was formed in 1947, when so many Palestinians lost their homes and all Palestinians lost their homeland.

Nearly sixty years from the creation of Israel, the real battle in the Arab-Israeli conflict isn't the military battle between the two peoples. It is the battle between ideology and pragmatism that rages on within both communities. I can quite steadfastly hold onto my concerns that I have about the state of Israel for the reasons I have given. It is easy for me. I am not a Palestinian. I do not live in the West Bank or Gaza. I am not a refugee in some foreign Arab country. But for a Palestinian to hold onto this position ... well how far does it lead to actually resolving the real and continued suffering of their people? In the present and foreseeable climate, does holding onto such a position actually do more harm than benefit to the Palestinian people? Well, quite possibly yes! Why? Because firstly, for reasons which ought not to make any sense to Americans, that multi-ethnic, multi-faith state that has become the most powerful nation on earth, has chosen to support the Jews and their aim to maintain a homeland for one ethnic community on land which just like theirs, also happens to be multi-faith, multi-ethnic. In this conflict over land, in this conflict between Palestinian and Jew, the Americans have supplied the Jews with an enormous arsenal of military hardware that has not only allowed Israel to become infinitely stronger than the Palestinians, but arguably stronger than the whole Arab world put together. In short, US military aid has been one of the main oxygen tanks that has allowed and continues to allow Israel to 'live' in the decades after its birth.

Secondly, in becoming the biggest military superpower in the region, Israel has not only been able to hold onto much of the territory it gained in the Arab-Israeli wars, it has built Jewish settlements on them. Not only have they built on land that officially forms the state of Israel, but also on the only remaining pieces of land the Palestinians control—the West Bank and Gaza. What other conclusion can one come to, other than that the building of these illegal Jewish settlements on the Palestinian territories is for the eventual appropriation from the Palestinians of their only remaining territory. Why else build and populate settlements on someone else's land? Over the decades, these Jewish settlements have grown dramatically, both inside Israel and in the Palestinian territories, whilst the Palestinian populations of these areas have shrunk. Land which less than a century ago was populated by Palestinians, has now become populated by Jews. The longer the Arab-Israeli dispute goes on, the more the Jewish population of the disputed territory increases and the more the Palestinian population of the disputed territory decreases. I have heard several Arab commentators refer to the phenomena as constituting the 'Palestinian Holocaust'. The Palestinian born Dr Salman Abu Sitta, for example, argues:

> The Palestinian Holocaust is unsurpassed in history. For a country to be occupied, emptied of its people, its physical and cultural landmarks obliterated, its destruction hailed as a miraculous act of God, all done according to a premeditated plan, meticulously executed, internationally supported, and still maintained today, is no doubt the ugliest crime of modern times.[4]

Provocative language indeed, but if the trend continues, if the dispute rages on and on, there may come a time when there is not a single Palestinian living on this disputed land. These demographic trends bring a whole new question into the debate—a question that is firmly directed at the Palestinians. Which is more important: a) holding onto your belief that Israel should not exist, that the whole of the land appropriated by Israel belongs to you, or b) your very survival, the very existence of a Palestinian community in Palestine? Does pragmatism prevail over ideology? When faced with these two competing principles, surely the survival of your own community is paramount and takes precedence over the ideological principle that Israel's existence is illegal. It is an awfully bitter pill to swallow, but in order to survive, it is a pill many Palestinians are realising they may have to take. A pill that has *the two-state solution* etched on it. This, in short, is the increasing reality, the longer the Arab–Israeli conflict continues, the longer the Palestinian Holocaust continues.

A further reality emerges the longer the dispute rages, one that Israel has been all too well aware of (and the reason why it has sought to colonise as much of the land it has captured as quickly as it is feasibly possible with Jewish civilian communities). This reality is that the more time passes, the more difficult it will be for Palestinians to reclaim lost land that has subsequently become saturated with Jewish settlements. Israel's actions have forced the Palestinians into the same position the Jews were in during the Diaspora, since the Palestinians can only reclaim their land by inflicting an enormous injustice on Jewish civilians who know no other home but Israel. How likely is it that the Western powers are going to either tolerate or be sympathetic to such a course of action given the enormous harm it would do to a civilian population?

How do these changes affect an outsider like myself, one who does not believe that Israel ought to have been created in the circumstances that it was, one who is therefore sympathetic to the Palestinian cause, but one who also believes that any solution must be pursued through an ethical framework. Well, if the Palestinian people consent to the two-state solution then how can outsiders like myself oppose their wishes? After all, they are the victims in this conflict. Their wishes are paramount. Under these circumstances I may have little difficulty in shifting from my original position to one that accepts Israel's existence under a two-state solution.

What might also force me to this 'compromise position' (if it hasn't already) is the point that I have raised above—of the ever-increasing reality that the whole of Palestine cannot be returned to the Palestinians except through measures that will bring about great injustices to civilian populations. Here, I have not moved to the centre position voluntarily. I have been forced into this compromise position. Israel's aggressive settlement policy on land that it has captured and occupied has arguably taken away all ethical ways of returning lost Palestinian lands to the Palestinians since the only remaining ways that the whole of the Palestinian lands appropriated by Israel can be returned to their previous owners and occupiers is through policies that would entail the large-scale displacement of Jewish civilian communities. Such actions would entail committing an enormous injustice to a Jewish civilian population in order to rectify an enormous injustice done to a Palestinian civilian population. Easy solutions to this conflict there are not.

Islam and the Muslim World

In 1993 a seminal text in the field of Cultural Studies was published, Gayatri Spivak's, *Outside in the Teaching Machine*.[5] Spivak is an Indian who teaches at a Western university. She is someone from the third world, an 'outsider', who is on the 'inside' of a first-world institution, its teaching machine. As a Muslim, I am part of the Muslim world but I am not from it, I am from the West. Did I travel to these Muslim lands as an 'insider' or an 'outsider'? Or was I neither? If Spivak is an 'outsider' on the 'inside', am I an 'insider' on the 'outside'? I suppose in many ways that is how I felt, a stranger, an outsider amongst people of my own faith, an insider-outsider. I apologise if all this sounds like mumbo jumbo, but I believe it's important in drawing the conclusions that I do in this section of the chapter, as to whether I am speaking on the topics as an 'insider' or an 'outsider'. I'll leave it to you to decide.

I'll deal with the Palestinian side of the Arab-Israeli conflict first (I am definitely an 'outsider' in relation to this issue). As I have repeated several times within this book, even the victim is constrained by ethical rules, moral boundaries through which he should formulate and execute his responses. Given the reasons that I have laid out as to why I do not believe in the modern state of Israel, it follows that I regard the Palestinians as the primary victims in this conflict. Although they are not the only victims; there have been innocent victims on every side of this conflict, including the Arab countries such as Jordan and Lebanon that have been obliged to take in large numbers of Palestinian refugees, and the wider Arab/Muslim world that feels itself morally obliged to protect one of its family in a Jewish-Palestinian war that it never started.

There are three possible avenues through which Palestinians can address their grievance; (a) through diplomacy, (b) through direct military warfare (a fair fight), or (c) through indirect military warfare (an unfair fight, a.k.a. terrorism/freedom fighting). Looking at these options one can say straight away that option (b) is no longer open to the Palestinians. American commentators and politicians can often be heard castigating the Palestinian paramilitaries for the cowardly way in which they target Jewish civilian populations. I agree. But in making Israel the region's military superpower, they (the United States) have removed from the Palestinians the option of direct military warfare. If Israel was once able to defeat several Arab countries in six days in direct warfare, I doubt that today it would take Israel longer than six hours to defeat any of the Palestinian paramilitary groups in direct warfare; such is her military strength (although Hezbollah might beg to differ given the events of the summer of 2006). By supplying Israel with so much military hardware, the United States has removed from the Palestinians their ability to take on Israel in direct military warfare with even the remotest expectation that they might win. The United States has therefore transformed option (b) from a 'fair-fight' scenario to an 'unfair-fight' scenario. Of the two military options that are available, a 'fair-fight' option now no longer exists. It might be pertinent at this point to ask the following questions: in this conflict between two peoples over land in which both have been long-term residents, why has the United States taken the position that it is better to empower one of the groups with a vast array of arms so that she is easily able to dominate the other, than to respond by attempting to arbitrate between them in a fair and even-handed manner? It is for reasons such as these that Arab nations quite rightly complain that the United States has failed to act as a fair and neutral arbiter in the conflict.

Irrespective of whether or not you think a 'fair fight' is moral (some might say that all war is evil), the removal of option (b) immediately places the whole conflict in a perilous situation, because now you have two options left and one of them really is evil.

I discussed in the last chapter the various ways in which indirect military warfare can be conducted. In recent times the Palestinian paramilitary groups have started to use suicide bombers, whose express and only purpose is usually to kill Jewish civilians. I absolutely recognise that the Israeli military is, on an almost daily basis, committing some of the most awful human rights abuses anywhere in the world. But it is wrong for the Palestinians to respond by specifically targeting and killing Jewish civilians. It is more than that; it is evil. It is also counterproductive because it achieves little except the predictable Israeli response of killing more Palestinians. Suicide bombings have not brought the prospect of a Palestinian state any nearer. They are simply prolonging the Palestinian Holocaust.[6]

Let's go back to our list of options. If option (b) has been taken out of the equation and option (c) is evil, then that just leaves option (a), diplomacy.

Of the two options, (a) diplomacy and (c) indirect warfare, a.k.a. terrorism/ freedom fighting, most readers would persuade the Palestinian people to go for option (a). I would do so as well. The only problem is this, if option (a) doesn't work, or doesn't appear to be working, then that only leaves the Palestinians with one remaining option, option (c). Unfortunately, Israeli-Palestinian diplomacy is a history of one momentous failure after another. The Arab-Israeli conflict is now well into its sixth decade, peace initiatives have come and gone and still the Palestinians have no land that they can properly call a home. It is very difficult to try to convince a people that the best way to resolve their grievances is through diplomacy when they have experienced nearly sixty years of failed diplomacy.

It isn't some religious ideology that drives so many Palestinians towards option (c), it is the conditions in which they live, it is the occupation of their land by Israel, it is the way in which Israel controls their economy, controls their everyday movements, controls every aspect of their lives and above all, it is the failure of option (a) that creates the despair that in turn fuels the support for option (c). I am not trying to condone such conduct. I will repeat again that such behaviour is evil. But is it not also evil for a people who have had a great injustice inflicted upon them to feel that they only have one option, option (c) available to them to rectify a legitimate grievance? Finally, one might add that it is the duty of the West, and Britain and the United States in particular (since they partly created this mess, and enable its continuation) to make sure that option (a) is made available to the Palestinians.

Writing for the *New Statesman* magazine in early 2003 the British Muslim, Ziauddin Sardar, made the following observation about contemporary Islam:

> In truth, while humane representations of Islam ease our conscience, they do little to address the problems within Islam itself. The problem with all varieties of Islam as it is practised today, not as it is envisaged by liberals, is that it has lost its humanity. Our religion has become a monster that devours all that is most humane and open-minded. Instead of retreating to an imagined liberal utopia, we Muslims need to ask some tough questions about our faith. What, for example, makes so many pious Muslims such nasty and intolerant individuals? Why is it that every time a country enforces the shariah—the so-called Islamic law—it retreats into medieval barbarity? Why do Muslims still insist on treating women as though they were an inferior race, sent to earth only to deprave and spread corruption? . . . It is easy

to dismiss the followers of all the non-liberal verities of Islam as fanatics and fundamentalists. It is much harder and much more painful to see them as a natural product of what contemporary Islam has become.[7]

Sardar is not a neo-Orientalist of the Naipaul variety. On the contrary, he is a leading British Muslim academic. He is someone who cares a great deal about his faith, someone who has spent a lifetime attacking misrepresentations of Islam in the West. His comments are a harsh and brutal appraisal of contemporary Islam (or maybe more accurately contemporary Muslims). There is also some truth in them. Religious bigotry is no less prominent in the Muslim community than it is in Christian, Jewish, Hindu or any other faith community. That does not explain why, as Sardar puts it, an increasing number of pious Muslims are turning out to be such nasty and intolerant individuals. What it does mean is that if we are to avoid a 'clash of civilisations' between the West and Islam, there must be a 'clash within civilisations'. For the Muslim world this specifically means a fight to reclaim its humanity from the terrorists and extremists. A fight to reclaim its soul from people who, much to the frustration of the rest of the Muslim *ummah*, have become the voice box of contemporary Islam. It is a fight, ultimately, to ensure that Islam and Muslim nations can be a force for good in the modern world. And that is needed not simply for the prosperity and well being of the 1.5 billion people that make up the Muslim *ummah*, it is needed for the prosperity and well being of the twenty-first century world community.

One of the central problems facing all Middle Eastern countries (those which I visited and those which I did not) can best be summed up in a simple question framed by the philosopher and British parliamentarian John Stuart Mill, "What are the legitimate powers which society has over the individual?" I do not know the exact and precise answer to this question. I know the answer is more likely to be found in a more democratic type of government than an autocratic one. I know that one of the reasons medieval barbarity emerges when the Shariah is implemented, is because the Taliban (and others) did not get this balance right. I know that the reason so many young and highly-educated Iranians and Arabs want to emigrate to the West is because their governments have not gotten this balance right. I know that one of the main underlying reasons for Muslim terrorism is that these governments have not got this balance right. And I know that the answer isn't to be found by simply and solely pointing the finger of blame at the West alone, although as things stand today, a great many Middle Eastern states do need to ask themselves whether it is right that the powerful Western nations have arguably more influence on the affairs of their country than their own people do. During the American War of Independence one of the biggest (maybe the biggest) grievance that the American colonies had with Great Britain was best summed up in another simple maxim, 'no taxation without representation'. It is the ironies of all ironies that the United States today has greater representation and greater influence in the corridors of power of many Middle Eastern states than the citizens of those countries, the taxpayers. I also know that this is not right.

The Prophet Muhammad once said, "The best of your rulers are those whom you love and who love you, who invoke God's blessings upon you and you invoke His blessings upon them. And the worst of your rulers are those whom you hate and who hate you and who you curse and who curse you."[8] If fair and transparent democratic elections were held right across the Middle East today, how many Muslim rulers could be confident that their rule would result in them falling into the first half of the maxim and not the latter half? If I were in their shoes, I wouldn't be overly confident.

The West

> Throughout the last century, the United Kingdom and the United States have stood together when liberty was assaulted and free people were tested. And now in this century our nations see clearly the dangers of our time, and we share a determination to meet them.
>
> President George Bush, April 2004

> I charge the white man with being the greatest murderer on earth . . . There is no place in this world that that man can go and say he created peace and harmony. Everywhere he's gone he's created havoc. Everywhere he's gone he's created destruction . . . I charge him with being the greatest kidnapper on this earth. I charge him with being the greatest murderer on this earth. I charge him with being the greatest robber and enslaver on this earth.
>
> Malcolm X

In order to avoid a potential 'clash of civilisations', the West (and the United States in particular) must with equal vigour assess and appraise its own conduct and its own attitudes towards the Arab and wider Muslim world. It must go through its own 'clash within civilisations'. For what merit is there in the West proclaiming itself to be the defender of the civilised world if Western governments act in an uncivilised manner? Gandhi once said, "The weak can never forgive. Forgiveness is the attribute of the strong". Maybe one of the things he was trying to stress in this statement is the imbalance of power between the strong and the weak. In dealings between strong and weak nations the balance of power inevitably favours the strong. It is the strong, not the poor, who have the greater ability to oppress and exploit. It is therefore the strong that are more often than not the greatest oppressors and mischief-makers. It is the strong who therefore have the most to apologise about and make amends for.

When the sun finally sets on the American empire and it is no longer the world's superpower, and historians and academics the world over debate its legacy and write its obituary, as they have done after the demise of every world power, many things will be written about it and its contribution to mankind. There will be much that it will be commended for. Amongst these things will be its great economic and industrial prowess. America's discoveries and achievements in science, engineering, medicine and technology will be applauded, as will be the many great writers and artists it produced. Its greatest achievement will almost certainly be, that true to its founding convictions, it was indeed a beacon to many of the world's oppressed. Faithful to the inscription on the Statue of Liberty, it will be written that for many of the world's millions, it did indeed lift the lamp beside the golden door and provide refuge to the tired and the poor, the huddled masses yearning to breathe free, as they were tossed up onto her teeming shore.

Yet there will also be many chapters of America's biography in which history will not treat it so kindly. Some of these chapters have already been written, such as the enslavement of black people during the early part American history and its continuing reluctance to effectively deal with the legacy of slavery. These things will come as no surprise to the reader. But it wasn't simply a section of its own people to whom the US government denied the unalienable rights enshrined in the opening to its Declaration of Independence, "We hold these truths to be self-evident: That all men are created equal, that they are endowed by their creator with certain unalienable rights; that amongst these are life, liberty and the pursuit of happiness". It will be written that in the further "pursuit of its own happiness", the United States sometimes flexed imperial muscles, and that sometimes, its increased happiness and prosperity was at the cost of the happiness and prosperity of other citizens of the world, and that sometimes it even muffled out the sound of the liberty bell in these faraway lands, particularly amongst undemocratic regimes where there existed large and valuable reserves of natural resources that the United States wanted. Nowhere will this be truer than of the American presence in the Middle East during the twentieth century. History will not say that its continual presence and interventions in the region throughout the course of that century were designed to spread the gospel of 'democracy and freedom'. History will record that its interventions were designed to secure its strategic interests in the region, even if it had the effect of denying the people of these lands the very same freedoms and rights that the United States considered sacrosanct. History will record, that in the same way the European imperial powers carved up Africa and then masked their economic exploitation of these lands by convincing themselves and the world that their occupation was in order to carry out the noble and honourable mission of teaching the savage natives of these lands the righteous doctrine of Christianity, America likewise persuaded itself and tried to persuade the outside world that its interventions in the region were also for noble and moral purposes, and not at all motivated by strategic geopolitical interests. And unless it changes, history will also record that America's increasing intransigence to either acknowledge, address or rectify the inequities that its foreign policy inflicted on the peoples of this region was a significant factor that led to a catastrophic but avoidable clash between two of the world's great civilisations.

EPILOGUE
IMAGINE: BEYOND GOOD AND EVIL

Part One: The Ghosts of Detroit Red

AS A CHILD, I vaguely remember attending an event held at one of the local halls in my area. There is very little I can now recall about the occasion, but I do remember that it was organised by an Afro-Caribbean group with some sort of political objectives that aimed at a radical solution to the issues concerning black youth in the United Kingdom. Such events were commonplace in the Afro-Caribbean community in those days. Blacks lived in some of the worst ghettoes in the United Kingdom and suffered some of the worst discrimination; this began with their entry into the education system and continued on into their employment. That is, if they were lucky enough to get employment. In the area in which I lived, very few blacks managed to get any sort of job, and although I was not from the Afro-Caribbean community, when I saw a flyer advertising the event in a local shop some weeks earlier, I decided to go along out of interest. As I said, I cannot remember much about the event. I do however, have one abiding memory, the only real memory of the event and the one that has stuck with me throughout my life. One of the speakers was a very elegant, smartly dressed young black woman, who spoke the English language in such an eloquent manner that you could listen to her all day. At one point in her speech she paused, turned to the audience, paused again, and then said that as a child growing up in this country her mother had taught her never to forget two things; "never trust a policeman and never, never allow a policeman into your house." The roof went off, the place erupted as everyone stood up to cheer what the speaker had just uttered. I was stunned, not so much by her comments, but more so by the joyous, almost ecstatic reaction of an audience that was quite clearly in universal agreement with what the charismatic speaker had just said. As I sat there listening to the remainder of her speech, I felt a real sadness come over me as a result of what I had witnessed. I could see where those remarks came from. I could equally see where the audience's response came from. I was under no illusions about the police force in those days; I had witnessed enough to know that the British police force included more than the odd bad apple. But they were still bad apples, and still the exception. To construct a reality, a stereotype, a myth, surrounding a whole group of people based around the actions of a minority, was not only deeply unfair, it was inaccurate and in this instance would simply lead to the further marginalisation of a community that was already one of the most marginalised and alienated in our society. The incident provided me with a powerful reminder of how easily negative stereotypes can arise amongst communities and groups within a society and among differing societies where there is little interaction, little understanding and little knowledge of the other. In this instance, a sizeable minority of police officers had passed off a whole race of people as being criminals. All blacks were now tarred with the same brush. In turn, the inner city black community was slowly beginning to pass off the entire police force as being anti-black, an enemy group who deliberately picked on them simply on the basis of their skin colour and who would be quite capable of planting some illicit substance on anyone foolish enough to allow the police into the house. The human need to pigeonhole 'others' into categories is strong in societies—we all do it—though very rarely is it to our benefit, more often than not it is to our detriment.

Maybe I don't look carefully enough, but I rarely see or hear of such events anymore. Though I have witnessed, over the years, a slow and steady rise in these types of events being organised and held by various Muslim groups. Like those black groups of the seventies and eighties, these radical Muslim groups often present radical solutions to our problems, offering their Muslim audience a utopia that is far removed from the reality of living in an inner city ghetto and even further removed from what they could offer if they ever managed to seize power.

The themes they explore are by and large the same; why has our community become alienated, marginalised, ghettoized? Why is it that we face discrimination from all sectors of society? The answer they say is because we are Muslim and Western society has it in for us because we are Muslim. The problems they speak of are not imaginary. They are real. They exist. I only need to look at the poor educational performances of Muslim children, or of the unemployment rates in my local area amongst young Muslim men. Combined with international developments (such as the War on Terror) these often institutionalised forms of discrimination effect the ideology of radical (for want of a better word) Muslim groups, creating a form of socio-schizophrenia, or cultural-paranoia—a loss of reality, in which the Muslim community appears as a perpetual victim singled out by the West as a threat that needs to be contained, that needs to be eradicated. Yet this socio-schizophrenia, this cultural-paranoia, can be found in the voices and in the fears of so many other communities around the world.

If one listens, it can be heard in the voices of some Chinese, Africans, Afro-Caribbeans, South Americans and even Indians—a belief that the West has singled them out, that it is seeking to eradicate their culture, their history, their identity—and wants them to behave and act more like white Westerners. They fear the effects of globalisation, they fear that the slimy tentacles of Western culture have seeped into their lands and their homes, and these tentacles are wrapped tightly around their community and squirted them with black poisonous ink that erases, eradicates and blanks out their history, their culture, their identity.

There is a great sense of irony; as I finish penning the last lines to this segment of the chapter, Britain has witnessed the London bombings. It has already resulted in an increase in police 'stop and search' of British Muslims and an increase in the search of Muslim-occupied households (which normally tend to be located in Muslim ghettoes) and, most seriously, an increase in the pre-charge detention of many hundreds of Muslims (most of whom are subsequently released without charge). When I started writing this epilogue, when I quoted that young black woman's comments, the London bombings had not occurred. I could never have imagined that as I come to write the final words to this section that so much could have happened, so much could have changed. Her words, when I wrote them, harkened back to another era, to a period of British social history long gone and so such words could not reasonably be expected to be repeated by any ethnic community. And yet I have this strange sense of déjà vu, of history repeating itself: police target Muslims because of racial stereotyping and in turn, Muslims become increasingly angry and resentful towards the police. For if things continue along as they are, with the plethora of anti-terror legislation that targets Muslims, I can see the day, not too far away, when some Muslim speaker will stand up and utter those same words, give the same advice to their community, as that young black woman did all those years ago.

In these uncertain times there is a great deal of pressure upon all of us, Muslim and non-Muslim, to sway towards one of two directions, to see the world in the black and white of one of two opposing camps. If there is one point I want to make in this book, it is to challenge this assertion, to question whether that hypothetical fork in the road, which has been placed before us by our leaders and counter-leaders, does indeed lead to one of two paths. What these people are telling us is that they know the meaning of 'boum' and 'ou-boum'. They do not. Having travelled on my great expedition, I am still no closer to understanding the meaning of 'boum' and 'ou-boum', but I will keep trying, that much I do know.

Part Two: The Fitna (tribulation) of Yusuf K: A Modern-Day Fable

ONCE UPON A time, there lived a young Arab student called Yusuf K.

Yusuf K came from one of these nouveau-riche families that we seem to find in increasing abundance amongst many of the sheikdoms and dictatordoms of the Arab world these days.

Yusuf's father was known to all as 'The Big J'. Nobody quite knew what The Big J's real name was. There was an ugly and slanderous rumour that used to circulate during The Big J's smaller days that he was in fact an illegal Pakistani immigrant who had mischievously entered the country just prior to the petro-dollar revolution. However, to prevent any libel action being taken against us, we must stress that this is simply an unsubstantiated rumour for which there exists no corroborative evidence (with the exception of a Pakistani birth certificate that mysteriously surfaced a few years ago; however, given that it was a Pakistani document, its authenticity must be treated with great caution).

The Big J was a very shrewd businessman who possessed an uncanny ability to spot a good business venture, but an even better ability to ensure that the right official was bribed at the right time.

By the time his only son (The Big J thought it a great personal tragedy that his remaining seven children from his three wives were all daughters) had reached his eighteenth birthday, his father had accumulated enough wealth to be able to comfortably send his son to one of the best universities in the land and thereafter, to the States, so that he could complete his studies by obtaining a post-graduate degree from one of these fashionable Ivy League universities (the current rage amongst the nouveau-riche of the Middle East).

It was The Big J's dream that upon his son's return from the States he would work in the family business for a few years (but not before a big party was held to welcome back the 'golden child', so that he could be thoroughly paraded amongst the important socialites of his home town). After his return, The Big J would also arrange Yusuf's marriage to a beautiful young Arab woman from a noble family (i.e., she had a father who was rich and had the right business and political connections). In addition to being beautiful and from the right family background, his future daughter-in-law also needed to have a strong academic background (he considered himself one of these 'modern types') and to share his belief that after a woman's studies were complete she should devote all her time to being a full-time wife and mother of about six children, preferably all boys (he considered himself one of these 'modern types' with 'old fashioned values'). After a few years working in the family business his son would enter politics to enjoy a successful career helping his country (and his father).

Finally, on his twentieth birthday, Yusuf did indeed manage to enter the best university in the land (after two re-sits and the bribery of a certain senior official at the university).

Yusuf would spend his days as a student missing lectures, listening to the right music and wearing the right clothes (so as to make himself appear very cool), reading the great works of literature, or at least giving the impression to those around him that he was reading such works (so as to make himself appear very learned), chasing girls (where looking 'cool' and 'learned' came in handy), smoking hookahs with his buddies whilst discussing Arab politics, taking the occasional recreational drug and dreaming about how to make the world a better place (he was a student after all).

One day, young Yusuf returned from his local music store having purchased a much sought after 'greatest hits' album by the Doors. He placed the CD next to his Monty Python DVD collection and settled down to finish reading a novel by Kafka when he suddenly decided the time had come for him to try a hallucinogenic drug so that the windows and doors of his perception could be flung wide open and he could see once and for all who was behind the faceless bureaucracy that was oppressing his people and his dreams of a Marxist-Thatcherite Islamic state—a high public expenditure, low-tax society with a strong Islamic ethos (but not so Islamic that it might curtail his un-Islamic recreational habits). You see, whilst Yusuf also wanted to enter politics, he did so for the far more noble purpose of creating a greater and better Arab society and not to ensure greater and better government contracts for his father's businesses.

So off Yusuf went to see his local dealer, a dodgy man with a crooked nose, handlebar moustache and funny accent, who always wore a distinctive purple overcoat and went by the name of Akaky Neva Samosa, or Mr Samosa to all his regular customers. His father, the very proud Logog Neva Samosa, was a well-respected inspector general who had disowned his son when he caught him smoking pot in his bedroom on his fifteenth birthday. Lost, abandoned, and without a home or a hope, Akaky soon came to the attention of his district's biggest and baddest hoodlum, the notorious and legendary 'Turkish Tee-Que' (whose own origins were baffling since he was not a Turk and hated all things Turkish). After their first uneasy meeting, rumour had it that Turkish Tee-Que was heard murmuring to himself, "he's an arrogant, egotistical, narcissistic . . . but hey! he can't be all good, I'm sure he's got his bad points as well". Mama didn't raise no fool, for Turkish Tee-Que saw within the boy Akaky, the enormous potential that his over-proud, overbearing and uncompromising father had so mercilessly overlooked, he saw the man that that boy could be. So he took the fifteen-year-old under his wing and spent several years teaching the parentless prodigy the ways of the 'dark side'. By his twenty-fifth birthday, Akaky or Mr Samosa as he had become both professionally and personally known, had risen to become the leading supplier of illegal narcotics to the rich and wealthy of his hometown, a feat achieved through a combination of the meticulous and steadfast learning of all that his master had taught him, developing a distinct dress sense and persona and cunningly targeting various high society functions—to which he had easy access by virtue of the high social class that he had originally belonged to. As a footnote, his teacher, Turkish Tee-Que, was viciously murdered just before Mr Samosa turned twenty-three—shot three times in the head whilst being a very naughty boy one afternoon in attending a sauna-come-brothel called Madame Hot 'n' Spicy (established in Damascus but with franchises throughout the Middle East, Europe and North America). His assassin? None other than Akaky Neva Samosa himself. Hey! He who lives by the sword dies by the sword, or alternatively, as Mr Samosa calmly uttered as the last bullet embedded itself into his former master, "mama didn't raise no fool".

Mr Samosa, always eager to assist a valued customer increase his portfolio in recreational drugs, offered Yusuf, at a reduced introductory rate, a new drug called, 'Lucy in the Sky with Diamonds'. Mr Samosa assured Yusuf that if he took the drug whilst rehearsing the line of a famous Arab poem backwards, it would result in the user experiencing an illusion in which he was being whisked away on a cornflake to a boat in a river surrounded by tangerine trees and marmalade skies and inhabited with people who walked around with kaleidoscope eyes.

Yusuf, eager to experiment now, whilst still in his youth, and certainly before he entered politics so that he could, with some level of sincerity and truthfulness, give vague answers to any probing questions a journalist might ask about drug use during his student years (drugs do after all effect the memory), paid Mr Samosa the discounted price and returned to his student digs.

Upon returning to his room, Yusuf locked the door, switched off the light and with the help of a glass of cold water he swallowed the single large tablet inscribed with the letters LSD.

Ten minutes later, he imagined he had turned into the worst thing imaginable for an over-proud Arab. Yes! He imagined he had turned into a Pakistani.

Yusuf then had the following hallucination:

'Hey Mr Balfour, hey Mr Britain, what you doing telling the whole world that you're gonna build a homeland for the Jews in Palestine? Yes, people do live here. Urr hello! The Palestinians live here. You know those funny-looking Arab type people with their chequered scarves. Yeh, I know the Jews used to live here as well, I know they want to come back, but you can't go about it this way, you can't just barge them to one side and say, 'we're in charge and we say the Jews live here as well'. Yeh I know they've been discriminated against, I know they've been persecuted for god knows how many centuries . . . No! No! No! I'm not being anti-Semitic, hey just hold on a second, don't go accusing 'me' of being prejudiced, look it wasn't me or the Palestinians that were ill-treating them, it was you Europeans. I'm not losing my temper, all I'm saying is that you just can't go about it this way. I know that you're this big colonial power and all that, but just think this thing through, if you go ahead with this, it's gonna cause some serious unrest in the region, it's not gonna solve your problems, you're gonna be opening up a Pandora's box. No I'm not being narrow-minded; don't talk to me like that. Oh you're gonna go ahead with it anyway. Oh I see, you're 'right', more like 'might is right'. Well, if you don't listen I'm gonna speak to your younger brother America, he's gonna grow up to be stronger than you. You'll see, he'll sort you out. Wait there I'll be back.

Hey America, hey America, can you help us out here, your big snooty brother's been at it again, you're not going to believe this, he's only gone and . . . hold on . . . hold on . . . what's happening here, why you talking to the Sauds of Arabia? Something fishy going on here. Agreement? What agreement? Black gold underneath the golden sands? Yeh I can keep a secret. What do you mean they're an uncivilised, backward race stuck in the seventh century, who can't even dig a hole in the ground without your help! You can't talk like that, that's my Muslim brothers you're talking about. Well, maybe they can't dig a hole in the ground without your help, but they're big holes, I mean . . . really big holes, and most of us are gonna need help with stuff like that. Anyway, it's not as if you're not getting paid or anything, I'm sure you'll get a fair price and all that, you know, 'free market economics', the *laissez faire* society. Is that a copy of the agreement you have there, lying there on that table next to the tissue box? I feel a sneeze coming on. Oops, sorry, did I accidentally pick up the wrong thing? Oh I see, I see . . . you're being compensated extremely well for your hole-digging services aren't you? So much for the free market, so much for open competition, so much for *laissez faire* economics. I don't see any other . . . hey no need to snatch, if you wanted it back you only needed to ask. Can I just say something? Well I'm gonna say it anyway. I know you're gonna build all these big fantastic oil wells for my brothers, I know they kind of need your 'expertise' to do complicated stuff like this, what with technology advancing since the seventh century and all that, but don't you kind of think this deal is a tad bit unfair to the ordinary Arab, sorry ordinary Saudi? I mean, I can see the House of Saud doing very well out of it and I can see you doing very well out of it . . . 'Commie', 'Commie', now don't go accusing me of being a 'communist'. I was only trying to point out the unfairness, the . . . well okay if you're gonna be like that I'll go 'n talk to someone else. You know what, I'll go and speak to my Saudi brothers and try and talk some sense into them.

Assalaamu alaikum brothers, how are you? Thank you for inviting me in. *Mashallah*, you know brothers, Arab hospitality, still the best in the world. Look, I hope you don't think I'm talking out of place or anything, but that oil agreement you made with the Americans. You know Americans, 'Mickey Mouse', 'CHIPS', 'The A Team' and all that. Well Americans . . . lovely people and all, always courteous whenever I go there, polite to a fault, but brothers . . . sometimes their government and some of their big companies are well . . . well . . . you know . . . you gotta be a bit careful with them, you know, that whole crazy capitalism breeds greed theory that's doing the rounds at the moment. Yes, yes brothers I hear you. I appreciate that they're your friends, that they've helped you in your aim to maintain stability in Arabia and that the warring tribes of Arabia have not seen stability for God knows how many years. Yes, as I was saying, I appreciate that these leaders in US industry and in US politics are your friends, as I said, don't think I'm being rude or speaking out of place here or anything, but you know what brothers, they're not really your friends. I mean, they're not really, are they? I mean . . . what I mean . . . is . . . that they're your business partners really, that's a more accurate term to describe them. Yes, yes, I hear you brothers, you consider them friends as well. Do you remember that really famous saying, the one that goes something like, "friends and money, oil and water"? Urr no, Shakespeare might have said something like that, but I was thinking more like Michael Corleone from *The Godfather*. Brothers listen, let me put this another way—I think they will be your friends, even your best friends as long as those oil wells keep pumping out that black gold and you keep selling it to them cheaply, but brothers you're gonna find that as soon as those oil wells dry up, so will your friendship and they will start saying that they don't wanna deal with you anymore because you suppress your women and you don't have democracy and you chop off people's hands and all kinds of other serious stuff. You get what I'm saying brothers? Brothers, I hope it never happens, but if by some remote chance you Arabs start bickering and fighting over the oil in the coming decades and say someone, hypothetically speaking of course brothers, but say some future Arab leader wearing a military uniform and a dodgy moustache decides he wants a lion's share of the oil for himself, then your business partners, sorry your friends, will certainly come to your aid. I accept that. I will even say that they will be prepared to pay the 'blood price' to defend 'their oil', sorry 'your oil'. But once it has vanished, once the oil has been sucked dry from the desert land and you start bickering amongst yourselves, for whatever reason, do you think they will come to your aid then brothers? Do you think the American government will be able to persuade their people that they should pay the 'blood price' so that you can continue to oppress your women and chop off people's hands? Quite frankly my dear, they won't give a damn. They'll be 'gone with the wind'. As I was saying brothers, they're not your friends, not really—they're just your business partners. No . . . no . . . no . . . I'm not insulting your intelligence . . . No . . . no . . . no . . . I'm not saying you oppress your women either, perish the thought brothers. Sorry . . . I didn't quite catch that . . . What? I'm a saint-worshipping deviant, like most Pakistanis, and should spend more time reading the Quran and improving my understanding of *tawhid* than idly wasting what precious time I have remaining on this earth buying Monty Python DVDs, analysing the lyrics of that puffta Morrissey, reading E. M. bloody Forster or that complete loony Kafka. Urr . . . Well . . . brothers . . . I suppose you're right . . . I mean, I should read the Quran more often and I should make more of an effort, you know, to improve my *iman* (faith) and my understanding of *tawhid* (the oneness of God) and all. I'm not disagreeing with you, although that Pakistani saint-worshipping jibe was a bit out of order. Yeh, I know you're kind of right in the substance of what you're saying. One can spend unnecessary time on things that aren't important, such as trying to understand the philosophy of Monty Python or over-analysing the lyrics of Morrissey, who by the way isn't a puffta, he's . . . he's . . . just . . . different. After all brothers, as you are helpfully trying to tell me, the pleasures of this world aren't going to save me from eternal damnation, are they? Oh I see from all those bags in the corner that you've been shopping in London again. No, no, I wasn't inferring anything brothers, perish that materialistic thought. Anyway, back to my point. I see what you're saying brothers. I mean, even that Oscar Wilde, now he was a bona fide puffta, famously said, "All art is quite useless". Now I'm losing track of my train of thought—Yeh brothers, I know I gotta do all these things, I know they are really important, but that doesn't mean I'm incapable of making . . . of making . . . you know, of making a valid point. No, no I didn't mean to offend. I know you've shown me that famous Arab hospitality. I do appreciate it. As I said brothers, I didn't mean to offend. I apologise. I was only trying to help. Okay, okay, I'm leaving, I was on my way to meeting your brethren in Palestine—(looking through the window) I can see Mr Britain is already there. I must be on my way. *Assalaamu alaikum.*

Hey Mr Britain wait up, wait up. Hey Mr Britain, O my God! O my God! Look at the mess you've created. See . . . see . . . look at the unrest you've caused, didn't I tell you? Didn't I tell you? Well . . . what you gonna do about it? You can't just let them kill and slaughter each other. This is awful, look at what they're doing to each other. What you gonna do about it? Yeah I know you got this big worldwide war going on at the moment, that your hands are kind of tied. But it seems like the Second Great War is nearly over and you gotta promise to sort out the mess when it's over. You promise? Hey, wait a minute; I think there is a message coming in through the wire . . . I think I can make it out . . . yes, yes, it's confirmed, the Germans have surrendered. Hooray, the war is over. Congratulations, you won. So what you now gonna do about Palestine? What you gonna do about the Holy Land? Holy Maloney, you're gonna walk away? What! What! You can't just create this mess and then walk off. Oh, the UN will sort it out will it? I see, that new body formed out of that dead toothless tiger the League of Nations will sort it out. It can't even sort itself out but it will sort out the problem of two significant populations claiming a single land to be theirs. Did you hear that Mr Britain, Mr Balfour, we now have a scenario where two populations are claiming a single land to be theirs? You helped create this scenario. Don't take this the wrong way Mr Britain, but you really balls-ed this one up didn't you? I mean what an enormous cock-up. Added to your colonial legacies in Northern Ireland, South Africa and Kashmir, your contribution to creating the twentieth-century's 'most impossible conflicts to resolve' is pretty impressive. And now that news of the horrors of the Holocaust is seeping out, the Jews are gonna be clamouring to get away from the West and back into Palestine in even greater numbers. It's gonna get a lot worse. Well done, Mr Britain. Anyway, I better be off. I can see my Arab brethren approaching; actually they seem to be approaching in quite large numbers. They seem serious . . . This seems serious.

Brothers, brothers, what seems to be the problem here, why you all approaching the land of Palestine in such a menacing manner? You want to reclaim the land back for your Palestinian brethren, back to what it was like before the Balfour Declaration and Aliyahs. Well hold on a second, you sure this is the right thing to do? After all, the United Nations have got involved. They're independent you know, they'll sort everything out. Yes . . . yes . . . you can stop laughing now. I said you can stop laughing. Listen, just listen for a moment. The UN will make sure there is an equitable division of the land. They will make sure that everyone's voice is heard. Oh I see . . . I see . . . how can you equitably divide land that belongs to the Palestinians? Why should the Palestinians, who have lived on this land continuously for thousands of years, divide the land with the Jews who, until a few decades ago, lived in Europe; the majority of whom were allowed to enter and settle on this land, not at the permission of the residents of the land, the Palestinians, but at the behest of their colonial ruler. Hmm . . . I see what you are saying brothers, I agree with a lot of what you are saying, but the Jews are here, they have the backing of the great powers of the West, they have the sympathy of the great powers of the West. Brothers, we know that they feel guilty about what they have done to the Jews, that this guilt thing is playing heavily on their consciences and this guilt thing will prevent them from looking at this escalating conflict in neutral terms, but you have to be careful here, because if you take matters into your own hands and try to take on the Jews in open warfare, I don't think the great powers of the West will stand by and allow it to happen, and you'll then have to deal with them as well and how you gonna deal with them? I mean . . . they're super-powers. I hear what you saying brothers, what they've done to our Palestinian brethren is well out of order and we can't just sit back and let this injustice continue . . . But . . . but . . . urr . . . urr . . . I don't know the answer ok? That Mr Balfour . . . he's really placed us in a pickle . . . Look we're not thinking about it objectively, no . . . no . . . no . . . I mean . . . I think we are thinking about it emotionally . . . well basically, what I'm trying to say is that we also have to look at it . . . practically, don't we? Yes, practically! I mean you can't just take things into your own hands in this way without thinking the whole thing through, we have to think about the possible con-sequences that could follow from such action, what you're suggesting . . . well . . . it doesn't seem right . . . it feels wrong. I have a bad feeling about this. Oh you know what you are doing, do you? You think you can sort them out, do you? Woosies to the side, leave it to the big boys hey! Bish, bash, bosh, problem solved, Palestine saved, all in the blink of an eye.

Blink. Blink.

Open eyes: O my God, what on earth happened here? Where has Palestine gone? It's almost disappeared . . . it's fallen off the map, been munched up by the new state of Israel. Look at what's left of it? Well done boys. You got battered. What a . . . what a . . . what a complete catastrophe. Didn't I say it was only a matter of time before America joined in and helped the Jews? You had no chance once they entered the fray and started supplying them with all that top-notch ammo. All those Jews who emigrated to America, that infamous Jewish lobby, putting their case to the power-makers of the world's new superpower, pleading their case to the movers and shakers, "please sir, can't you see a few thousand innocent Jews in Palestine are being attacked by all those big bad Arab nations, please sir, please help us, please help, at least give us some arms so that we can fight back and defend ourselves". Nobody was there to put the Palestinian case forward. Even if one of your reps had been there, in those corridors of power, what sympathy would you guys have got? I can just hear those Yanks in DC looking down at you, wagging their finger at you and saying to you, "You wanted a fight with the Jews over the disputed territory, we didn't want you to fight, we pushed for a diplomatic resolution, but NO! You wanted to fight for the land, you started that fight when we were pushing for a diplomatic solution and you lost that fight, so tough! Finders keepers, losers weepers". Brothers, pardon my language, but you've really screwed up big time. With 'Am-ri-ka' behind them, that new Jewish state has one hell of an ally. Let me just go and talk to that ally.

Am-ri-ka, Am-ri-ka, hey Mr US of A. 'Houston, we have a problem'. Wow! That is a serious amount of military hardware you guys are selling to the Jews of Israel. Wow! Man you guys are selling them some top-notch gear. Look at what they're doing with it, they're using it to oppress Palestinian resistance and with it Palestinian life. Well of course they're gonna fight back. Duh! What do you expect, they've lost their homeland. Did you seriously expect them to get off the floor, wipe the dust off their hands and say, 'Oh well, we just lost our home, our heritage, our identity, never mind, let's just perish here in the desert heat?' Urr hello ... they've had their land taken away from them. Why should some Palestinian child, born in Palestine, with his destiny now rotting away in some dump of a refugee camp in some far-fetched corner of a no-man's land in some distant Arab country, sit back and accept the fact that some big belly middle-class American, wearing a diamond crusted Star of David around his neck and with a Big Mac in one hand and a Coca-Cola in the other, who was not born in Israel, can't even trace his heritage back here apart from citing some story thousands of years old, has a greater right to live on that land than him, the land where he, his parents, his grandparents, his great grandparents, his great great grandparents (and so on) were born? Does the inequity in this need to be spelt out? There is something really, really morally repugnant about the way in which Zionist ideology has led to immigrant Jews migrating to the Holy Land and their wanting to create a Jewish homeland on a land already occupied by Muslims and Christians. Can't you see that

America? Can't you see the injustice? You don't see it, do you? You don't see the inequity in the Zionist vision? You don't see what most of the rest of the world sees? You've grown up to have the same bad traits as your elder brother, 'might is right, might is always right'. You don't see Palestinian lives rotting away in Gaza, the West Bank or the refugee camps of Arab nations. You're not listening, are you? You just keep on selling them those arms. You don't see that inequity either, do you? Your military hardware being used so aggressively against the Palestinian people, suffocating them, suppressing them, killing them—not just combatants, but civilians, women and children, killed by Israeli forces using heavy-handed tactics and 'made in the US of A' military hardware. Yes they fight back. No, it's not just suicide bombers. It's also top notch US military hardware verses sticks and stones. F-16s versus a two-inch piece of broken brick found next to that donkey grazing by the well. Yes I've had my say. Urr . . . I see . . . you want to have your say as well. Well, yes I will listen. No, no, I'm calm; I don't need to take a seat or anything. I'm all ears. Urr . . . aha . . . yes . . . yes . . . umm . . . mmm . . . oh . . . urr . . . I see . . . I see what you're saying. Yes I know, by 1948 there were many hundreds of thousands of Jews present in Palestine, by that stage there was a significant Jewish civilian population present and living on the land, and yes, whatever the rights and wrongs of them being there, when you have a large number of Arab armies descend on Palestine to drive out the Jews, when you have the Mufti of Jerusalem uttering statements such as, "I declare a holy war my Muslim brothers! Murder the Jews! Murder them all!" you can't seriously expect the United States to sit back and allow the Arab armies to walk into Palestine and put at risk the lives of hundreds of thousands of Jews. Well yeah, I suppose it was unrealistic to expect the United States to idly sit by whilst the lives of hundreds of thousands of Jewish civilians are put in danger by Arab states who feel the best way to handle the complex situation in Palestine in 1948 was to drive the Jews into the sea. No, I guess you're right, that is not the best way to deal with the situation. Yes, I suppose you also have a point that if you didn't supply Israel with so much arms and military hardware, then before you can say, *Fiddler on the Roof*, you'd have a number of Arab nations descending on Israel, with aggressive intent, again placing at risk the lives of hundreds of thousands of Jewish civilians. Yes, I acknowledge all that, but don't you see that this almost intractable situation has largely been created by your histories. No, not yours personally, but by the history of Mr Balfour, of Mr Hitler and Nazi Germany, of the Catholic Church, of fascism, of anti-Semitic Europe, of a less tolerant Christianity of a by-gone age and of so many other histories that have blended together and have resulted in the creation of a Zionist ideology that urges Jews to return to Jerusalem to create a Jewish homeland. You guys simply don't seem to care, or don't care enough that so many innocent Palestinians have suffered enormously, having lost their homeland, their heritage, their future, so that millions of Jews can live their lives free from Western persecution and Western anti-Semitism. You don't care because you choose to look at the conflict through another set of spectacles: 'We must protect the Jews, we must protect Israel, we must ensure its security'. You forget the fact that Israel was created on an injustice, and in protecting Israel's security, for all the valid reasons that you have cited, you also protect that injustice, and that, my friends, is the problem; that, my friends, is the real injustice.

Wow! Wow! Am-ri-ka, what on earth you doing now? Houston, we have a problem, Houston we have one mother of a problem. What on earth are you and the Soviet Union doing? What ideological race? What Cold War? You're not just making deals with the Sauds of Arabia, you're making deals with as many oil-rich Arab sheikhdoms as possible. You're making deals with the whole post-colonial world. Oh I see, communism is bad, communism is a threat to the world, communism must be defeated. Right, ok, ok, just say for the moment that I'm with you on that one—how exactly does propping up dictators and monarchs spread the gospel of Western liberal democracy in the region? How does that exactly defeat the communist threat? How does it show that parliamentary democracy is the best form of government? Oh I see—it prevents such nations from falling to the communist threat. What, even if such regimes oppress their people? What do you mean 'yes'? What do you mean that is a price well worth paying? Right ok, let me get this one straight, you and the Soviets are quite happy to prop-up corrupt third world dictators, ply them with aid, let them oppress their people, turn a blind-eye to such things, so long as they don't go to the 'other side', the 'dark side'? That is a price worth paying? It is better that a third world people be ruled by a corrupt dictator supported by the West, than a corrupt dictator supported by the Soviets. What . . . do you do quality checks on the torture cells of Western-backed third world dictators to ensure that they don't inflict quite as much pain on their political dissidents as their Soviet counterparts? Is that what's in it for them? "Ooo! How much better it is to be oppressed by a dictator that supports Am-ri-ka than one supported by those infidel commies. Oh please sir, please, we would rather be tortured by an American-backed dictator than one who is a commie lover." It surprises me that the Cold War wasn't called the Hot War, because you guys seem to be blowing a lot of hot air about the moral virtuousness of your cause. I'm gonna talk to my Muslim brothers to see if I can get more sense from them.

Brothers, brothers, I know what you're gonna say, but just hear me out on this one. Right, I know you gotta make sure that your kingdoms and sheikhdoms and dictatordoms need to have stability, need to have security, both from external and internal threats. You guys are no different from the rest of the world in that respect. Brothers, you really gotta listen to your people more, listen to their hopes and dreams and aspirations, you gotta give them a greater voice in how their country is run. I mean, all that aid you getting from the West, it's got more strings attached to it than a giant harp. You guys might be giving the impression to some of your people that countries like Am-ri-ka have more of a say in how the internal affairs of your country are run than their own citizens; that the wishes of Am-ri-ka are more important than their wishes. That's why some of them might be seriously grieved, that's why they might start seriously criticising you and wanting regime change. That is all I am trying say. What, I see . . . I see . . . who am I to comment on how your country is run? Well that is true. What? Oh . . . I see . . . I'm a nobody annexed from his motherland, dumped in a foreign land and left to breed in some no-hope Western ghetto, the product of a mongrel culture, mongrel history, someone with no identity or noble lineage. Urr . . . right . . . You are right in one sense, that I don't have any right to dictate to you how you should run the affairs of your country, after all, I'm only a mongrel from the ghetto, as you say, but then who is the United States to tell you how you should run your country? Anyway, using your analogy, aren't they mongrels as well, aren't they a mongrel nation who have done very well for themselves? But I get the message, what is a nobody like me doing, telling you great monarchs and dictators how you should run the affairs of your state. I leave you, but be warned, your people are not stupid, they know when their rulers are trying to pull the wool over their eyes.

What! What! Oh my God, you're fighting amongst yourselves. Iran, Iraq, stop it . . . stop it. I don't care who started it, stop it. Look how many of your people are dying. Why are you killing each other? America, America, I know I've not been too kind in some of the things I've said about you, but can you please, please help us. Iran and Iraq are fighting each other, killing each other. Can't you at least use your diplomatic powers to ensure a peaceful resolution to the conflict? Oh my God, what are you doing, why are you arming Iraq? Are you aware that their leader is crazy? I don't believe it, we come to you to ask for help, hoping you can channel all your energies into finding a peaceful resolution and you do the opposite, you make sure that the killing goes on. Look at what that stupid son of a super-gun Saddam is doing, he's using chemical weapons, you're still gonna arm him? This is crazy. The whole world has gone crazy. You're all at it. Muslim and non-Muslim. Why are you helping them kill each other? This is sick, you're all making money off two nations hell-bent on killing each other. Look America, you're the all-powerful all-wise one, I don't expect you to side with Khomeini's Iran, I know you don't see eye-to-eye with him, but Holy Maloney, why side with Saddam, he's an evil murderous dictator, you know this, you know this. But you don't care, is this what freedom was about? The freedom to support whatever despotic ruler one thinks will best serve one's interests? Oh thank God it's over. Thank God it's finally finished.

What! Stupid Saddam, he's done it again, he's invaded Kuwait. What the!!! America ... America ... urr ... what? Heh! 'Saddam's an evil man who uses chemical weapons and invades other nations ... he must be defeated ...' Oh don't give me that bull★★★★ Mr America, you don't care about the Kuwaitis, you only care about your oil, you don't seriously expect the world to buy that garbage? Oh you do, do you? Oh deary me, you're right, the whole world has bought it. This is not some sort of moral crusade you're on Mr America, why can't you be honest with yourself? You're doing this to protect the oil fields, period. Period. Yesterday Saddam was one of your bestest buddies, today he's one of your worstest baddies. Oh at least it will free the people of Kuwait from his murderous grip. At least one good thing will come out of it.

Now that you've freed Kuwait, at least leave Saudi. I mean there is no point in you being there, is there? Why are you still there? Oh I get it, you need to be there, you need to have US forces based in the Holy Land in order to deter Saddam from attacking. Oh this is really gonna cheese people off. Don't you realise Mr America that this further US presence in the region might be viewed by 'you' as maintaining stability and security in the region, but it will be seen by Middle Easterners as yet another encroachment onto their lands in order to protect your interests. Which, technically speaking, is true. That is why you're here, because it is in your strategic interests to ensure that the prevailing undemocratic status quo in the region is not disrupted, that the prevailing undemocratic status quo remains stable and secure, irrespective of what the leaders of the prevailing undemocratic status quo might be doing to their people. What about Iraq, all those sanctions you've imposed, I see the ordinary Iraqis suffering, I see children, young children, dying because of your sanctions, but I don't see Saddam being affected that much, he still seems that normal jubilant, unapologetic murderous dictator suffering from illusions of grandeur, the same as he always was.

I'm going mad here, why is nobody listening? Mr Am-ri-ka, can you not see the bigger picture here? You're seriously cheesing off Muslims because of your support for Israel, you're seriously cheesing off Muslims because their leaders seem to listen to you more than they listen to their own people, you're seriously cheesing off Muslims because you've got your finger in every Arab pie, you're seriously cheesing off Muslims because your ineffective sanctions are killing tens of thousands of Muslims whilst Saddam and his playboy sons are free to roam about in their playboy mansions. Why is it so difficult for you to see that you are seriously cheesing us off? And you Muslim leaders, can you not see that you have arguably the greatest source of human and material labour in the world and yet almost none of you are able to utilise it properly, man you're cheesing us all off. Will you stop forever licking America's arse? Listen to your people, listen to their grievances, otherwise one day some of them may do something we all regret.

Boom!!! Boom!!! Boom!!! What was that? What on earth was that? Three explosions, no . . . no . . . three planes flying into two towers and one Pentagon. Thousands dead. Awful indiscriminate loss of human life. Who's responsible? Muslims. Can't be. Islam doesn't condone such things; even a Muslim with the intelligence level of a mentally challenged amoeba would know that. Gosh! I don't believe it, it is Muslims. Did you say something Mr America? Yes I'm still here. No, No, of course I wouldn't condone such acts. Yes, absolutely, you have the right to seek redress against the perpetrators of such acts, you have the support and goodwill of the whole global community. Maybe something good can come out of this, maybe it needed something like this for us to come to our senses. Oh you agree. Well it's good we agree on something. Finally.

No . . . No . . . No . . . please let this not be true. What are you saying Mr Bush? Oh no, you've got it all wrong . . . no . . . no . . . no . . . you were not attacked because these people wanted to change your values. No . . . no . . . no . . . Mr Bin Laden, Mr Mullah Omar and the nineteen hijackers did not all sit in a cave together and hold a conversation going something like; "Hey Bin Laden, hear this one, those Americans have freedom in their country, it's disgusting isn't it? Yeah it is, I mean it is so repulsive it makes me want to puke. Hey wait, I even hear they believe in the 'rule of law', No! Oh how repugnant is that . . . how sick can a people be? Hey, get this one . . . wait for it . . . they even believe in . . . 'democracy'. Never! Oh such depravity amongst a people, how evil is that? I mean it is so sick and so evil that they should hold these values and they offend us so much that I think we should bomb them! Yeah (the rest of the room applauds), let's kill them for holding these values, because if we kill them for holding these values, then they might start thinking, 'they are killing us because we hold evil values, we must therefore change our values, we must end democracy and freedom and live like the Taliban'". This is crazy. What are you doing Mr Bush? Oh you're going to war against Afghanistan and Iraq in order to introduce 'regime change'. Innocent people will die you know, it will upset a lot of people. Oh God, can't you control your military, you're torturing suspects in Guantanamo Bay, you're humiliating suspects in Iraq, the whole world is looking at you. Is this what freedom is about? Is this the so-called *War against Terror*? Who's terrorising whom? For God's sake get a grip on Iraq, the insurrections, the instability, get a grip. And you want me to pick which side I'm on? Hold on, you want to spread the gospel of democracy throughout the whole of the Middle East. Urr . . . correct me if I'm wrong but aren't you telling us that it is the 'Muslim extremists' that are trying to change your values. Urr . . . correct me if I'm wrong, but in spreading the gospel of democracy aren't you trying to change these people's lives, aren't you trying to change their values? This doesn't make sense. I give up. I give up. Who do I believe? What should I believe? BOOM! Bombs in Madrid. BOOM! Bombs in London. The whole world is gone mad. Boom boom, boom boom, bo-oum ou-boum, bo-oum ou-boum, what does all this mean anymore?

Yusuf awoke from his hallucination terrified and in a cold sweat. He had been horrified by what he'd seen and immediately promised himself never to take drugs again. The idea of him being a Pakistani was simply too much for him to take.

But Yusuf didn't know that he had not in fact experienced a hallucination at all, for that dodgy Mr Samosa had inadvertently sold him one of his 'duff' tablets (called *Biggus Trickus* and sold only to unsuspecting tourists). Young Yusuf K had simply fallen into a deep sleep, the after-effects of a dodgy kebab he'd had a few hours earlier. Yusuf had also forgotten to switch off the TV before taking the tablet and whilst his nightmare vision of being a Pakistani was being played out for him by his mind, a documentary on twentieth-century Middle East history by an award-winning British Pakistani journalist was quietly showing on the TV in the far corner of his room and had somehow managed to seep into his dream.

So the moral of our story is, never buy drugs from a man who calls himself Mr Samosa and before you listen to the Doors you should listen to the Beatles, because *Lucy in the Sky with Diamonds* was never about drugs. No seriously, there is a moral to our modern day fable. It is simple and is simply this, 'you reap what you sow'. As to whether the moral applies to Yusuf K, The Big J, Logog Neva Samosa, Turkish Tee-Que or the events contained in Yusuf's hallucination/dream, I'll leave that for you to decide.

THE END

Post script: Yusuf K went on to become a successful politician, but he lacked backbone and courage and ended up being the bent and corrupt politician that his father had always wished for. Yusuf's blueprint for that utopian Marxist-Thatcherite Islamic state lies lost somewhere in some student dormitory, waiting to be picked up by some young bright Arab with courage and integrity, who can take that blueprint, substantially revise it and then present it to his people as a dream that they can genuinely believe in. Maybe it is not quite 'the end!'

ENDNOTES

Prologue: From the Marabar to the Tora Bora Caves

1. Nigel Messenger, *York Advanced Notes; A Passage to India* (London: York Press, 1991).
2. For diehard Smiths fans I'm aware that the much analysed line, "burn down the disco, hang the blessed DJ, because the music that they play, it says nothing to me about my life", is most commonly thought to refer to the state of eighties British pop music and not Margaret Thatcher.
3. Monica Ali, *Brick Lane* (London: Doubleday, 2002), pages 92–93.
4. Meaning 'the enemy'.

4. Careless Whispers in the State of Grace
(Tehran–Qom–Esfahan)

1. Muhammad Haykal, *The Life of Muhammad*, translated by Ismail Ragi A. al-Faruqi (Kuala Lumpur: American Trust Publications, 1976), page xxvii.
2. Karen Armstrong, *Muhammad: A Biography of the Prophet* (New York: Harper Collins, 1992), page 164.
3. Maxime Rodinson, *Muhammad* (London: Tauris Parke, 2002), pages xvi–xvii.
4. It is customary for Muslims to say "God bless him and grant him peace" after the name of the Prophet Muhammad is spoken. I have written this here but have omitted it in other instances assuming that Muslims will automatically invoke this blessing.

5. Coca-Colonisation
(Esfahan)

1. V. S. Naipaul, *Beyond Belief: Islamic Excursions among the Converted People* (London: Abacus, 2000).
2. V. S. Naipaul, *Among the Believers: An Islamic Journey* (London: Penguin Books, 1981).
3. Ibid., page 8.
4. Quotation printed on the unnumbered inside page of Naipaul, *Beyond Belief*.

5. Edward Said, *Orientalism* (London: Vintage Books, 1979).

6. Naipaul, *Beyond Belief*, page 1.

7. Umar Faruq Abdallah, *Islam and the Cultural Imperative*, Nawawi Foundation Paper, http://www.nawawi.org/downloads/article3.pdf

6. Purple Rain Where the Streets Have No Name (Esfahan)

1. Gordon Robison, *Divide, not Conquer*, Mideast Analysis.com, http://www.mideastanalysis.com/Articles.php?item = divide-not-conquer

2. Even before the Revolution Iran was accused of helping various insurgency groups: "In 1974 Iran had begun supplying weapons to Kurdish nationalists in northern Iraq, enabling them to stage a revolt against the Iraqi government. In order to halt the rebellion, Iraq in 1975 compromised on a dispute with Iran regarding the border on the Shatt al-Arab estuary. In exchange, Iran stopped supplying arms to the Kurds." See: 'Iran-Iraq war', http://militaryhistory.about.com/gi/dynamic/offsite.htm?site = http%3A%2F%2Fmembers.tripod.com%2FAl_3irakia%2Firaniraq.htm

3. Jim Garamone, "Iraq and the Use of Chemical Weapons", American Forces Information Service, http://www.defenselink.mil/news/Jan2003/n01232003_200301234.html

4. Stephen R. Shalom, "The United States and the Iran-Iraq War", *Z magazine*, http://www.zmag.org/zmag/articles/ShalomIranIraq.html

5. Mansour Farhang, "The Iran-Iraq war: The feud, the tragedy, the spoils", *World Policy Journal* 2 (Fall 1985).

6. "The Iran-Contra Affair", The American-Israeli Cooperative Enterprise, Jewish Virtual Library, http://www.jewishvirtuallibrary.org/jsource/US-Israel/Iran_ Contra_Affair.html

7. Jane Hunter, "Israeli Arms Sales to Iran", *Washington Report on Middle East Affairs*, http://www.washington-report.org/backissues/1186/8611002.html

8. *Time*, 25 July 1983, page 28.

9. Jeremy Scahill, "The Saddam in Rumsfeld's Closet", Znet, http://www.zmag.org/content/showarticle.cfm?ItemID = 2177

10. Ibid.

11. For example, see Michael Dobbs "US Had Key Role in Iraq Buildup," *Washington Post*, December 30, 2002: http://www.washingtonpost.com/ac2/wp-dyn/A52241-2002Dec29?language = printer

12. Shalom, "United States and the Iran-Iraq War".

13. See, Stephen Kinzer, *All the Shah's Men: The Hidden Story of the CIA's Coup in Iran* (London: John Wiley & Sons Inc, 2003).

14. Shalom, "The United States and the Iran-Iraq War".

7. Martyrs Blood Stains the Stairway to Heaven (Esfahan-Shiraz)

1. Islamic Republic of Iran Broadcasting, http://www.irib.com/worldservice/moharram/lesson3.htm

2. One other academic that I spoke to would repeat this claim of racial discrimination within academia under the Shah. As I am only the story-teller in this instance I cannot vouch for the veracity of such an assertion, although it does not sound completely implausible to me, hence its inclusion within the book. I was further persuaded to cite this twice-repeated allegation because Azar Nafisi's best seller, *Reading Lolita in Tehran: A Memoir in Books* (London: Forth Estate, 2004), a book that explores academia in Iran under the ayatollahs and has become an enormously popular choice amongst book club readers in the United States over the past few years, seems to overlook this somewhat less attractive feature of Iranian academia under the Shah.

9. Smooth Criminals on the Road to Damascus (Shiraz-Tehran-Damascus)

1. John Simpson, *Strange Places, Questionable People* (London: Pan Books, 1998), page 219.

2. Otherwise known as physical contact between a man and a woman when they ... err ... that thing you're thinking right now, yeah that's it!

10. Madame Tells a Tale of Two Cities (Damascus)

1. "Brummie" is a term used to describe people who originate from Birmingham, England.

11. The Continuing Adventures of Man's Spare Rib
(Damascus)

1. Katherine Bullock, *Rethinking Muslim Women and the Veil: Challenging Historical and Modern Stereotypes* (London: Institute of Islamic Thought, 2002), page 219.

2. Naomi Wolf, *The Beauty Myth* (London: Vintage, 1991), page 10.

3. Ibid., page 9.

12. The Gospel of Descartes
(Damascus)

1. In the Middle East tea is served without milk and much to my surprise (considering I dislike tea immensely) it doesn't taste too bad.

2. It was the anti-Semitism that the Jews suffered for many centuries in the West that gave rise to secular Zionism, which argued for a safe haven for Jews and was the driving force behind the creation of the modern state of Israel.

13. The Shame of Midnight's Children
(Damascus-Beirut)

1. Now that Saddam has been toppled, the border crossing with Iraq may become easier to cross.

2. Salman Rushdie, *Midnight's Children* (London: Jonathan Cape Ltd, 1981).

3. Noam Chomsky, *Power and Terror: Post 9/11 Talks and Interviews* (London: Seven Stories Press, 2003), page 52.

4. Edward Said, "Rushdie and the Whale", *Observer*, 14 February 1989.

5. Ziauddin Sardar and Merryl Wyn Davies, *Distorted Imagination: Lessons from the Rushdie Affair* (London: Grey Seal, 1990), page 165.

6. Salman Rushdie, "In Good Faith", from *Imaginary Homelands: Essays and Criticism 1981–1991* (London: Granta Books, 1991), page 397.

7. Anita Desai in the Introduction to *Midnight's Children* (London: Everyman's Library, 1995), page ix.

8. Salman Rushdie, "The New Empire within Britain" from *Imaginary Homelands: Essays and Criticism: 1981–1991* (London: Granta, 1991), pages 131–132.

9. Akbar S. Ahmed, *Discovering Islam: Making Sense of Muslim History and Society* (London: Routledge, 1988), page 5.

10. Ziauddin Sardar, *Desperately Seeking Paradise: Journeys of a Sceptical Muslim* (London: Granta, 2004) page 278.

11. Paul Brians, *Notes on Salman Rushdie: The Satanic Verses*, http://www.wsu.edu/~brians/anglophone/satanic_verses/

12. Ismail Isa Patel summarises the history of pre-modern Western scholarship on the Prophet in the following terms: "The father of anti-Islamic polemics was John of Damascus (675–749), and he began the tradition of ridiculing Islam and the Prophet (peace be upon him). He claimed, in his book *De Haeresbius*, that the Quran was not revealed but created by the Prophet (peace be upon him), and that he was helped by a Christian monk, Bahira, to use the Old and New Testament to create a new scripture. He also claimed that the Prophet (peace be upon him) created verses of the Quran to fulfil his own wants, and these were usually to do with lust and sexual deviancy. Others followed John of Damascus in spreading ideas that portrayed Islam as an inferior religion, such as Peter the Venerable (1094–1156) and Martin Luther (1483–1546), works by figures as well-known as Chaucer, Gower and Dante also contained anti-Islamic elements. All of these figures added to the myths surrounding Islam; the revelations received by the Prophet (peace be upon him) were claimed to be no more than epileptic fits, and eventually the Prophet (peace be upon him) was seen as simply the disciple of Satan and the anti-Christ. The language of these works always referred to the Prophet (peace be upon him) as the 'impostor', the 'pretender', and the 'deceiver'—soon he was referred to as 'Mahound', the devil incarnate ..." See: http://www.trueislaam. free-online. co.uk/rushdie.htm

13. Salman Rushdie, *The Satanic Verses* (London: Vintage, 1998), pages 364–365.

14. Ibid., page 386.

15. Paul Brians, *Notes on Salman Rushdie: The Satanic Verses*, http://www.wsu.edu/~brians/anglophone/satanic_verses/

16. Ibid.

17. Ziauddin Sardar and Merryl Wyn Davies, *Distorted Imagination*, page 7.

18. Ibid., page 4.

19. Haykal, *Life of Muhammad*, page 105.

20. W. Montgomery Watt, *Muhammad: Prophet and Statesman* (Oxford: Oxford University Press, 1964), page 61.

21. The only other argument he forwards in his book is that a particular verse of the Quran can be interpreted in a particular way so as to give a particular interpretation that is consistent with the satanic verses story.

22. Rodinson, *Muhammad*, page 106.

23. Salman Rushdie, "In Good Faith", from *Imaginary Homelands: Essays and Criticism 1981–1991* (London: Granta Books, 1991), page 408.

24. From an address delivered in Kings College Chapel, Cambridge, on 14 February 1993.

25. Salman Rushdie, "In Good Faith", page 395.

26. Richard Webster, "Reconsidering the Rushdie Affair: Freedom, Censorship and American Foreign Policy", http://www.richardwebster.net/therushdieaffairreconsidered.html

27. Sardar, *Desperately Seeking Paradise*, page 282.

28. Salman Rushdie, "In Good Faith", page 396.

29. Professor Paul Brians, *Notes on Salman Rushdie: The Satanic Verses*, http://www.wsu.edu/~brians/anglophone/satanic_verses/

30. Hanif Kureishi, *The Black Album* (London: Faber and Faber, 1996), page 183.

31. Ibid.

32. Salman Rushdie, "Is Nothing Sacred?" from *Imaginary Homelands: Essays and Criticism 1981–1991* (London: Granta Books, 1991), page 420.

33. Webster, "Reconsidering the Rushdie Affair".

34. Michael Dummett, "Foreign Affairs: The Friends of Salman Rushdie", *Atlantic Monthly*, vol. 273, no. 3, 1994, page 30.

14. Finding Hermes Footprints: A Critique of Pure Dogma?
(Beirut)

1. Striving; scholarly endeavour; competence to infer expert legal rulings from foundational proofs within or without a particular school of law.

2. The battle lines are not as clear-cut or as refined as I appear to be suggesting (they never are). Within the two extremes of hard-line reformists and hard-line reaffirmationists there are a whole spectrum of different ideological positions.

3. Sayyid Qutb, *Milestones* (Lahore: Kazi Publications, 1993), page 17.

4. Mohammed Abed al-Jabri, *Arab-Islamic Philosophy: A Contemporary Critique*, translated by Aziz Abbassi (Austin: University of Texas Press, 1999), page 11.

5. Ibid., pages 6–7.

6. Leila Ahmed, *Women and Gender in Islam: Historical Roots of a Modern Debate* (New Haven: Yale University Press, 1992).

7. Aftab Ahmad Malik, "The State We Are In", in Aftab Ahmad Malik (ed.) *The State We Are In: Identity, Terror and the Law of Jihad* (Bristol: Amal Press, 2006), pages 24–25.

15. Social(ist) Unrest on Animal Farm
(Beirut)

1. On the morning I was due to leave Amman for Aqaba, an overnight snowstorm closed all the motorways. My flight to the United Kingdom would depart from Amman in two days—I couldn't go to Aqaba. I never did get to relax on a beach with a picturesque view of the clear blue water!

17. Float Like a Butterfly Stung by a Bee
(Amman)

1. The *qibla* is the direction that Muslims face when praying, this being the direction towards the Ka'ba in the holy city of Mecca in Saudi Arabia.

18. Ballad of a Thin Man's Son
(Amman)

1. Internet research on this point unearthed an article by Brent E. Sasley for the respected academic journal *Middle East Review of International Affairs*. In an article entitled, "Changes and continuities in Jordanian foreign policy" (vol. 6, no. 1, March 2002), the author makes the following comment about King Abdullah, "He is considered moderate and cautious like his father, but Jordanians also talk about his poor Arabic and are very much aware of his lack of experience." Link at, http://meria.idc.ac.il/journal/2002/issue1/jv6nla3.html

2. http://www.state.gov/g/drl/rls/hrrpt/2004/41724.htm

3. "God's Order to Kill Americans: Usamah Bin-Laden's 1998 Fatwa" in Adam Parfrey (ed), *Extreme Islam: Anti-American Propaganda of Muslim Fundamentalism* (Los Angeles: Feral House, 2001), pages 290–292.

4. Ibid., page 304.

5. Ibid., page 305.

6. Bruce Lawrence (ed.), *Messages to the World: The Statements of Osama Bin Laden* (London: Verso, 2005).

7. Ibid., pages xviii–xix.

19. Two Tribes: How Does a Rose Grow from Concrete? (al-Quds)

1. I don't know about Lebanon, although I can't see them being too sympathetic towards Israel.

21. Somewhere over the Rainbow: The End of History? (The Promised Land)

1. *The Muslim News*, Friday, 24 January 2003.

2. While I hope that this won't be considered a bold statement, I do hope that once the reader has read the section, they will appreciate and recognise (even if they disagree with me on the arguments that I put forward in support of my view) that such a statement is not intended to be anti-Semitic. (In fact, I believe in a utopian vision of Palestinians and Israelis; Muslims, Jews and Christians, living together in peaceful co-existence on land that they have all occupied for many centuries.) It is often said, yet bears repeating: 'criticism of Israel does not equal anti-Semitism'. However, I am acutely aware that sound bites such as mine can be misinterpreted by those who are sympathetic or neutral to Israel's existence and then portrayed as a reflection of underlying anti-Jewish sentiments—hence the lengthy endnote.

I do not support or condone any form of Arab/Muslim/Palestinian aggression that attempts to drive the Jews of Israel into the sea or seeks to destroy Israel and all its Jewish inhabitants. I do not condone or overlook the many atrocities that the Jewish citizens of the Israeli state have had to endure from various Palestinian paramilitary groups. There have been atrocities and injustices committed against both Jews and Palestinians. Each side has had its aggressors and each side has had its victims. Certainly everyone could agree that, with bigotry and prejudice rife on both sides of the debate, articulating the grievances each side feels about the 'other' without alienating or offending the 'other' community is difficult, no matter how diplomatically one expresses an argument or opinion.

Beyond the statement itself, it must also be noted that reservations over the modern Israeli state have always existed within some parts of the Jewish community. From the very birth of the state of Israel, a number of Jews, both secular and orthodox, questioned the ethics of its existence, because of its potential impact on the Arab-Palestinian population. As Aftab A. Malik notes, even prominent Jews had their reservations about the establishment of the state of Israel:

> Some of the most distinguished Jews in the world protested against the formation of Israel . . . A letter sent by a host of Jewish intellectuals, including Albert Einstein, to the *New York Times* in 1948 regarded the emergence of Israel as among "the most disturbing political phenomena of our times."

(Aftab Ahmad Malik, ed. "The Betrayal of Tradition: Zionism's Challenge to Jews and Muslims," in *With God on Our Side: Politics and Theology of the War on Terrorism* [Bristol: Amal Press, 2005] page 141.)

Malik further explains,

> Amongst the prime reasons for their opposition was that the establishment of a Jewish state in Palestine would inevitably result in conflict with the population, which had been living there for centuries. Judah Magnes proclaimed "the Jews have more than a claim upon the world for justice [. . .]. But as far as I am concerned, I am not ready to try to achieve justice to the Jew through injustice to the Arab." Albert Einstein wrote that he would "rather see reasonable agreement with the Arabs on the basis of living together in peace than the creation of a Jewish state." (Ibid.)

Even Israel's first prime minister, David Ben Gurion, acknowledged the way in which, from an Arab/Palestinian viewpoint, Israel's existence could be seen as an injustice;

> If I were an Arab leader, I would never sign an agreement with Israel. It is normal; we have taken their country. It is true God promised it to us, but how could that interest them? Our God is not theirs. There has been Anti-Semitism, the Nazis, Hitler, Auschwitz, but was that their fault? They see but one thing: we have come and we have stolen their country. Why would they accept that?" (Ibid., pages 161–165)

Unfortunately, I must add that my travels exposed a nasty underbelly of anti-Semitic discourse in the Middle East, only some of which I have detailed in this book. Most worrying was that some of the most irrational, bigoted and downright absurd opinions on Jewish people originated from people who were normal, well-adjusted and likeable human beings in all other respects. As a Muslim, I find this anti-Semitism extremely disheartening. Aftab A. Malik, quoted above, quite rightly comments,

> Jewish Law embodies the notion of compassion and justice as well as displaying a sense of human honor (*Kavod habriyot*), which stresses that a society must ensure equal dignity. It also asserts that "God is the parent of humanity" and by extension, the whole of mankind "are all members of a

single extended family." This is also very similar to the Islamic tradition which states that because of God's love of humankind, He conferred dignity upon all His Creation. As God confirms in the Qur'an, "We have bestowed dignity on the children of Adam and conferred on them special favors [...]". This divine favor is without qualification, inalienable and applies to the whole of mankind. (Ibid., pages 150–151)

He goes on to conclude that,

> Anti-Semitism in the Muslim world is very much a recent phenomenon. Rather than being ancient and religiously sanctioned, it is with a certain reading of Islam, one that is highly politicized, and emotionally driven, that is leading Muslims to equate all Jews as Zionists, and in effect, dismissing Islam's traditional outlook of the Jews. (Ibid., page 145)

3. Especially when you consider that every Jew has a right to live in Israel irrespective of whether their ancestry could be traced back to those Jews that were sent into exile all those thousands of years ago and irrespective of whether they had suffered from anti-Semitism.

4. Salman Abu Sitta, *Palestinian Right to Return: Sacred, Legal and Possible*, 2nd ed. (London: Palestinian Return Centre, 1999), page 64.

5. Gayatri Chakravorty Spivak, *Outside in the Teaching Machine* (London: Routledge, 1993).

6. Palestinians might also wish to pause for a moment and think about the types of rulers these politico-military organisations might throw up. My greatest fear is that once the Palestinians get their own state, Israeli oppression of the Palestinian people will be replaced by a Palestinian leadership whose method of dispute resolution is one of violent repression, leaving ordinary Palestinians no better off than they were under the Israelis. Israeli oppression of the Palestinian masses replaced by Palestinian oppression of the Palestinian masses. Some time ago I went on a march in London that (amongst other things) aimed to highlight Israeli aggression against Palestinians. Palestinian groups of numerous persuasions had collectively gathered to voice their opposition to Israel. They ranged from Islamic fundamentalist groups that wanted to create an Islamic state in Palestine to secular socialist/Marxist groups. Crushed in amongst these groups I commented to my friend how remarkable it was to see such a diverse range of groups so united on an issue. The sight did also make me wonder how tolerant these groups would be of each other in a Palestinian state.

7. Ziauddin Sardar, "The Agony of a 21st-century Muslim", *New Statesman*, 17 February 2003.

8. Reported in "Kitab al-Imara", *Sahih Muslim*.

SELECT BIBLIOGRAPHY

Abdallah, Umar Faruq. *Islam and the Cultural Imperative*. Nawawi Foundation. <http://www.nawawi.org/downloads/article3.pdf>

Abed al-Jabri, Mohammed. *Arab-Islamic Philosophy: A Contemporary Critique*. Translated by Aziz Abbassi. Austin: University of Texas Press, 1999.

Abu Sitta, Salman. *Palestinian Right to Return: Sacred, Legal and Possible*. 2nd ed. London: Palestinian Return Centre, 1999.

Ahmed, Akbar S. *Discovering Islam: Making Sense of Muslim History and Society*. London: Routledge, 1988.

Ahmed, Leila. *Women and Gender in Islam*. New Haven: Yale University Press, 1992.

Ali, Monica. *Brick Lane*. London: Doubleday, 2003.

Ali, Tariq. *Clash of the Fundamentalisms*. London: Verso, 2002.

Armstrong, Karen. *Islam: A Short History*. London: Phoenix Press, 2001.

_____. *Muhammad: A Biography of the Prophet*. New York: Harper Collins, 1992.

_____. *Muhammad: Prophet for our Time*. London: Harper Press, 2006.

Azzam, Abd al-Rahman. *The Eternal Message of Muhammad*. Cambridge: Islamic Texts Society, 1993.

Barlas, Asma. *Believing Women in Islam: Unreading Patriarchal Interpretations of the Quran*. Austin: University of Texas Press, 2002.

Brians, Paul. *Notes on Salman Rushdie: The Satanic Verses*. <http://www.wsu.edu/~brians/anglophone/satanic_verses/>

Bullock, Katherine. *Rethinking Muslim Women and the Veil: Challenging Historical and Modern Stereotypes*. London: Institute of Islamic Thought, 2002.

Chomsky, Noam. *Power and Terror: Post 9/11 Talks and Interviews*. London: Seven Stories Press, 2003.

Cohen-Sherbok, Dan and Dawoud el-Alami. *The Palestine-Israeli Conflict: A Beginners Guide*. Oxford: Oneworld Publications, 2001.

Dobbs, Michael. "US Had Key Role in Iraq Buildup", *Washington Post*. December 30, 2002. http://www.washingtonpost.com/ac2/wp-dyn/A522412002Dec29?language = printer Dummett, Michael. "Foreign Affairs: The Friends of Salman Rushdie". *Atlantic Monthly* 273, no. 3 (1994).

Esposito, John L. *Islam: The Straight Path*. Oxford: Oxford University Press, 1994.

Farhang, Mansour. "The Iran-Iraq War: The Feud, the Tragedy, the Spoils". *World Policy Journal* 2 (Fall 1985).

Forster, E. M. *A Passage to India*. London: Everyman's Library, 1991.

Garamone, Jim. "Iraq and the Use of Chemical Weapons", *American Forces Information Service*. <http://www.defenselink.mil/news/Jan2003/n01232003_200301234.html>

Haykal, Muhammad. *The Life of Muhammad*. Translated by Ismail Ragi A. al-Faruqi. Kuala Lumpur: American Trust Publications, 1976.

Hunter, Jane. "Israeli Arms Sales to Iran". *Washington Report on Middle East Affairs*. <http://www.washington-report.org/backissues/1186/8611002.html>

Kafka, Franz. *Collected Stories*. New York: Everyman's Library, 1993.

_____. *The Trial*. New York: Everyman's Library, 1992.

Kinzer, Stephen. *All the Shah's Men: The Hidden Story of the CIA's Coup in Iran*. London: John Wiley & Sons, 2003.

Kureishi, Hanif. *The Black Album*. London: Faber and Faber, 1996.

Lapidus, Ira M. *A History of Islamic Societies*. Cambridge: Cambridge University Press, 1988.

Lawrence, Bruce, ed. *Messages to the World: The Statements of Osama Bin Laden*. London: Verso, 2005.

Lings, Martin. *Muhammad, His Life Based on the Earliest Sources*. Lahore: Suhail Academy, 2005.

Mahfouz, Naguib. *The Cairo Trilogy*. London: Everyman's Library, 2001.

Malik, Aftab Ahmad, ed. *The State We Are In: Identity, Terror and the Law of Jihad*. Bristol: Amal Press, 2006.

_____. *With God on Our Side: Politics and Theology of the War on Terrorism*. Bristol: Amal Press, 2005.

Nafisi, Azar. *Reading Lolita in Tehran, A Memoir in Books*. London: Forth Estate, 2004.

Naipaul, V. S. *Among the Believers: An Islamic Journey*. London: Penguin Books, 1981.

_____. *Beyond Belief: Islamic Excursions among the Converted People*. London: Abacus, 2000.

Parfrey, Adam, ed. *Extreme Islam: Anti-American Propaganda of Muslim Fundamentalism*. Los Angeles: Feral House, 2001.

Qutb, Sayyid. *Milestones*. Lahore: Kazi Publications, 1993.

Raabi'ah, "The Forgotten Ones". *Muslim News*. Friday 24 January 2003.

Robison, Gordon. "Divide, not Conquer". <http://www.mideastanalysis.com/Articles.php?item = divide-not-conquer>

Rodinson, Maxime. *Muhammad*. London: Tauris Parke, 2002.

Rogerson, Barnaby. *The Prophet Muhammad: A Biography*. London: Little Brown, 2003.

Roy, Arundhati. *The God of Small Things*. London: Flamingo, 1998.

Rushdie, Salman. *Imaginary Homelands: Essays and Criticism 1981–1991*. London: Granta Books, 1991.

_____. *Midnight's Children*. London: Jonathan Cape Ltd, 1981.

_____. *The Satanic Verses*. London: Vintage, 1998.

_____. *Step Across this Line: Collected Non-fiction 1992–2002*. London: Vintage, 2002.

Sacco, Joe. *Palestine*. London: Jonathon Cape, 2003.

Said, Edward. *Orientalism*. London: Vintage Books, 1979.

_____. "Rushdie and the Whale". *Observer*. 14 February 1989.

Salahi, Adil. *Muhammad, Man and Prophet*. Markfield: Islamic Foundation, 2002.

Saleh, Mohsen M. Translated by Hassan A. Ibrahim. *The Palestinian Issue: Its Background and Development up to 2000*. Kuala Lumpur: Petra, 2001.

Sardar, Ziauddin. "The Agony of a 21st-century Muslim". *New Statesman*. 17 February 2003.

_____. *Desperately Seeking Paradise: Journeys of a Sceptical Muslim*. London: Granta Books, 2004.

Sardar, Ziauddin and Merryl Wyn Davies. *Distorted Imagination: Lessons from the Rushdie Affair*. London: Grey Seal, 1990.

Scahill, Jeremy. "The Saddam in Rumsfelds Closet", *Znet*. <http://www.zmag.org/content/showarticle.cfm?ItemID = 2177>

Shalom, Stephen. "The United States and the Iran-Iraq War". *Z magazine*. <http://www.zmag.org/zmag/articles/ShalomIranIraq.html>

Simpson, John. *Strange Places: Questionable People*. London: Pan Books, 1998.

Smale, David. *Salman Rushdie: Midnight's Children / The Satanic Verses: A Reader's Guide to Essential Criticism*. Houndmills: Palgrave Macmillan, 2001.

Smith, Charles, D. *Palestine and the Arab-Israeli Conflict*. 3rd ed. Houndmills: Macmillan Press, 1996.

Spivak, Gayatri. *Outside in the Teaching Machine*. London: Routledge, 1993.

Watt, W. Montgomery. *Muhammad: Prophet and Statesman*. Oxford: Oxford University Press, 1964.

Webster, Richard. "Reconsidering the Rushdie Affair: Freedom, Censorship and American Foreign Policy". <http://www.richardwebster.net/therushdieaffairreconsidered.html>

Wolf, Naomi. *The Beauty Myth*. London: Vintage, 1991.

INDEX